Directory of FORMULA ONE CARS

£9.95

Directory of FORMULA ONE CARS

1966-1986

ANTHONY PRITCHARD
Photographs by Nigel Snowdon

Aston Publications
Sole distributors for the USA
Motorbooks International
Publishers & Wholesalers Inc.

Published in 1986 by Aston Publications Limited,
Bourne End House, Harvest Hill
Bourne End, Bucks. SL8 5JJ

ISBN 0 946627 02 9

Sole distributors to the
U.K. Book Trade
Springfield Books Ltd.,
Norman Road, Denby Dale,
Huddersfield,
West Yorkshire, HD8 8TH

Designed by Chris Hand

Filmset and printed in England by
BAS Printers Limited, Over Wallop, Hampshire

Contents

Introduction

For five years, from 1961 to 1965, the 1500 cc unsupercharged Formula One had encouraged a breed of 'kit car' builders, in the main relying on the Coventry Climax V-8 engine; it had produced racing that drivers regarded as tame and cars that were slower than their sports/racing contemporaries and spectators were bored. This all changed with the introduction of the 3000 cc Formula One for 1966, a return to power that revitalized Grand Prix racing.

Initially it seemed that there would be difficulties over the supply of power units and that the 'kit car' breed of constructors, relying on readily available proprietary engines, would disappear. In addition the number of teams competing when the Formula started was very small. Since then the number of teams competing has just about doubled, and the number of rounds in the World Championship has increased by around 50 per cent. There are two principal reasons for the increase in the sport's popularity. The sheer spectacle and speed of modern Grand Prix racing coupled with the commercial promotion of the sport has encouraged sponsorship on a massive scale and resulted in world-wide television coverage.

Equally important was the development of the Ford-Cosworth DFV engine first seen in the Lotus 49s in the Dutch GP in 1967. From 1968 this engine was readily available to any constructor who could afford the price, and with the exception of Ferrari its use became almost universal. While Lotus, McLaren and, later, Brabham and Williams were the leading Cosworth users and were also leaders of technical innovation, other constructors using the same engines were constantly short of money, some racing only briefly, some cheerfully cribbing the successful designs of their more competitive rivals and always scrabbling for places at the back of the grid.

During the 20 years of the Formula only three constructors have won Championship races powered by their own engines, Ferrari, BRM and Renault, and the only others to use their own engines, albeit unsuccessfully, were Alfa Romeo, Matra and Tecno. Whilst Matra enjoyed a good run of success in 1968–69, the cars that won races were powered by Cosworth engines and victory for a Matra engine came only when installed in a Ligier chassis. Cosworth also built their own car, but this was never raced.

In reality the long run of Cosworth domination ended with Rosberg's win in the 1982 World Championship at the wheel of a Williams, but Alboretto drove a Cosworth-powered Tyrrell to victory at

Detroit in 1983. It was not until the end of 1985 that 3-litre unsupercharged engines were finally banned and during that time Cosworth had won a total of 155 Grands Prix.

Although there had traditionally been retained in the Grand Prix Formulae of both 1961–65 and 1966 onwards a supercharged alternative, no team raced a supercharged car during either period. It was only through the advanced technical development work of Renault that the 1500 cc turbocharged engine became a serious and viable proposition. Renault first raced their turbocharged car at Silverstone in July 1977 and the team finally withdrew from racing at the end of 1985 without having won the World Championship.

During these years, however, racing had been transformed largely as a result of Renault's pioneering work. Ferrari has raced turbocharged cars since 1981, from 1982 Brabham has raced turbocharged BMW-powered cars and the turbocharged engine has become universal. With McLaren using the Porsche-designed TAG engine, Honda supplying engines to Williams and Renault, notwithstanding their own withdrawal from racing, continuing to supply engines to Lotus, Ligier and Tyrrell, racing has never been so fast or so exciting. Now, with the fatal high-speed accident of Elio de Angelis during testing at the Paul Ricard circuit, consideration is being given to the limiting of power outputs so as to restrict speed.

Throughout the last ten years there have been constant wrangles and arguments over interpretation of the rules, constant changes to the rules and a battle for power between FISA, the governing body of the sport, and FOCA, the Formula One Constructors' Association. Many of these constant disputes have no place in this book, but where they are relevant they are referred to in the text.

Since the inception of the 3-litre Formula, 52 different constructors have built Formula One cars and the aim of this book is to provide a convenient identifying guide with brief notes on design, development and racing performances. For a full account of racing during the last 20 years, the reader is directed to that superb annual, *Autocourse*, and to the weekly magazines *Autosport* and *Motoring News*. For a detailed and comprehensive review of technical developments, Doug Nye's *Autocourse History of the Grand Prix Car* is the answer. John Blunsden's *The Power to Win*, dealing with the Cosworth DFV engine, is equally important in its narrower field.

Alfa Romeo
(Italy)

No company has a more distinguished racing record than Alfa Romeo, an involvement that can be traced back to pre-World War I days and with immense success enjoyed by the P2 cars in the twenties, the Monza and Monoposto in the thirties and the Tipo 158 and 159 Alfettas that were the dominant force in early post-war motor racing. Alfa Romeo withdrew from Grand Prix racing at the end of 1951, dabbled for two seasons with the futuristic 'Disco Volante' sports/racing cars and then withdrew from racing completely. In 1963 Alfa Romeo formed a new racing organization, Autodelta, separate from the factory and headed by ex-Ferrari engineer Carlo Chiti. Autodelta was originally based at Udine, but in 1964 moved to Settimo Milanese. Here the team developed competition versions of Alfa Romeo production cars and from 1967 built and raced the long line of Tipo 33 sports/racing cars that never achieved much in the way of substantial success.

By 1968 Alfa Romeo was showing interest in Formula One by making available to Cooper one of the Autodelta V-8 engines, but this was unraced. The V-8 Alfa engines were raced in McLaren and March cars in 1970–71 without success. Next in development came the flat-12 3-litre engine of 2995.125 cc (77 × 53.6 mm) first used in sports car racing in 1973 and progressively developed for Formula One. Initially the engine was installed in a Lola of Graham Hill's Embassy team, but was adopted by Brabham for 1976. For four seasons Brabhams raced with the flat-12 (and, later, V-12) engines, but without achieving much in the way of success. During 1979, however, the first of the new line of Alfa Romeo Formula One cars made its racing appearance.

Tipo 177 and 179 – 1979

Alfa's racing efforts in 1979 were part of their preparation for a full onslaught in 1980 and the team made its first appearance at the Belgian GP at Zolder. The first car, the Tipo 177, was very much a development hack that had been running and steadily developed since 1978. It featured a riveted aluminium chassis, with front suspension by upper rocking arms, lower wishbones and inboard-mounted coil spring/damper units and, at the rear, parallel lower links, single top links, twin radius rods and outboard coil spring/damper units. The Tipo 115–12 flat-12 engine, said to develop 520 bhp at 12,000 rpm, was used in conjunction with an Alfa Romeo 5-speed gearbox. It was a bulky, bulbous-looking car finished in the handsome dark red colour adopted by Autodelta and went surprisingly well in the hands of Bruno Giacomelli. Giacomelli took a mid-position on the grid in Belgium and ran steadily in the race until he was shunted up the back by de Angelis (Shadow).

Giacomelli and the Alfa reappeared at the French GP at Dijon, running at the tail of the field, but finishing, and then did not run again until the Italian GP at Monza, where the new Tipo 179, the definitive car to be raced in 1980, appeared. The power unit was now the Tipo 1260 V-12 with the same cylinder dimensions as the flat-12, slightly lower power output, but much more compact. There was a completely new chassis with the cockpit well to the front, 'wing' aerodynamics designed by Robert Choulet of SERA, the Paris-based wind tunnel facility, inboard-mounted rear suspension that incorporated lower wishbones and a general appearance similar to that of the contemporary Arrows A2. The wheelbase was 9 ft 0 in., front track 5 ft 7.7 in. and rear track 5 ft 1.8 in. At Monza the new car was driven by Giacomelli, while Vittorio Brambilla drove the old 177. For the Canadian GP Autodelta brought along two 179s, but there was an argument as to whether the Alfas had to take part in pre-race qualifying, and eventually one car, driven by Brambilla, started the race. In the United States GP Brambilla failed to qualify along with the five other slowest in practice and only Giacomelli started. There was nothing worthwhile gained in these early outings, but the whole team was still very new.

Tipo 179 – 1980

During 1980 Autodelta raced a total of seven different chassis, Giacomelli was joined in the team by French driver Patrick Depailler and the team was in receipt of Marlboro sponsorship. As the season progressed the cars were substantially modified. Initially they appeared with outboard rear brakes and modified rear suspension, and early in the season the aerodynamics were improved and the monocoque was stiffened. Carbon-fibre body panels were adopted, as were titanium suspension components. Apart from a fifth place by Giacomelli in the Argentine, no success was gained and tragedy struck when Depailler crashed with fatal results during testing at Hockenheim, possibly as a result of suspension failure. Giacomelli with the only car entered finished fifth in the German GP, retired in Austria and was joined by Brambilla (who had earlier driven a third Alfa Romeo entered in Spain) for the European races and by de Cesaris in Canada and the United States. The remainder of the year proved a complete blank for Autodelta except for the United States GP, where Giacomelli took pole position on the grid and led until eliminated by ignition failure. There were high hopes for 1981.

Tipo 179C – 1981

Autodelta, by dint of adopting Williams-style underwings, had adjusted to the era of sliding skirts and produced exceptional times during winter testing only to be faced with the 1981 ban on sliding skirts. Giacomelli was joined by Mario Andretti, but it was to prove another year of complete failure. Carlo Chiti experimented with hydropneumatic lowering suspension, but it proved hopeless and was soon abandoned. The team's best performances were a fourth by Andretti in the US (West) GP at Long Beach, the first round in the Championship, another fourth by Giacomelli in Canada and a third place by Giacomelli in the Ceasar's Palace GP at Las Vegas in October. These results meant that Alfa ranked along with the under-financed also-rans and clearly the situation was becoming hopeless. At the British GP at Silverstone the team had introduced the revised (it is not possible to say improved) 179C/D car, about 5 cm lower and with modified rear suspension. Shortly afterwards the team was joined by Gérard Ducarouge (who had left Ligier) and his first step had been to introduce Ligier-style side pods that moved the centre of pressure more to the rear.

Tipo 182 – 1982

For 1982 Autodelta introduced the new Tipo 182 with carbon-fibre

1. Bruno Giacomelli with the V-12 Alfa Romeo Tipo 177 in the 1979 Belgian Grand Prix at Zolder. He was eliminated in an accident with the Shadow of de Angelis.

monocoque manufactured (and largely designed) by the British Advanced Composite Components company. The new car was much lighter and aerodynamics had been improved, but it was only too obvious that Autodelta would have to introduce a turbocharged engine if the team were to become competitive. Inevitably Autodelta enjoyed yet another unsuccessful year with only three finishes in the first six. Much of the team's flair was displayed by Andrea de Cesaris, an exceptionally fast driver, but who has written off so many Formula One cars that he is virtually unemployable. De Cesaris took pole position in the United States GP (West) and led before he shunted his Alfa into a wall, and later he finished third at Monaco (after running out of fuel) and sixth in Canada (again out of fuel), whilst Giacomelli took fifth place at Hockenheim. Developments during the year had included the narrower 182B monocoque that was first seen in Belgium. In practice at Imola the team revealed a Tipo 179 fitted with the new V-8 1496 cc (74 × 43.5 mm) turbocharged engine claimed to develop 600 bhp at 11,500 rpm. This was driven by Giorgia Francia, but an oil pipe ruptured and the car caught fire. It was not until Monza that the Tipo 182, combining the existing chassis with the turbocharged engine, was driven in practice by de Cesaris.

Tipo 183T – 1983

For 1983 operation of Alfa Romeos was taken over by the Euroracing Team of Milan run by Paolo Pavanello, but Autodelta remained responsible for manufacture of the cars and engines. The T182s, fitted

2. The turbocharged Alfa Romeo 184T was heavy on fuel, unreliable and lacked the sheer power of the front runners. Eddie Cheever is seen in the 1984 Austrian Grand Prix in which he retired with engine trouble.

with Italian Sylo turbochargers, modified to comply with the new flat-bottom rules and fitted with shorter side pods, were driven by de Cesaris and Mauro Baldi. Steady development took place throughout the year, but the team made a major blunder at the French GP. The qualifying time in the first session set by de Cesaris was disallowed because of an empty fire extinguisher bottle (which would give a minimal weight advantage) and, allegedly, the whole situation had been engineered to enable the team to dismiss Ducarouge, who immediately joined Lotus! A reduction in fuel consumption permitted fuel cell capacity to be reduced to 225 litres, the rear suspension was revised and there were constant engine improvements during the year. Alfa Romeo had little to be proud of at the end of the year, but in fact it had proved the best enjoyed by the team; de Cesaris succeeded in finishing second both at Hockenheim and Kyalami and had actually led the Belgian race at Spa for 18 laps.

Tipo 184T – 1984

Euroracing continued the struggle in 1984 with sponsorship from the very successful Benetton knitwear company and adopted Benetton's bright green livery. The cars were the improved Tipo 184T with pushrod front suspension and pullrod rear suspension and were driven by Riccardo Patrese and Eddie Cheever. The team looked as though it had all the makings for a successful year, but it was not to be. The cars were simply not fast enough to cope with the opposition and the best results of a very poor year were third by Patrese in the Italian GP and fourth places by Cheever in Brazil and by Patrese in South Africa. Perhaps the most significant event was the removal of Carlo Chiti, who had been running Autodelta for so many years without substantial success, and his replacement by Giovanni Tonti, formerly with the Lancia Prototype team.

Tipo 185T – 1985

For 1985 Patrese and Cheever both remained with Euroracing and the team managed to retain its Benetton sponsorship. John Gentry joined Eurocracing from Toleman and Autodelta's contribution was now limited to engines and gearboxes. Gentry redesigned the suspension and the cars were now designated the 185T, but the British designer left before the start of the season to join Renault. It soon became apparent that all was not well with the new suspension and the Alfa engines were too thirsty to comply with the 195-litre fuel capacity limit and remain competitive. Tonti was obliged to scrap two of the 185T chassis, convert the third back to 1984 184T specification and bring back two of the 1984 cars. Throughout the year Cheever's driving was dispirited, at Monaco Patrese collided with Piquet's

Brabham and put both cars out of the race and in South Africa the Alfas collided and eliminated each other on the first lap! It was obviously the end of a sad story and Alfa Romeo disappeared from the racing scene at the end of the year after six seasons of fruitless effort and continuing failure.

Amon

(United Kingdom)

1974

New Zealand driver Chris Amon proved himself one of the fastest Grand Prix drivers of the late sixties and the early seventies, but his entire racing career was overshadowed by bad luck tinged with an element of bad judgement. After three years with Ferrari, in 1967–69, he left the team when it was just about to introduce a new and successful model and his following seasons with March (1970), Matra (1971–72) and Tecno (1973) failed to bring him a Championship Grand Prix victory.

To outside observers it seemed almost inevitable that when he decided to build his own Formula One contender for 1974 that the venture would be plagued by misfortune. The Amon AF101 was designed by Gordon Fowell and largely financed by John Dalton, one-time amateur Aston Martin and Austin-Healey driver. Amon's team endeavoured to build a car that was a little more sophisticated than average, inspired by Lotus design principles, and with good develop-

3. Chris Amon's efforts to run a Formula One team under his own name were doomed to failure. Here he is at Monza where he failed to qualify as a starter in the 1974 Italian Grand Prix.

ment potential. The result was a design that was over-complex and could not be made raceworthy before the team's money ran out. There was a 16-gauge monocoque with the fuel cells between the engine and the driver's seat (which, as a result, was well to the front of the car) and completely surrounded by the deformable structure which continued along the cockpit sides. Torsion bar suspension was fitted front and rear and there were inboard front brakes driven by constant-velocity-jointed shafts. The light blue-painted Amon sported distinctive and very aerodynamic bodywork; the nose itself was an aerofoil section working in harmony with the wing mounted above it.

The Amon was scheduled to make its debut in the Race of Champions in March, but non-started after crashing when it lost a wheel during testing at Goodwood. By the time the Amon was first raced in Spain stronger front wishbones had been fitted and there was a reprofiled nose without the wing above it. Amon was one of the slowest drivers in practice and retired when a brake-shaft broke. From then onwards the team was plagued by continuing misfortune. Amon did not run the new car again until the German Grand Prix in August, but it was pathetically slow in practice, was badly damaged when reserve driver Larry Perkins collided with the guard rail and failed to qualify as a starter. After another five weeks of development work Chris Amon reappeared with the AF101 at Monza, but it was still too slow to qualify. By this stage Amon had lost all interest in the project and he drove a works BRM in the last two races of the season; nothing more was heard of the Amon Formula One car.

Arrows

(United Kingdom)

FA1 and A1 – 1978

During the winter of 1977–78 Alan Rees, Jack Oliver, designer Tony Southgate and their draughtsman Dave Wass all quitted the ailing Shadow organization and set up their own Formula One équipe with financial support from Franco Ambrosio. In the space of two months Southgate designed the FA1 Arrows, closely inspired by the design of the DN9 car that he had just completed for Shadow. The basis of the design was a ground-effect wing car with twin wing sections attached to the sides of the monocoque. At the front suspension was by upper rocking arms, lower wishbones and inboard coil spring/damper units. For the rear suspension Southgate used a layout of parallel lower links, single top links, twin radius rods and outboard coil spring/damper units. The power unit was the inevitable Ford-Cosworth DFV used in conjunction with the Hewland FGA400 5-speed gearbox. The wheelbase was 8 ft 6 in., front track 5 ft 5 in. and rear track 5 ft 0 in. The drivers were Patrese and Stommelen and the team was sponsored by the Warsteiner brewery.

There had been a frantic rush to complete the design, for if Arrows was to qualify in 1979 for membership of the Formula One Constructors' Association, they could miss only one of the year's non-European GPs. The team missed the Argentine GP, ran a single car for Patrese in Brazil and competed with two cars at the remainder of the year's races. It was inevitable that with a new design from a small team not much in the way of success could be expected, but Patrese took a sixth place in the United States GP (West) at Long Beach, a sixth again at Monaco and, the team's best performance of the year, a second in Sweden.

In the meanwhile Don Nichols had taken High Court proceedings against his former employees and obtained judgement that the Arrows had been designed from Shadow's copyright drawings and an injunction preventing the team from racing the FA1. Tony Southgate had been only too well aware of the way that the wind was blowing and had already designed a further new A1 car that was raced in the Austrian GP. The new A1 featured inboard rear suspension, longer 8 ft 10 in. wheelbase and 1 in. wider front and rear track. Only Patrese ran in Austria, colliding with Ertl, and another collision with Pironi followed at Zandvoort. Patrese's wild driving was initially blamed for the tragic death of Ronnie Peterson at Monza, for it was said that the Arrows hit Hunt's McLaren, which in turn shunted the Lotus into the path of Brambilla's Surtees, and he was not allowed to compete at Watkins Glen, where the sole Arrows starter was Stommelen. Both entries ran in Canada, but Stommelen failed to qualify, while Patrese took an encouraging fourth place.

A1B and A2 – 1979

Initially in 1979 the Arrows team raced the 1978 cars in improved form with revised rear suspension, new skirts, side pods and with larger brakes. Tony Southgate was also developing the A2, which was distinctly unconventional in that the entire engine and gearbox were angled upwards, enabling the fitting of full-width aerodynamic underfloor sections. Whereas the A1B was now uncompetitive and overweight, the A2 soon proved a sad disappointment, for it suffered directional handling problems on the slower circuits and suffered badly from porpoising. As a result the drivers, Patrese and Jochen Mass, started the season with the A1B, moved on to the A2 and back again to the A1B when the new car proved so unacceptable. It was a very dismal year for the team and the best performances were a fifth place by Patrese at Zolder and sixth places by Mass at Monaco, Zolder and Hockenheim.

A3 – 1980

By the first race of the 1980 season, The Argentine GP, Tony Southgate had ready two of his new A3 cars with very short wheelbase (at 8 ft 6 in., the shortest of any Formula One car of the time), front track of 5 ft 8 in., rear track of 5 ft 3 in., shrouded gearbox and much improved directional handling (although the cars were plagued by a persistent understeer). The drivers remained Patrese and Mass. During the year a number of attempts were made to improve the handling and aerodynamics, but with limited success, and Southgate left the team, so that Dave Wass became solely responsible for design. The best performances of the year were second by Patrese at Long Beach and second by Mass in the Spanish race, but this was the GP from which Alfa Romeo, Ferrari and Renault withdrew following the dispute between FISA and FOCA and the race did not count as a round in the World Championship. Mass crashed on an oil slick in practice for the Austrian GP, non-starting as a result, and his place was taken by Mike Thackwell at Zandvoort and Manfred Winkelhock at Monza, but both failed to qualify as starters.

A3 – 1981

By this stage Arrows' fortunes were at a very low ebb, for their continuing lack of success meant that the team had great difficulty in

4. The Arrows team has survived in Formula One, although it has never achieved substantial success. Riccardo Patrese drove this A3 in the 1980 Belgian Grand Prix, but retired when he spun off.

obtaining adequate sponsorship and was constantly in financial difficulty. Arrows continued to race the A3, with the rear suspension modified and the balance and handling of the car much improved. Patrese remained with the team and he was joined by young Siegfried Stohr. At the beginning of the year FOCA ran the South African GP as the last race for skirted cars, without entries from Alfa Romeo, Ferrari and Renault and on a non-Championship basis. Patrese drove a steady race to finish sixth and in the first of the Championship series, the United States GP (West) at Long Beach, took pole position on the grid and led for the first 25 laps. A third place for Patrese followed in Brazil. A bizarre accident followed at Zolder. Patrese's engine stalled on the grid, chief mechanic Dave Luckett jumped over the barrier with an air line and was working on the back of the car when the green light came on for the start. Team-mate Stohr jockeying for position hit Luckett and the back of Patrese's stricken car with the result that the mechanic suffered severe injuries. Luckett of course should not have been on the grid and there should have been a yellow flag displayed by Patrese's car to indicate that it had stalled. In Canada and at the Caesar's Palace GP at Las Vegas the team entered Jacques Villeneuve, but he failed to qualify at both races and Arrows was completely out of the picture for most the year.

A4 and A5 – 1982

For 1982 Wass introduced the new A4, a wing-car with the emphasis on achieving the maximum downforce and front and rear suspension by upper rocking arms, lower wishbones and inboard coil spring/damper units. The wheelbase was 8 ft 9.5 in., front track 5 ft 10 in.

5. Thiery Boutsen with the turbocharged BMW-powered Arrows A8 in the 1985 Dutch Grand Prix.

and rear track 5 ft 4 in. Five of these were built during the year, but the team also built the A5, a one-off copy of the Williams FWO8. A number of different drivers handled the cars during the year, including Brian Henton (South Africa, Brazil and Long Beach), Patrick Tambay (South Africa), Mauro Baldi (throughout the year) and Marc Surer (Zolder onwards), but the only places gained were a fifth by Surer in Canada, sixth places by Baldi at Zandvoort and in Austria and sixth by Surer at Hockenheim. It was hardly worth the effort.

A6 – 1983

Nevertheless Arrows struggled on in 1983 with the A6 design complying with the flat-bottom rule and running again on Goodyear tyres after a period on Pirellis. The A5 was converted to the specification and four new cars were built. The new cars featured front suspension by double wishbones, pull-rods and with inboard springs and rear suspension by upper rocking arms, lower wishbones and inboard springs. The wheelbase was 8 ft 10 in., front track 6 ft 0 in. and rear track 5 ft 2 in. By this time a turbocharged engine was vital for success and Arrows were still struggling with the Cosworth DFV. The drivers were Surer and Chico Serra, although Alan Jones was brought back from retirement to drive for the team at Long Beach (Arrows could not afford to retain his services) and Thierry Boutsen joined the team at Detroit. The sole fruits of the season were fifth places by Surer at Long Beach and sixth places in Brazil and at San Marino.

A7 – 1984

For 1984 Jack Oliver succeeded in negotiating for the supply to the team of BMW 4-cylinder 1500 cc (89.2 × 60 mm) turbocharged engines. Unfortunately this move did not launch Arrows into the forefront of racing as the engines were in the same kit as supplied to ATS and fell far short in power and development terms of the engines supplied to Brabham. New cars were built to take the BMW engines, broadly following the design of the A6, but with shorter 8 ft 8 in. wheelbase, narrower 5 ft 8 in. front track and wider 5 ft 3in. rear track. Team drivers remained Boutsen and Surer. At that start of the year Arrows continued to race the A6 cars, but the first of the A7s appeared at Zolder and it was not until Dallas in July that the team fielded two of the turbocharged cars. Success continued to elude the team and the sum at the end of another miserable year was sixth by Boutsen at Imola with a Cosworth-powered car and fifth with BMW power in Austria.

A8 – 1985

Dave Wass's new design for 1985 featured a moulded carbon-composite monocoque, suspension by top and bottom wishbones with pushrods at the front and pullrods at the rear. Wheelbase had been increased to 9 ft 3 in., with front track of 5 ft 10 in. and rear track of 5 ft 5 in. The BMW engines were tuned by Heini Mader and featured an exhaust system rising through the rear suspension as on the BMW-powered Brabhams. The drivers were Gerhard Berger and Boutsen and throughout the year the team's strongest card was its reliability, resulting in a fine second place by Boutsen at Imola, where first on the road Prost was disqualified and fuel consumption problems plagued the field; later in the year Boutsen finished fourth at the new Nürburgring, sixth at Brands Hatch and sixth at Kyalami (here Berger took fifth place). Berger was sixth in Australia.

A8 – 1986

Despite rumours to the contrary BMW continued the supply of turbocharged engines to the Arrows team in 1986 and in the early part of the year the A8s continued to be raced with Surer and Boutsen at the wheel. No success was gained and although a new 1986 car had appeared, it was only too clear that Arrows, after nine seasons amongst the also-rans, had only limited chances of survival in Formula One.

ATS

(West Germany)

When the specialist wheel company, ATS, headed by Hans Gunther Schmid, entered Formula One in 1977, it embarked on perhaps the least successful racing career of any Formula One entrant, a programme that lasted eight years spent at the back of the grid amongst the also-rans and with a reputation second to none for poor organization and management.

PC4 – 1977

ATS entered racing by the acquisition of the cars formerly raced by the Penske team. The team first appeared at the United States GP (West) in April, and Jarier, starting from the fifth row of the grid, took an encouraging sixth place. Jarier failed to qualify in Spain, finished at the tail of the field at Monaco, Belgium and Sweden and retired at Dijon; Hans Heyer was also entered in Germany and Hans Binder was entered in three races, but no further success was gained and the team missed the races outside Europe.

HS1 – 1978

For 1978 Schmid bought the March Formula One team and, in so doing, their membership of the Formula One Constructors' Association. During the early part of the year the ATS team raced the HS1, a development by Robin Herd (of March) of the existing Penske design. In the first five races of the year the cars were driven by Jarier and Jochen Mass, but no success was gained and at Monaco both cars failed to qualify. Thereafter Jarier was dropped from the team (but appeared again at the Nürburgring, where he failed to qualify) and Mass was entered along with a number of other drivers of varying ability, Alberto Colombo (entered twice and failed to qualify twice), Keke Rosberg, who at least turned in some encouraging performances, Hans Binder and Michael Bleekemolen.

In practice at Zandvoort the ATS team brought out the new D1 'wing' car designed by John Gentry. The new car featured revised rear suspension, much wider front and rear track and new bodywork. Mass crashed the first D1 in testing at Silverstone and put himself out of racing with a broken leg. The D1 was finally driven in the last two races of the season, the Canadian and United States GPs, by Rosberg.

D2 and D3 – 1979

Schmid engaged Fred Opert and Vic Elford to manage the team in 1979 and Giacomo Caliri was commissioned to develop the D2. The main changes were to the aerodynamics and the adoption of inboard rear springs. Throughout the year the team entered a single car for Hans-Joachim Stuck, but it proved yet another dismal catalogue of

6. ATS were never front-runners and became increasingly disorganized as season succeeded season. Here Slim Borgudd drives the HGS1 in the 1981 Italian Grand Prix. He spun off into retirement.

failure (on occasions Stuck did not even qualify). Three of the D2 cars were built, but in Austria ATS revealed the D3, outwardly very similar to its predecessor but with new monocoque and suspension and designed by Nigel Stroud – Caliri had been sacked from the team by the time of the Belgian GP. The best performance of the year was a stalwart drive by Stuck into fifth place in the wet at Watkins Glen.

D3 and D4 – 1980

For 1980 Gustav Brunner was brought into the team and updated the cars to D4 specification, with shorter wheelbase, wider track, other minor changes and more than a passing resemblance to the Williams FWO7, and team management was now the responsibility of Jo Ramirez. There were two D3s updated to D4 specification and six new D4s. Mark Surer and Jan Lammers started the season in D3s in the Argentine and Mark Surer drove the first of the D4s at Kyalami, where he crashed heavily in practice, breaking his legs and writing off the first of the new cars. Surer was fit to drive again by the French race at the end of June, ATS continued to enter only one car and Lammers went off to drive for Ensign. Although ATS reliability improved

7. The 1984 ATS D7 was the last of the line before the team withdrew from racing at the end of the year. Here the BMW-powered car is driven in the Dutch Grand Prix by the late Manfred Winkelhock.

as the season progressed, no Championship points were scored and it was all looking rather hopeless, a typical also-ran with no design or management initiative and no likelihood of improvement.

D4 and HGS1 – 1981

During the early part of 1981 ATS continued to race the D4 with Jan Lammers at the wheel. For the European races ATS secured sponsorship from ABBA and entered a second car with Swedish drummer Slim Borgudd at the wheel at Imola. By the Belgian race ATS were back to a single car for Borgudd, but it was the new HGS1 designed by Hervé Guilpin, an improvement on its predecessor and a typical design of its period with no innovative design features. After running the D4 again at Monaco (where Borgudd failed to qualify), the HGS1 reappeared in Spain and raced for the remainder of the year, but the only Championship points gained was a sixth place in the British GP.

D5 – 1982

Alastair Caldwell assumed team management for the following season and ATS raced modified versions of the HGS1, now known as the D5, entering a pair of cars for Manfred Winkelhock and Eliseo Salazar. Once again the cars proved neither conspicuously quick nor notably reliable, but Salazar finished fifth in the very thinly supported San Marino GP at Imola (Winkelhock was sixth on the road but disqualified because his car was under the minimum weight at the finish) and Winkelhock was promoted from seventh to fifth place in the Brazilian race after the disqualification of leaders on the road Piquet and Rosberg.

D6 – 1983

For 1983 ATS succeeded in obtaining BMW turbocharged engines, and while it seemed that there were several other teams that would have been worthier recipients of turbocharged engines, BMW's interest was their wish to support German driver Manfred Winkelhock, who had done well in the past with BMW-powered Formula Two cars. Brunner devised the new D6 with carbon-fibre monocoque, Hewland gearbox modified by ATS to suit the BMW engine and front and rear suspension by double wishbones, pullrods and inboard springs. The wheelbase was 8 ft 8 in., front track 5 ft 9 in. and rear track 5 ft 4 in. Three of these cars were built during the year. Although several other teams, notably Arrows, Ligier, McLaren, Tyrrell and Williams, were still struggling with Cosworth power, the team was so hopelessly organized that Winkelhock failed to finish in the first six at any race, finished only four times out of fifteen starts, failed to qualify in Germany and was disqualified at Zandvoort.

D6 and D7 – 1984

In 1984 ATS raced one of the D6 cars and a pair of D7s, slightly modified versions of the 1983 cars. The season started badly in Brazil, where Winkelhock was disqualified because the mechanics had pushed the car on the circuit during practice (he would probably have been allowed to start if Schmid had not lost his temper with the organizers) and the D6 was written off by Winkelhock in practice at Monaco. The team did not even finish until Winkelhock took eighth place in Canada in June. In a number of races ATS entered a second car for Gerhard Berger and he scored the team's best performance, a sixth place at Monza.

At the end of the year BMW withdrew supplies of engines and the long, fraught dreary story of ATS was at an end.

Bellasi

(Italy)

Swiss amateur Silvio Moser commissioned this private venture Formula One car from Italian constructor Vittorio Bellasi, who had previously built a number of rather flimsy-looking Formula Three cars. The Bellasi featured a simple riveted aluminium monocoque with tubular sub-frame carrying the radiator and front suspension. The suspension was derived from that of the Brabham BT24 raced by Moser in 1969 and the Cosworth DFV engine and the gearbox came from the same source (Moser had replaced the usual Repco engine in the BT24).

The Bellasi was rather bulky, heavy and uncompetitive. Moser first drove the car at Zandvoort in 1970, but failed to qualify, started from the back of the grid in Austria (he retired because of a holed radiator) and failed to qualify at Monza. A year elapsed without the car being raced and Moser tried again, without success, to qualify at Monza in 1971. The Bellasi is now in Tom Wheatcroft's collection at the Donington circuit.

Brabham
(United Kingdom)

Brabham cars were built by Motor Racing Developments, a business run jointly by driver Jack Brabham and designer Ron Tauranac with support from the Australian Repco company. During the years of the 1500 cc Grand Prix Formula the Climax-powered cars were entered by the Brabham Racing Organization. Tauranac had no direct interest in this company and as a result was none too interested in building a new team of Formula One cars. This problem was resolved only in November 1965, by a new agreement between Brabham and Tauranac, as a result of which the cars were henceforth entered under the banner of Motor Racing Developments (MRD).

BT19 and BT20 – 1966

Jack Brabham had already solved the problem of finding an engine to power the new car, a 3-litre version of the Oldsmobile F85 developed by the Australian Repco company for Tasman racing. The Oldsmobile had been evolved as a 3.5-litre V-8 production unit by General Motors, but then abandoned after a costly development programme. Frank Hallam (the chief engineer) and Phil Irving (development engineer) chose the Oldsmobile because the block could be adapted for capacities ranging from 2.5 to 4.4-litres and because it had considerable development potential.

The aluminium block was stiffened by a steel tie-plate between the crankcase and sump, and the centre-camshaft operating the overhead valves by long push-rods was replaced by a single overhead camshaft per bank of cylinders; there was a new Laystall crankshaft running in five bearings; the bores had Repco cast liners; and there were Repco pistons and Daimler con-rods. Additional stiffening was provided by a ribbed sump with a depth of 3.25 in. The 2.5-litre Repco engine first ran in March 1965, and it was at about this time that Brabham requested the company to produce a Grand Prix version. Repco evolved the type 620 with a capacity of 2994 cc (88.9 × 60.3 mm) and, with Lucas fuel injection, developing about 285 bhp at 8000 rpm.

There was a frantic rush to get a car ready in time for the South African GP, a non-Championship race in 1966, but the first of the new Formula and held on 2 January. Like both Cooper and Lotus, the MRD organization had constructed a chassis to take the still-born flat-16 1500 cc Coventry-Climax engine that had never reached the race track. This was the BT19, which was hastily adapted to suit the needs of the new Formula. Tauranac had consistently avoided succumbing to the fashion of building monocoque chassis initiated by Lotus in 1962 and, in the interests of simplicity and ease of repair (coupled with adequate rigidity), the BT19 retained a multi-tubular space-frame, but with oval-section tubes round the cockpit area to provide additional strengthening at this critical point.

At the front there were unequal-length double wishbones, consisting of an upper transverse link and trailing radius rod and a lower one-piece tubular wishbone, and outboard coil spring/damper units. The rear suspension consisted of single upper links, reversed lower wishbones, twin radius rods and coil spring/damper units. Originally 13 in. wheels with 10.5 in. disc brakes were fitted, but the team later substituted 15 in. rear wheels with 11 in. disc brakes. Transmission was

8. Brabham proved the dominant make in 1966–67. At Monaco in 1967 Jack Brabham drove this old BT19 car with the first centre-exhaust 740 Repco engine. Brabham retired on the first lap because of a broken con-rod, but team-mate Hulme won the race.

initially by a Hewland HD 5-speed gearbox, but this was later replaced by the stronger DG unit. The wheelbase was 7 ft 8 in., front track 4 ft 5.5 in. and rear track 4 ft 6 in.

In the early part of the season, while Brabham drove the BT19, number two driver Denis Hulme had to make do with a 1964–65 1500 cc chassis powered by the 'Tasman' 2.75-litre version of the Coventry-Climax FPF engine. Initially little success came MRD's way, although Brabham took pole position in South Africa and led until the fuel injection pump seized, and scored a win in the thinly supported International Trophy at Silverstone. The next development was the BT20, which appeared at the French GP. The BT20 was constructed from round-section tubing throughout, the main lower chassis members were revised, the cockpit area was stengthened by twin side-tubes and the suspension, although basically similar, had revised geometry to suit 15 in. wheels front and rear. Initially 12 in. brake discs were fitted, but smaller 11 in. discs were later substituted. In appearance there was little to distinguish the cars apart from the fact that the BT20 had two small engine covers (instead of the BT19's one-piece cowling) and a revised exhaust system curling round the upper radius arms (on the BT19 the exhausts ran tortuously between the pairs of radius arms). The BT20 had sligtly longer 7 ft 9.5 in. wheelbase, wider 4 ft 9.5 in. front track and 4 ft 6.75 in. rear track.

It was at this point in the season that the MRD team hit winning form and Brabham forged ahead to win from Parkes (Ferrari) and team-mate Hulme. This was the first of a series of wins and Jack Brabham took first places at Brands Hatch (Hulme was second), Zandvoort and the Nürburgring. Hulme took third place at Monza, and at Mexico City Brabham and Hulme were second and third behind Surtees's Cooper-Maserati. Jack Brabham convincingly won his third World Championship with a total of 42 points.

BT19, BT20 and BT24 – 1967

For 1967 Repco developed the 40-series cylinder heads with the exhausts in the vee of the engine and the inlet ports on the outside. Otherwise the cars were unchanged at the start of the season. Jack Brabham won the Spring Cup at Oulton Park with a car fitted with the 640 engine (that is the 1966 block and 1967 heads) and took second place in the International Trophy at Silverstone with a 1966 620-engined car. At Monaco Brabham drove the original BT19 with the full 1967 740 engine having the new cylinder heads, redesigned aluminium alloy crankcase and a power output of 330 bhp at 8000 rpm. Brabham retired on the first lap, but Hulme won the race with a 620-powered car. Driving these same cars Brabham and Hulme took second and third places in the Dutch GP behind Clark's new Lotus 49.

In the transporter at Zandvoort was Tauranac's latest car, the BT24, which made its debut in the Belgian race with Brabham at the wheel. The new car was derived from the Formula Two-chassised BT23A raced in the Tasman series and was lighter and more compact than its predecessors. Although the wheelbase was unchanged, the front track was slightly narrower and the rear track slightly wider, there were new cast magnesium front suspension uprights, a lightweight Formula Two Hewland FT200 gearbox (insufficiently robust and replaced by the usual DG300 after the Spa race) and a detachable nose-cone. The Belgian GP was a bad race for the team and both entries (Hulme drove the BT19) retired with oil scavenge pump failure.

During the remainder of the season the Brabhams were no match for the Lotus opposition, but scored well when the 49s ran into problems. With BT24s Brabham and Hulme took the first two places in the French GP on the Bugatti Circuit at Le Mans, Hulme finished second at Silverstone, won the German GP (Brabham was second) and Brabham and Hulme were again first and second in the Canadian GP. At Monza Jack Brabham tried in practice only a BT24 fitted with a bubble cockpit canopy and gearbox cover and in a closely fought race he finished second to Surtees's Honda. After third place by Hulme at Watkins Glen (Brabham was fifth), Brabham and Hulme finished second and third in Mexico. Hulme took the World Championship with 51 points to Jack's 46 points. It had been great while it lasted, but it seemed most unlikely that the Brabhams could prove a match for the ever-improving Lotus 49s and be capable of beating other new Ford-powered cars destined to appear in 1968.

BT26 – 1968

Denis Hulme left to drive for fellow New Zealander Bruce McLaren in 1968 and his place in the Brabham team was taken by Jochen Rindt. At the South African race Brabham fielded BT24s and Rindt finished third. For the European season Tauranac developed the BT26, a lighter and stronger car with alloy sheet panelling instead of tubular triangulation, smaller-gauge thinner-section tubing, a longer 7 ft 11 in. wheelbase and 5 in. wider track. In most other respects, power unit apart, the BT26 closely resembled its 1967 predecessors. The engine, however, was the new Repco 860 with a lighter cylinder block that could only be used in 2.5- and 3-litre forms, new crankshaft, nitrided gear train, twin overhead camshafts per bank of cylinders and a power output of 375 bhp at 9000 rpm. Unfortunately the new engine proved hopelessly unreliable, and with a distance of around 12,000 miles separating the team's racing activities and Repco's engineering department, there was little scope for 'feed-back' of information and eradication of the engine's shortcomings.

Initially only one BT26 was ready and in the first races Jochen Rindt drove a BT24. In the Belgian race at Spa MRD introduced a rear aerofoil on the BT26, an innovation shared by Ferrari at the same race. It was a dreadful season for the team, at most races both entries retired and the only performances worthy of mention were Rindt's pole position on the grid in the French GP at Rouen (he retired in the race) and third and fifth places by Rindt and Brabham in the rain-soaked German GP.

BT26A – 1969

For the 1969 season the Brabham team retained the BT26 cars; the power unit was now the Ford V-8, new glass-fibre bodywork designed by Robin Herd was fitted and in this form the model was known as the BT26A. Jack Brabham was joined by young Belgian driver Jacky Ickx and the team received sponsorship from the Gulf Oil Corporation. A third, dark blue BT26A was driven by Piers Courage for private entrant Frank Williams, but this entry was looked upon without much favour by MRD. MRD had declined to sell a car to a potential Formula One rival and Williams had acquired his BT26 under the pretext that

9. In 1969 Frank Williams entered a Ford-powered BT26A Brabham for Piers Courage seen here on his way to second place at Monaco.

it was to be used for Formula 5000 racing.

The BT26As appeared in South Africa with fixed front and rear aerofoils, but both retired after the rear aerofoils broke. At the beginning of the European season Jack Brabham won the International Trophy at Silverstone and although Courage drove Williams's car to second at Monaco, the works cars were not in the running again until the French GP at Clermont-Ferrand, where Ickx finished third. By this time Jack had been sidelined by a broken ankle suffered in a practice crash and the team was entering just the one car. Ickx took second place in the British GP at Silverstone and followed this up with victories in the German GP and also the very unimportant Gold Cup race at Oulton Park. Jack was back behind the wheel at Monza, but both entries fell by the wayside. Ickx won in Canada after a long battle with Stewart (Matra), Courage brought his now much-modified car across the line second at Watkins Glen and Ickx and Brabham finished second and third in Mexico. Ickx finished second in the World Championship.

BT33 – 1970

For 1970 Ron Tauranac produced a new Ford-powered contender, the BT33, the first monocoque Formula One Brabham to comply with the new regulation that fuel tanks must be sheathed. This was inspired by the team's only previous monocoque design (the 1968 Indianapolis BT25) and directly derived from the BT26, which had been a 'half-way' house between a space-frame and a monocoque. Ickx returned to the Ferrari team, for whom he had driven in 1968, Brabham lost its Gulf Oil sponsorship and the team raced on a very small budget. Only a single turquoise and yellow car for Jack Brabham was entered in 1970, but a second, white-painted BT33 sponsored by the magazine *Auto Motor und Sport* was run by the works for young German driver Rolf Stommelen.

Jack Brabham made a brilliant start to the season by winning the South African GP at record speed. At Monaco he was so very close to another victory when he slid into the barriers at the Gasworks hairpin on the last lap, partly because of failing brakes, and rejoined to finish second to Rindt (Lotus). Stommelen finished fifth at Spa and Jack took third place in the French GP – and then suffered his second big disappointment of the year at Brands Hatch. The Australian slipped into the lead ahead of Rindt's Lotus and stayed in front only to run out of fuel on the last lap and coast across the line in second place. The remainder of the season proved disappointing and the best performances were both by Stommelen, fifth in the German GP and third in Austria.

BT33 and BT34 – 1971

At the end of 1970 Jack Brabham retired from racing and returned to Australia, but Ron Tauranac soldiered on with the team for one more season. Graham Hill was team leader and although Dave Charlton drove for Brabham at Kyalami, for the rest of the year the number two driver was young Australian Tim Schenken. Although the team continued to rely on the BT33 at Brands Hatch in March Tauranac revealed his latest development, the novel 'lobster-claw' BT34, so-called because there were twin radiators on either side at the front between the 'claws' of which the aerofoil was mounted. By shielding the front tyres, air flow was improved, and although later design practice dictated that the radiators should not be at the front of the car, many other designers later adopted full-width nose cones. The BT34, of which only one example was built, was basically a derivative of the BT33, but other changes included increased front and rear track (5 ft 2 in. and 5 ft 3 in. respectively); this car had a rather square appearance resulting from the use of rectangular side fuel tanks which

10. Graham Hill with the one-off Brabham BT34 in practice for the 1971 Monaco Grand Prix. In the race he was eliminated when he collided with the barriers on the second lap.

Tauranac was able to have made from a single sheet of steel with only one seam and which, in his view, were less likely to deform in the event of an accident.

It proved a bitterly unsuccessful year for the team and the only real success was Hill's win with the BT34 in the International Trophy at Silverstone. Throughout the year a number of minor changes were made to the cars. The BT33 was fitted with the slightly modified rear suspension of the BT34 and the lighter Hewland FG300 gearbox. High-mounted ram-type air boxes were adopted at the French GP and Schenken's BT33 was fitted with a full-width nose in the Austrian race. The best performances of the year were a sixth place by Schenken in Germany and a third by Schenken in Austria (Hill was fifth).

BT33, BT 34 and BT37 – 1972

At the end of 1971 MRD was sold to Bernie Ecclestone, who had raced Cooper 500 cars in the Fifties, entered a brace of Grand Prix Connaughts after they had been auctioned off and had latterly acted as Jochen Rindt's racing manager. The team was now managed by Keith Greene and design and development work rested with former

11. Carlos Reutemann on his way to victory in the 1974 Austrian Grand Prix with the Gordon Murray-designed Brabham BT44.

McLaren man Ralph Bellamy and Gordon Murray. Graham Hill drove a modified BT33 early in the season, switching to the new BT37 at Jarama, while team-mate Carlos Reutemann drove the BT34 with modified bodywork in the Argentine and South Africa and was then seen with a BT37 from Nivelles onwards. For much of the season the team entered a third car for Wilson Fittipaldi. The BT37 was derived from the BT34, but featured a conventional radiator at the front and complied with the deformable structure tank protection regulations.

The Brabham team was without major sponsorhip and in their unadorned white finish looked neat and effective. There was not much success gained, although Reutemann won the non-Championship Brazilian GP at Interlagos. The best performances were sixth by Hill at the Nürburgring, fifth by Hill at Monza and fourth by Reutemann in Canada.

Another Brabham development in 1972 was the construction of the BT39 prototype car to take the Weslake Type 190 V-12 engine (a derivative of the Gurney-Weslake V-12 used in the Eagle) and based on the BT38 Formula Two monocoque. The engine proved insufficiently powerful and the project was quickly abandoned.

BT37 and BT42 – 1973

For 1973 Bellamy left to join Lotus and design responsibility was assumed by young Gordon Murray, who has remained in charge ever since. Two BT37 cars were raced early in the season, but at the Race of Champions the team introduced the BT42 that incorporated all Murray's advanced ideas. The basis of the new car was a monocoque of triangular pyramid section with simple fuel system (three tanks only) and very short wheelbase (at 7 ft 10 in. it was the shortest of all the contenders, but the Tyrrell's wheelbase was only .5 in. longer). Track was also narrow, 4 ft 9.5 in. at the front and 4 ft 9 in. at the rear. Murray retained twin radiators ahead of the front wheels faired into a streamlined full-width nose. The result was a car of compact, low and distinctive shape with frontal area substantially lower than that of many of the Brabham's rivals. Suspension was conventional, at the front by double wishbones and outboard coil springs and at the rear by parallel lower links, single top links, twin radius rods and outboard springs.

Brabham's successes were limited in 1973, partly because the team was still very much in the learning curve and there were problems of stiffness and suspension geometry that remained unresolved; and partly because the team's drivers were not the most experienced or able. The first of the new cars was written off when John Watson crashed heavily at Stirling's Bend at Brands Hatch after the throttles had jammed open; he broke both legs and put himself out of racing until June. The regular drivers were Reutemann and Wilson Fittipaldi, whilst a third car was entered for Andrea de Adamich with Ceramica Pagnossin sponsorship. De Adamich wrote off BT37/1 in Spain when he lost a wheel as a result of hub failure and at Silverstone, Scheckter (McLaren) initiated a multi-car crash that resulted in de Adamich being trapped in his car with two broken legs and BT42/4 becoming another write-off. By the Nürburgring his place had been taken by Rolf Stommelen and Watson reappeared in the United States. The best performances during the year were a fourth by de Adamich (BT37) at Zolder, and all by Reutemann, fourth in Sweden, third in France, fourth in Austria, sixth at Monza and third at Watkins Glen.

BT44 – 1974

Over the winter months Murray evolved the improved BT44 car with unchanged dimensions, slightly modified bodywork to improve aerodynamics, additional stiffening and much improved front suspension incorporating pullrod rising rate linkages, while, initially, the rear suspension remained unchanged. Carlos Reutemann remained with the team, but he was partnered by the unknown Richard Robarts. Robarts soon revealed that he was struggling; in Spain his place was taken by Rikki von Opel (another young man with more financial backing than ability), but von Opel failed to qualify at two races and gave way to Carlos Pace at Brands Hatch. The Brazilian Pace soon settled into the team and showed his ability. The BT42s had been sold off and were raced as private entries and without doubt the only serious private contender was John Watson with the Hexagon-entered car.

Reutemann led the Argentine GP until he ran out of fuel (the result of a refuelling error on the morning of the race), briefly led in Brazil before dropping back because of tyre problems and scored an excellent first win in South Africa. At Monaco Watson took sixth place with the Hexagon BT42 and Reutemann finished sixth at Brands Hatch. A third for Reutemann followed at the Nürburgring, Reutemann won a hard-fought Austrian GP, Pace was fifth at Monza and the team rounded off the year with a brilliant one-two at Watkins Glen, Reutemann leading Pace across the line. Brabham was going places again.

BT44B – 1975

Reutemann and Pace stayed with Brabham for 1975 and Murray was content to race the slightly modified BT44B cars with slightly narrower front track, strengthened monocoques and more aerodynamic bodywork. Throughout the year Murray's main efforts were concentrated on aerodynamic improvements. The biggest change, however, was that Brabham now had major sponsorship from Martini & Rossi.

The Brabhams led the Argentine GP in the opening laps and Reutemann eventually finished third. Then Pace scored a brilliant win on home territory in the Brazilian GP, Reutemann was second at Kyalami and third in Spain (the race was stopped after 29 laps), Pace third at Monaco, and Reutemann third at Zolder, second in Sweden and third at Zandvoort (Pace was fourth). Pace was classified second in the British GP abandoned after 56 laps because of a torrential downpour – the results stood as at the end of lap 55, when most of the drivers, including Pace, had crashed. Reutemann scored his only Grand Prix victory of the year at the Nürburgring and subsequently finished fourth at Monza. Reutemann was third in the Drivers' Championship and Brabham, thanks to so many consistent performances, second to Ferrari in the Constructor's Cup.

BT45 – 1976

For some while Ecclestone had been negotiating with Autodelta to use their Tipo 115 flat-12 engine of 2995 cc (77 × 53.6 mm) which had been primarily developed for sports car racing. It was a bulky engine that was destined to develop around 510 bhp at 12,000 rpm towards the end of the 1976 season and in theory offered a distinct power advantage over the familiar Cosworth DFV. While Autodelta were working intensively to adapt the flat-12 to Formula One use and throughout the year concentrated on improving reliability and reducing fuel consumption and weight, Murray had evolved a new chassis to take the engine. The BT45 featured a very wide monocoque, the widest permitted by the regulations; the engine could not be used as a stressed member so two pontoons ran rearwards surmounted at their extremities by tall, slim cold air boxes. The Alfa engine was used initially in conjunction with the Hewland FG400 5-speed gearbox. At the front and rear suspension was basically similar to that of the BT44B. Wheelbase was increased to 8 ft 2 in., and the car was all of 60 lb heavier than its predecessor.

Although Brabham received the engines free of charged from Autodelta and there was increased sponsorship from Martini, the team and the drivers, Reutemann and Pace, faced an uphill struggle to make the cars competitive. In Spain Reutemann and Pace managed fourth and sixth places and already the cars had been much lightened. At Monaco Pace's car was fitted with a 6-speed gearbox and this was soon adopted on both cars. Pace finished fourth in the French GP on the Paul Ricard circuit, where the cars appeared with rising-rate front suspension, deep skirting round the perimeter of the monocoque and other detail changes. The BT45s showed devastating straight-line speed and Pace was timed on the Mistral straight at 177.37 mph – in the race he finished fourth. At the Nürburgring Pace again finished fourth and sixth place went to Rolf Stommelen with the spare works car after a court injunction had prevented him from driving a RAM Racing-entered BT44B. After the Dutch GP Reutemann left the team to drive for Ferrari and his place was taken initially by Stommelen and for the last three races of the year by Australian Larry Perkins. No further finishes in the points were gained that year.

BT45 and BT45B – 1977

At the start of the 1977 season the team continued to field the BT45 cars, now somewhat reduced in weight, much developed and with power output now around 520 bhp. The drivers were Carlos Pace and John Watson. In the Argentine the Brabhams set the pace but Watson retired because of broken suspension mountings and because of heat exhaustion Pace dropped back to finish second to Scheckter's Wolf. The BT45B appeared at Kyalami and was a much improved car with the engine 1.5 in. lower in the chassis, the Brabham/Alfa Romeo 6-speed gearbox and parallel link rear suspension. Pace finished at the tail of the field with the new car after a pit stop and Watson with an original BT45 was sixth. This was Pace's last race for the team as, sadly, he was killed in a crash in a light aircraft. His place in the team was taking by Hans-Joachim Stuck. Apart from a third place in the Race of Champions by Watson, Stuck finished sixth in Spain and sixth in Belgium, Watson was fifth in Sweden and second in the French GP – but the cars had been showing tremendous form and Watson had only lost out in the French race through running out of fuel. At Silverstone Stuck finished fifth, he was third at Hockenheim and third in Austria. Throughout the year the cars had showed immense promise, but too many things had gone wrong, and as the season progressed Watson's frustration became more and more obvious.

BT45C, BT46 and BT46B – 1978

The 1978 season revealed a series of dramatic Brabham innovations from designer Gordon Murray. The most significant development was the surface-cooled BT46 with triangular monocoque and very small frontal area. The cooling of water and oil was achieved through two water and two oil surface heat exchangers mounted within the monocoque and the liquid flowing through a double-skinned channel and finned outer surface. Other features of this revolutionary design were digital read-out displays for the main instruments, an on-board air jacking system to speed up wheel changes during practice and a lighter gearbox. Sadly the cooling system did not work, the car overheated, and so at the beginning of the year Brabham was forced to race the BT45C cars, which sported very slim full-width front radiators. Niki Lauda joined the team from Ferrari, bringing with him as sponsor the

12. Niki Lauda won the 1978 Swedish Grand Prix with the controversial BT46 fan car. Although the win was allowed to stand, the fan car was subsequently banned.

Parmalat Italian dairy food company, and Watson remained with Brabham.

In the Argentine Lauda took an excellent second place, he finished third in Brazil and by the South African race in March Murray had ready revised versions of the BT46. These were now in conventional form with nose radiators. Watson finished third at Kyalami, Lauda was second at Monaco with Watson fourth and Watson was fifth in Spain. At the Swedish GP at Anderstorp Murray unveiled another dramatic development, the BT46B 'fan car'. The water radiator was mounted horizontally on top of the engine, the engine and gearbox were sealed off from outside air by flexible skirts and at the rear of the car a large fan driven from the gearbox sucked the air out from the engine bay. It was a brilliant concept in that it both achieved the slim frontal area that Murray had planned for the BT46 originally and also glued the car firmly to the road. Watson retired early in the race, but Lauda went on to a fine victory over 30 seconds ahead of Patrese's Arrows. Although the win was allowed to stand, following protests from other teams the CSI banned the 'fan car' from Formula One.

As a result Murray was forced to abandon the BT47, a more sophisticated version of the 'fan car' theme, and for the rest of the year the team raced the BT46s. During the year Brabham achieved a good measure of success with fourth place by Watson in the French GP, second and third places by Lauda and Watson at Brands Hatch, third and fourth places by Lauda and Watson at Zandvoort and, in the restarted Italian GP, Lauda and Watson were first and second. The year had been one of domination by the Lotus 79 and Mario Andretti and Brabham's uphill struggle to remain competitive had resulted in fourth place in the Drivers' Championship for Lauda and third place in the Constructors' Cup.

BT48 and BT49 – 1979

While Murray concentrated on the development of a new ground-effect design for the 1979 season, Alfa Romeo developed the new V-12 Tipo 1260 engine developing 525 bhp at 12,300 rpm and still used in conjunction with the Brabham/Alfa Romeo gearbox. The new BT48 took the engine as a stressed member, the monocoque was constructed from aluminium-alloy sheet with carbon fibre composite structural panels (Murray was the first to use these on a Formula One car) and front and rear suspension by pull-rod-operated double wishbones and inboard coil spring/damper units. Both the Brabham and the new Lotus 80 featured full-length underwings. Drivers were Niki Lauda and Nelson Piquet.

In the Argentine (where Piquet drove a BT46) the BT48 was discoverd to be suffering from the most appalling handling and porpoising problems and Brabham spent much of the year struggling to sort out both a new chassis and new engine. By the Brazilian GP the team had two BT48s prepared with new skirts in a honeycomb material, improved fuel systems and conventional rear wings to replace the low wings fitted at Buenos Aires. That the cars were improving was clear when Lauda and Piquet finished sixth and seventh in South Africa. The main problem was the engines, and although the Brabhams were often quick in qualifying, the Alfa side of the business rarely lasted race distance. The sum total of success in Championship races by the Alfa-powered cars was two fourth places, by Piquet at Zandvoort and by Lauda at Monza. In addition Lauda won a battle with Villeneuve's Ferrari to take victory in the non-Championship Imola race.

As the Brabham became increasingly depressed with these successive failures and it became known that Alfa Romeo were embarking on their own racing programme, the team decided to switch back to Ford DFV power. In a very short space of time three BT49 cars were built, two converted from BT48 specification and one from scratch. The new cars looked very much like their predecessors, but there had been substantial changes behind the cockpit. In Canada Niki Lauda, unexpectedly, decided to retire from racing and young Argentinian Riccardo Zunino was hastily brought into the team. In the last two races of the year no success was gained, but at least Brabham knew that they were on the right lines of development.

BT49 and BT49B – 1980

For Brabham the year was to prove the best since Ecclestone had taken over the team, and although the Williams FW07B and Alan Jones were to prove the dominant combination, Piquet enjoyed a fine run of success and took second place in the Drivers' Championship. Zunino remained with the team without achieving anything in the way of success until the French GP and his place was then taken by Hector Rebaque who was sponsored by Pemex, the Mexican national petrol corporation. Piquet started the season well with a second place in the Argentine, fourth in South Africa and scored a fine win at Long Beach. At Long Beach Brabham revealed their new 5/6-speed gearbox designed by American Pete Weismann, and when the cars ran with this transmission they were known as the BT49B. This gearbox was soon abandoned. Piquet finished third at Monaco, fourth in the French GP, second in the British race, fourth at Hockenheim, fifth in Austria and won at Zandvoort and Monza.

BT49C – 1981

For 1981 Brabham relied on the BT49C, a lighter, neater version of the 1980 car featuring greater use of carbon fibre composite panels and no sliding skirts. During the year the team revealed the BMW turbo-powered BT50 at Silverstone, but that was under development for 1982. Brabham drivers remained Nelson Piquet, who was to win his first Drivers' Championship by a narrow margin, and Hector Rebaque. At the start of the season Piquet finished second in the South African GP, held as a non-Championship race, and victory went to Carlos Reutemann at the wheel of a Williams, his closest challenger throughout the year. Piquet was beaten into third place by the Williams entries of Jones and Reutemann at Long Beach and was out of the running in Brazil because of a bad choice of tyres. The first of Piquet's victories came in the Argentine and in the San Marino GP at Imola. There was constant dissension throughout the season over the question of skirts and in South America the BT49 was fitted with a system of soft air-springs so that the aerodynamic load dropped the car to a ground effective position at speed, but as the car slowed on returning to the pits it rose to comply with the 6 cm ground clearance rule imposed in 1981.

In the French GP Piquet finished third, he scored a fine victory in the German GP at Hockenheim, was third again in Austria, second in Holland, sixth at Monza, fifth in Canada and fifth in the Caesar's Palace GP at Las Vegas. Piquet won the Championship by one point, 50 points to the 49 of Reutemann and 46 of the other Williams driver Alan Jones. In the Constructors' Cup Williams, with two strong drivers, were convincing winners with 95 points to the 61 of Brabham.

BT49D and BT50 – 1982

Back in 1980 Bernie Ecclestone had first come to terms with BMW to run Formula One cars powered by the German turbocharged engines

13. Nelson Piquet with the Ford-powered Brabham BT49C in the 1981 Austrian Grand Prix. Piquet won the World Championship that year by the margin of a single point.

and the fruits of their co-operation were first seen in 1982. The BMW M12/13 was a 4-cylinder 1499 cc (89.2 × 60 mm) with Bosch fuel and ingnition systems, a KKK turbocharger and a power output at this stage in its development of 570 bhp at 10,800 rpm. It was used in conjunction with the Brabham/Alfa Romeo gearbox. Murray's design to take the new engine was the BT50, derived from the BT49C, but with a 1 in. longer wheelbase (9 ft 0 in.), a larger 48-gallon fuel cell concealed by the curving rear bodywork and only marginally heavier than the BT49C. In addition the team had prepared the BT49D Cosworth-powered cars with carbon fibre brake discs, water-cooled braking systems and one-piece bodywork. Piquet was joined in the Brabham team by Riccardo Patrese.

At the first race of the season at Kyalami Brabham ran the BMW-powered BT50s, but both were eliminated. The team reverted to the BT49Ds in Brazil, and although Piquet finished first on the road, he was disqualified because the water-cooled brake system meant that the car was below the minimum weight at the end of a race and was only within limits when it had been topped up – it was the start of another long and bitter wrangle. At Long Beach Patrese was classified third after Villeneuve had been disqualified because the dimensions of his rear aerofoil infringed the rules. The Brabham team missed the Imola race because of a dispute between FISA (the governing body of the sport) and FOCA (the Constructors' association). Piquet took fifth place at Zolder with a BMW-powered car and Patrese won at Monaco with a BT49D. One car of each type ran at Detroit and Montreal and Piquet scored a very unexpected win in the Canadian race and thereafter only BMW-powered cars were entered. A fine second place for Piquet followed at Zandvoort and Piquet took a fourth place in the Swiss GP held at Dijon, but there were no other Championship points gained during what was primarily a season of development.

BT52 – 1983

During 1982 Murray had developed a new ground-effect car for the coming season, but this, typed the BT51, had to be abandoned when skirts were banned altogether at the end of 1982 and the flat-bottom rule was introduced. Murray produced another completely new design, the BT52, which was unveiled in March. The monocoque combined a lower section constructed from aluminium panelling with a moulded carbon fibre composite upper section. A magnesium casting at the front of the monocoque carried the inboard coil spring/damper units operated by a double wishbone and pushrod system. The BMW engine was mounted on a steel frame and aluminium plate bolted to the rear of the monocoque. The bellhousing was integral with the casing of the new Brabham gearbox using Hewland internals and also acted as the engine oil tank. Rear suspension was by double wishbone and push-rods. Carbon fibre brake discs were used and the radiators were mounted just ahead of the rear wheels. With no need to consider the problems of ground effects, the BT52 was delightfully sleek and slim and it was apparent that with a fuel capacity of only 42 gallons Brabham would be pursuing the policy of refuelling stops that they had initiated in 1982. The BT52 had a wheelbase of 9 ft 3 in., front track of 5 ft 9 in. and rear track of 5 ft 4 in.

It was to prove a dramatically successful year for the team and Piquet won the Brazilian, Italian and European (Brands Hatch) GPs, with second places in the French, Monaco and British races, together with a third place in Austria and fourths in Belgium and at Detroit. In addition Patrese won the last round of the Championship in South Africa. Piquet snatched the World Championship with 59 points to the 57 of Renault driver Alain Prost, but Brabham were only third in the Constructors' Cup behind Ferrari and Renault. From the British GP onwards the team had raced the improved BT52B cars with improved aerodynamics, many minor changes to the monocoque and a distinctive change of livery from primarily white with blue to primarily blue with white.

14. Nelson Piquet, 1983 World Champion, and the Brabham BT52B which he drove to victory that year in the Grand Prix of Europe at Brands Hatch.

BT53 and BT53B – 1984

Few changes were made to the cars for 1984, when they were known as BT53s, but there were larger fuel cells now that pit stops to refuel were banned. Although the power of the BMW engine was now claimed to be as much as 850 bhp, the Brabhams, now driven by Piquet and Teo Fabi, found themselves very much playing second fiddle to the new TAG-engined McLarens of Prost and Lauda. The Brabhams still displayed a sufficient turn of speed for Piquet to take pole position and lead the race at Kyalami, but they were always in trouble and it was not until the Canadian GP that they managed to combine speed with reliability, and here Piquet, fastest in practice, scored his first victory of the year and followed it up a week later with another win at Detroit.

By the British GP Murray had evolved the improved BT53B, with new rear wing, aerodynamics, radiators and rear suspension amongst myriad other changes. By the Austrian race Brabham had reverted to the BT53, now fitted with the BT53B rear suspension and rear body underwings. The team's fortunes improved in Austria, where Piquet finished second and Fabi took fourth place. Fabi finished fifth at Zandvoort, Piquet was third on the new Nürburgring and rounded off the season with sixth place in Portugal. He took fifth place in the World Championship with 29 points. Corrado Fabi, Teo's younger brother, had deputized at Monaco, Montreal and Dallas, when Teo had conflicting CART commitments in the United States, and Manfred Winkelhock deputized in Portugal when Teo had to rush home because of his father's death.

BT54 – 1985

Murray produced yet a further revised car for 1985, the BT54, still with aluminium outer skin stiffened by a moulded carbon-composite scuttle and tank top and with very slick lines. The front suspension, still by pushrod-operated double wishbones, was suspended from the bulkhead at the front of the monocoque in accordance with Murray's usual practice and a similar layout was adopted at the rear. Piquet stayed with the team and he was now partnered by François Hesnault. Hesnault failed to qualify at Monaco and his place in the team with effect from the postponed Belgian GP was taken by Marc Surer. The team was now sponsored by Olivetti. The Brabhams were running on Pirelli tyres, and throughout the year these seemed markedly inferior to the rival Goodyears. The team's only real success was in the French GP, which Piquet won in appalling hot weather, but he also managed a sixth place at Detroit, a fourth at Silverstone, a second at Monza and a fifth in the postponed Belgian GP at Spa. Surer took sixth places at Silverstone and in Austria and a fourth place at Monza. He was also in second place in the European GP at Brands Hatch when his car caught fire as a result of turbocharger failure.

BT55 – 1986

For 1986 Murray produced one of the most radical Formula One designs with an all-composite carbon-fibre and Kevlar monocoque produced as a one-piece seamless structure of exceptionally shallow construction. When the car was raced it looked conspicuously lower and longer than its rivals and had extermely low drag characteristics. The suspension was redesigned so that the coil spring/damper units were mounted further inboard with pullrod operation at the front and pushrod at the rear. The BMW engine, now claimed to provide 1100 bhp for qualifying and 900 bhp in race trim, was inclined 72 degrees to the left and used with a new 7-speed transversely mounted gearbox produced in the United States by Peter Weismann, as originally conceived, it appears that the driver was to be much more inclined than when the cars were raced, but the seat had to be moved nearer the vertical because of visibility problems. The drivers were Riccardo Patrese and Elio de Angelis,

From the start of the season the cars were plagued by development problems and at the time of writing had displayed considerable potential but little real form. They were out of contention during the first four rounds of the Championship and then de Angelis was fatally injured in a high-speed accident duing the testing at the Paul Ricard circuit. Patrese drove the sole Brabham entry at Spa, but thereafter he was joined by Derek Warwick, out of Formula One since Renault's retirement from racing.

BRM

(United Kingdom)

Throughout the years of the old 1500 cc Grand Prix Formula there had been a constant battle for surpremacy between BRM and Lotus. Although the Coventry Climax-powered cars of Colin Chapman had proved marginally more successful (two World Championships to the one of the Bourne team), there was little to choose between the two teams in terms of technical development, performance or team organization. Team Lotus embarked on the new Formula with a long wait before their new engine would be ready, while BRM, riding high on its earlier successes and with greater technical and engineering independence, was already well advanced with a new but very complex design that it was thought would soon become a race-winner.

At the beginning of the 1966 season BRM raced the familiar 1964–65 monocoque cars with front and rear double wishbone suspension, 6-speed gearbox and the four overhead camshaft, centre-exhaust V-8 engine featuring Lucas fuel injection, increased in capacity to 1930 cc and developing around 220 bhp.

P261 and P83 H-16 – 1966

BRM missed the non-Championship South African Grand Prix, but shortly afterwards competed with great success in the Tasman races, where the 2-litre version of the V-8 P261 was seen for the first time.

The first European outing in 1966 for the dark green cars was at Monaco, where 2-litre models were entered for Hill, and the team also brought along for practice only the first of their new 3-litre cars. Chief engineer Tony Rudd's latest design, designated the P83, was a very ambitious 2988 cc (69.85 × 49.89 mm) H-16 project consisting, in effect, of two of the 8-cylinder engines geared together and mounted in a slightly larger and rather more robust version of 1965 chassis. The banks of eight cylinders were now horizontally opposed and mounted on top of one another. The cylinder heads of the upper and lower halves of the engine were cast together, but the design retained the 1965 valves and similar camshafts (but, of course, with different firing sequence); the two nitrided flat crankshafts ran in plain bearings and there was a light alloy crankcase. Lucas fuel injection was fitted and on a compression ration of 11:1 power output was around 400 bhp at 11,000 rpm. In this initial form the H-16 fired as two 8-cylinder engines, but the firing sequence was later changed. Transmission was by a 6-speed gearbox with gear selection by a flexible cable system with special interlocking mechanism.

The H-16 engine was bolted directly to the rear bulkhead of the light alloy monocoque and this also carried the gearbox and rear suspension by means of long upper and lower arms. At the rear the suspension consisted of upper transverse links, lower wishbones, radius rods and coil spring/damper units, while at the front there were upper rocking arms, lower wishbones and inboard-mounted coil spring/damper units. BRM rack and pinion steering was fitted, there were 14 in. wheels front and rear and Girling disc brakes, at the front mounted slightly inboard of the hubs to provide adequate cooling. The wheelbase of the P83 was 7 ft 10 in., front and rear track was 4 ft 8.5 in. and although they claimed that the dry weight was 1184 lb, it was probably much higher.

At Monaco Stewart and Hill finished first and third with Bondurant's private V-8 car in fourth place. At Spa, the notorious race in which so many drivers went off on the first lap, Stewart crashed heavily and

Hill and Bondurant, both of whom had spun off, stayed to help rescue Stewart, trapped in his car, rather than rejoin the race. Later in the year Hill finished third in the British GP, second in the Dutch race (Stewart was fourth) and fourth at the Nürburgring.

By the Italian GP at Monza the BRM team had produced a version of the H-16 with the firing sequence revised so that it fired as a 16-cylinder engine (as opposed to two eights). Both cars retired very early in the race. Some indication that development of the H 16 was making progress was revealed at Oulton Park, where both Hill and Stewart led the Gold Cup race before retiring with engine trouble.

P261 and P83 H-16 – 1967

For 1967 Graham Hill left to become joint number one driver for Team Lotus, and Stewart was now partnered by Mike Spence. In addition, a third BRM was entered at most races under the banner of the Reg Parnell Racing Team for Chris Irwin (Tim Parnell usually managed BRM Tasman entries).

It proved another dismal year for the team with failure succeeding failure. By the Spring Cup race at Oulton Park the H-16s had completely redesigned rear suspension. A fabricated sheet steel structure above the gearbox located the upper wishbones, and there was a lower transverse tubular link running below the drive-shafts and attached to radius rods. This new suspension was fully adjustable to provide different rear wheel angles. There were now thick, perforated brake discs and the rear brakes were mounted slightly inboard of the hubs.

The best performance of the year was in the Belgian GP at Spa, where Stewart took the lead after the Lotus 49s had run into problems, but because of gear-selector problems fell back to finish second to Gurney's Eagle. Stewart finished third with a V-8 car in the French GP on the Bugatti circuit and Spence with the H-16 was fifth in the Canadian, Italian and Mexican races. The last appearance of the H-16 was in the 1968 South African GP.

This was not quite the end of the H-16 story, however, for BRM continued development work on a purely experimental basis. When the team revealed its latest V-12 cars in 1969, it also exhibited a much lighter version of the H-16 with four valves per cylinder (a total of 64!) and a claimed power output of around 450 bhp.

P126, P133 and P138 V-12 cars – 1968

In the 1967 Canadian GP a new V-12 BRM engine had powered Bruce McLaren's new McLaren M5A and for 1968 BRM decided to adopt themselves this 2999.5 (74.6 × 57.2 mm) 60-degree V-12 of comparatively unsophisticated design; it featured light alloy cylinder block and heads and twin overhead camshafts per bank of cylinders driven by a single roller chain from the front of the crankshaft; there were two valves per cylinder, single-plug ignition fired from a distributor on the front of the left bank of cylinders with the inlet ports between the pairs of camshafts and the exhausts on the outsides of the engine. Lucas fuel injection was fitted and, on a compression ratio of 12:1, an initial power output of 365 bhp at 10,500 rpm was claimed. BRM sold the V-12 engine readily and other users included the Cooper team and John Wyer's Mirage sports cars.

Although development of the V-12 engine had been under way for some considerable time, the decision to use it in the works Formula One cars was not made until a late stage and the new chassis had to be built in a hurry. BRM decided to entrust the design and construction of the first cars to Len Terry, a freelance designer who had previously been with Lotus. The result was the P126, a full aluminium-alloy monocoque with a small tubular structure at the rear to carry the suspension. At the front, suspension was by upper rocking arms, lower wishbones and inboard-mounted coil spring/damper units, while at the rear Terry chose to use single upper links, twin parallel lower links, twin radius arms and the usual outboard coil spring/damper units. Transmission was by a Hewland DG300 5-speed gearbox (the first time BRM had not used their own transmission). The wheelbase was 8 ft 0 in., front track 4 ft 10 in. and rear track 4 ft 9 in.

In all Terry built three cars; the first two were completed to Tasman specification with a 2.5-litre version of the V-12 engine in time for shipment to New Zealand in late 1967, while the third P126 was completed to Formula One specification and made its debut in the South African

15. The H-16 BRM was far too complicated and far too heavy; successes were few, but here Jackie Stewart is on his way to second place in the 1967 Belgian Grand Prix at Spa.

GP. Subsequently the two Tasman cars were rebuilt to Formula One specification and later, but very similar, cars built by BRM at Bourne were known as the P133.

Obviously the V-12 was a much simpler and potentially much more reliable prospect than its over-complicated predecessor, so prospects of success were reasonable. The drivers in 1968 were Pedro Rodriguez, who had been lured away from the Cooper team, and Mike Spence, but, sadly, the latter was killed at the wheel of a Lotus 56 gas-turbine car during practice at Indianapolis and his place in the team was taken by Dickie Attwood. Early in the season Rodriguez finished second in the Race of Champions at Brands Hatch and Attwood took a second place at Monoco, while Rodriguez finished second at Spa after a race-long battle with McLaren and third in the wet at Zandvoort. Although aerofoils had not yet been adopted on the works cars, the Parnell-entered P126 driven by Piers Courage at the Nürburgring was fitted with a small fixed aerofoil above the engine.

By the Italian GP BRM had ready a development of Len Terry's original design known as the P138 and differing in that the monocoque

16. Mechanics' nightmare – the H-16 BRM engine.

was extended backwards from the rear bulkhead to carry the suspension mountings (thereby doing away with the tubular structure) and with BRM's own 5-speed gearbox. At this race Attwood was dropped from the team in favour of American driver Bobbie Unser, very experienced in USAC racing but who had never competed in a Grand Prix. Unser was very slow in practice on the Friday and flew off immediately afterwards to compete in the Hoosier 100 race in the States. He returned to compete at Monza on the Sunday only to discover that not only he had lapped too slowly to gain a place on the grid, but that the organizers had disqualified him on the grounds that no driver is allowed to compete in two International races within 24 hours.

Sole starter Rodriguez retired at Monza, but Courage finished fourth with the Parnell car and Rodriguez rounded off the season with a third place in Canada and a fourth in Mexico.

P126, P133 and P139 V-12 cars – 1969

For 1969 BRM signed up John Surtees and Jack Oliver, while Rodriguez drove an old P126 car for Parnell during the early part of the year. A new 48-valve engine with the exhausts in the vee was ready

17. John Surtees in the pits at Silverstone in 1969 with the hopelessly unsuccessful BRM P139 with modified monocoque and 48-valve engine.

at the start of the year and was claimed, with wild optimism, to develop 452 bhp at 10,500 rpm.

It was a year of total failure, with the best performance in the early part of the year fifth place by Surtees in Spain. At the Dutch GP the BRM team introduced yet another development of the V-12 theme, the P139, with a monocoque tapering in very close to the engine at the rear, new hubs and 13 in. front wheels, but this did not run in the race. It was another hopeless outing for the team. Oliver (P133) retired early in the race and Surtees (P138) finished ninth, three laps in arrears.

In an effort to reorganize the team and make the cars competitive, BRM scratched its entries from the French GP. During a short but intense period of activity, Tony Rudd, who had been with the team for 19 years, was asked to resign. Rudd was replaced by three people: Aubrey Woods (who developed the 1500 cc V-8 BRM engine and later worked for Eagle) became chief engineer, Tony Southgate, largely as a result of Surtees's persuasion, took control of chassis design and Tim Parnell was appointed team manager. By the British GP the P139 had been redesigned with a roomier, more bulbous cockpit and additional strengthening so that it now had a cylindrical appearance. Despite these strenuous efforts to make the team more competitive, the BRM mechanics at Silverstone still looked unhappy and disinterested and the cars performed abysmally. Surtees retired the P139 on the first lap when the front suspension collapsed and Oliver (with a P133) was eliminated by transmission failure. During the remainder of the season the only worthwhile performance was a third place by Surtees at Watkins Glen.

P153 – 1970

Despite the failures of 1969 BRM embarked on the following season with optimism, a new car designed by Tony Southgate and substantial sponsorship from the Yardley perfumery company. The latest P153 had a new, lower and more bulbous monocoque, a very low, flatter nose-cone, front suspension by unequal-length double wishbones and inclined outboard-mounted coil spring/damper units, and, at the rear, single upper links, reversed lower wishbones and twin radius rods. Front and rear there were 13 in. wheels and 10.5 in. Girling ventilated disc brakes. Jack Oliver stayed with BRM, Pedro Rodriguez rejoined the team and at most races a third car was entered for young Canadian driver George Eaton, who was paying for his Formula One seat.

After a poor start to the season came the break that the BRM team had so long awaited. In the Belgian GP at Spa, Rodriguez took the lead on lap five and went on to score the team's first Grand Prix victory since Stewart's at Monaco in 1966. BRM won nothing else during the

18. Jo Siffert in the 1971 British Grand Prix with the P160 BRM fitted with 'shovel' nose and fairings ahead of the front wheels. He finished ninth after a pit stop.

year, but Rodriguez finished fourth in the Austrian GP, fourth in Canada and was leading the United States GP and all set for victory when an unscheduled fuel stop caused him to drop back to second place.

P160 and P180 – 1971

Years of despair had been succeeded by a season of hope and 1971 was to prove one of the most gratifying in BRMs long history. The team developed the P160 car, closely related to the P153, but improved in almost every respect. The monocoque was lower and wider (after the first two cars had been completed it was realized that they would be too wide to comply with 1972 regulations and so the width of subsequent cars was slightly reduced), the gearbox was more compact, lighter half-shafts were fitted and from Zandvoort onwards the P160s were fitted with a new 'shovel' nose style. Rodriguez was now joined in the team by Jo Siffert (also a team-mate at John Wyer's Gulf-Porsche team) and Howden Ganley (who was privately sponsored).

In the early part of the year Rodriguez won the Spring Cup at Oulton Park, finished fourth in the Spanish GP and fourth in the *Daily Express* Trophy at Silverstone. Rodriguez drove a fine race in the rain-soaked Dutch GP to finish second to Ickx's Ferrari and Siffert took fourth place in the French GP.

The following weekend BRM suffered a tragic and vital loss when Rodriguez crashed a sports Ferrari at the Norisring in Germany and suffered terrible burns, to which he succumbed almost immediately. At the British race only two BRMs were entered, for Siffert and Ganley (the latter was still having to make do with an old P153 car), and during practice Siffert tried his P160 fitted with wheel-width nose-cone and ram air-box – neither modification was used in the race. Siffert held second place for a considerable distance but after a pit stop to sort out a rough-running engine finished ninth.

So far in 1971 Yardley-BRM had shown a great deal of promise but achieved little in the way of success. This situation was remedied by two victories in succession, at the Österreichring, where Jo Siffert led throughout to win at 132.30 mph and set a new lap record, and at Monza, where newcomer to the team Peter Gethin had to fight hard for the lead and won by a hundredth of a second from Peterson's March. These two races represented the acme of BRM achievement during the years of the 3-litre Formula and from this point onwards the team went into a steady decline through a combination of bad management and the failure to maintain an adequate development programme. On the strength of his consistent performances throughout 1971, Siffert finished fourth equal in the World Championship, but his career came to a tragic end only three weeks after the United States race when he crashed his P160 with fatal results in the Rothmans World Championships Victory race at Brands Hatch.

P153B, P160B and P180 – 1972

In December Louis Stanley (Sir Alfred Owen's brother-in-law and *de facto* BRM chief) held a press conference at the Paul Ricard circuit in France. It was announced that henceforth BRM would be sponsored by the Marlboro tobacco company. The team started the season with a five-car entry, a 'first-string' consisting of Jean-Pierre Beltoise, Peter Gethin and Howden Ganley and a 'second-string' formed by Alex Soler-Roig (racing under the banner of Marlboro-BRM-España), who gave up after two expensive crashes early in the season, and Helmut Marko (Marlboro-BRM-Austria), who retired from racing following an eye injury suffered in the French race. The sixth car should have been driven by Gijs van Lennep (Marlboro-BRM-Holland), but the Dutch driver failed to raise enough cash to finance his entry.

During 1972 the BRM team raced almost as many different cars as they had drivers. The first-string drivers started the year with the P160B, an improved version of the 1971 model, but with a narrower monocoque constructed from heavier 16-gauge alloy, a wider cockpit, revised suspension geometry, 2 in. wider track, high ram air-box and improved brakes. At the French Grand Prix the BRM team produced the P160C, which had the even wider-track P180 suspension. The second-string drivers had to make do with the old P153B, that is, the 1970 car updated by the fitting of P160 suspension.

Tony Southgate had also evolved the P180, which, engine and transmission apart, was a completely new car. It was of very low construction and the monocoque had a completely flat underside. By mounting twin radiators either side of the gearbox it was possible to achieve a very low nose-line and the rear of the car was enclosed by the bodywork, which ducted air to the radiators and over the aerofoil. The cockpit was more enclosed than on other Formula One cars and had a detachable glass-fibre top panel through which the steering wheel protruded. Two of the new cars were built, but they were withdrawn for further development after only a couple of races. By the latter part of the season the P180 had much improved handling as a result of changes in the weight distribution and other modifications, and Beltoise drove one of these cars in the last three rounds of the Championship.

Apart from one freak victory, the red and white Marlboro-sponsored BRMs were hopelessly unsuccessful and the team's 1972 record consists of a succession of retirements and mediocre placings. At the rain-soaked Monaco race Beltoise, anticipating the fall of the flag, accelerated through from the second row of the starting grid to take a lead that was to prove unassailable. Throwing a vast cloud of spray in the path of Ickx's pursuing Ferrari, Beltoise went on to win the slowest Monaco GP since 1950. It was a truly freak victory, a glorious moment for the French driver and British team that was never to be repeated. During the remainder of the season's Championship races the team's only finishes in the first six were a fourth place by Ganley with a P160C at the Nürburgring, a sixth by Ganley in Austria and sixth place by Gethin at Monza. At the end of the season Beltoise with the P180 scored an unexpected win in the John Player Challenge Trophy at Brands Hatch.

P160E – 1973

Development of the P180 was now abandoned, Tony Southgate had departed to join the Shadow team and Marlboro-BRM staggered into another season with the V-12 car in further modified P160E form. Despite a strong team of drivers comprising Clay Regazzoni, Beltoise and Niki Lauda, it was a season of complete failure and as the year progressed the team's sponsors became increasingly disillusioned. It seemed, if anything, that the cars were less powerful than two years previously

19. BRM's only success in 1972 was Beltoise's win with the P160B in the rain-soaked Monaco Grand Prix.

and fast lap times from BRM drivers were rare. The best performances were fourth by Beltoise in Canada and fifth in Spain, Holland and Austria, fifth by Lauda in Belgium and sixth by Regazzoni in Brazil and Austria.

P201 – 1974

For 1974 BRM designer Mike Pilbeam produced the new P201 car of more compact, more aerodynamic design, but with increased wheelbase and track; revised steering and suspension geometry resulted in lighter handling characteristics and the car also had better straight-line speed. BRM were claiming 460 bhp at 11,000 rpm for the V-12 engine, the same output as for the Ford V-8, but it was only too obvious that this was wildly optimistic. The first of the P201 cars did not appear until the South African race and the second much later in the season at the French GP, so BRM continued to race the old P160E during the first six months of the year. Marlboro now sponsored the McLaren team, but the BRMs, which in 1974 were painted a rather delicate shade of green, received some sponsorship from the Motul oil concern. Initially the team fielded cars for Jean-Pierre Beltoise and Henri Pescarolo. Although the BRMs were amongst the also-rans, Beltoise achieved some reasonable places: fifth in the Argentine a second with the P201 on its debut at Kyalami (mainly thanks to the retirement of many of the faster cars) and fifth in the Belgian GP at Nivelles.

P201 – 1975

At the end of 1974 the Rubery Owen Organization finally lost all patience and resolved to wind the team up. Louis Stanley decided to take over the team personally; many of the staff left the organization, including team manager Parnell and designer Pilbeam. The cars became known as the 'Stanley-BRM' and staggered on into 1975 with no proper development programme and no hope of success. At the Argentine and Brazilian GPs a single P201 was entered for Mike Wilds, but he retired in both races. Although many critics were favourably impressed with Wilds' driving of the underpowered BRM, this was not a view shared by Louis Stanley. Stanley announced that Wild was to be rested becasue of a wrist injury, which was *le patron's* frank way of saying that he was replacing him, and Bob Evans drove regularly for the team until the French GP. The P201 was abysmally slow and its best performance was a sixth place in the Race of Champions at Brands Hatch. Persistent problems with the lubrication system of the V-12 engine resulted in the team scratching from the British Grand Prix, and when the P201 reappeared at the Österreichring it retired on the second lap of the race. At Monza the BRM failed to leave the starting grid because of electrical trouble. BRM did not contest the last two rounds of the Championship on the western side of the Atlantic.

P201 – 1976

That the BRM was dead but still wouldn't lie down was revealed at the first of the 1976 races at Interlagos in Brazil, where a modified P201 was entered for Ian Ashley – it retired on the third lap with oil pump failure after having started from the back row of the grid! BRM did not race again in 1976 and Louis Stanley subsequently stated that the entry of the P201 at Interlagos had been made solely to maintain BRMs unbroken record of racing every year since 1950.

P207 – 1977

BRM returned to racing in 1977 with the new P207 car designed by Len Terry and sponsored by Rotary Watches. This bulky, frankly uncompetitive-looking car sported a new blue and white colour finish, the old familiar V-12 engine and a smaller and lighter gearbox. The driver was to be Larry Perkins, who had done testing for the team in 1976. BRM failed to reach the Argentine race because the P207 was delivered to the airline in a crate too big to fit the aircraft's hold and at Interlagos it retired with overheating after completing only a single lap.

Conclusion

By 1978 the end had come, and although a modified P207C was run for Teddy Pilette in a number of minor events, it was all over. Sub-

20. By 1974 BRM was no longer a serious contender, but the team did achieve one good place during the year, a second by Beltoise in the South African Grand Prix at Kyalami.

sequently, in 1980 and 1982, John Jordan, who had bought most of the BRM equipment, ran cars as Jordan-BRMs in British events. BRM had first competed in Grand Prix racing in 1950 and in all the long time that the name was active it had enjoyed only four seasons of substantial success, during the years of the 1500 cc GP Formula, from the appearance of the first V-8 car in 1962 until the end of the Formula in 1965.

Connew

(United Kingdom)

A completely amateur and not completely unsuccessful car, designed and built by a 24-year-old Peter Connew with assistance from friends in a lock-up garage in East London. The original PC1 monocoque built in 18-gauge L72 aluminium was abandoned and replaced by the PC2 fabricated in 16-gauge NS4 aluminium. Front suspension was by double wishbones and inboard-mounted coil springs; rear suspension was by double wishbones and inboard-mounted coil springs, initially without radius rods. A Ford DFV engine was installed and there was a Hewland 5-speed and reverse gearbox. There was a chisel-nose body with front-mounted radiator inclined five degrees from the horizontal, eliminating turbulence under the car.

Design work started in March 1970, construction in September 1970

21. The Connew represented a brave effort to build a Formula One car on a shoe-string. Francois Migault drove the car in the 1972 Austrian Grand Prix, but retired because of collapsed rear suspension.

and the car was ready to race by 1972. After several failures to start, the Connew was driven by François Migault in the 1972 Austrian GP and was in 17th position when a rear suspension pick-up point broke. The Connew non-started at the Rothmans 50,000 Formule Libre race at Brands Hatch in August and pulled out of the John Player Challenge Trophy at Brands Hatch at the end of October (where the driver was David Purley) when the engine stopped because the wire to the electric cut-out button became disconnected. It was driven by Pierre Soukry with Chevrolet V-8 engine in a couple of Formula 5000 events in 1973 and crashed by Tony Trimmer as the result of rear damper failure.

Cooper
(United Kingdom)

During the first year of the new Formula, Cooper fortunes showed a marked upsurge. Cooper had not enjoyed any real success since Bruce McLaren had won the 1962 Monaco GP and Jack Brabham's victories in the 1959 and 1960 World Championships were now merely history. Following Charles Cooper's death in 1964, the Cooper company had been sold to the Chipstead Group of companies headed by Jonathan Sieff. This resulted in new impetus, new finance and, because Chipstead were British Maserati concessionaires, the availability of Maserati engines for 1966 Grand Prix racing.

T81 – 1966

The Maserati engine was an all-alloy 60-degree V-12 of 2989 cc (70.4 × 64 mm) with twin overhead camshafts per bank of cylinders, and although many features were new, the basic design dated back to the 2500 cc V-12 engines raced experimentally by Maserati in 1957. Lucas port-type fuel injection with the inlet ports between the camshafts on each cylinder head was featured and ignition was of the Lucas transistor type with twin plugs per cylinder. This engine was rather on the heavy side, but its claimed power output of 360 bhp at 9500 rpm would have been more than enough to be competitive. Unfortunately, this output claim was some 40 bhp optimistic, the engines were very unreliable and by mid-1967 they were being bodged together rather than properly repaired because the Modena factory could not always supply spare parts. Transmission was by a ZF gearbox/final drive combined unit and the drive to the rear wheels was through sliding joint drive-shafts.

For the new T81 designer Derrick White had evolved a conventional, strong, but rather bulky Lotus-style 'bathtub' monocoque chassis of riveted aluminium with fabricated steel bulkheads and the sides of the engine bay in sheet steel. Flexible fuel tanks were inserted along the length of the structure into boxes formed by the sides of the chassis. At the front, the suspension was by fabricated sheet steel upper rocking arms compressing inboard-mounted coil spring/damper units and wide-based lower wishbones. The rear suspension consisted of upper rocking arms, outboard coil spring/damper units, lower wishbones and twin radius rods each side – an utterly conventional but nevertheless very effective layout. The disc brakes were mounted inboard of the hubs and driven by stub axles. The smooth, rather delicate nose of the T81 contrasted with the crammed engine compartment, over which no cover was fitted. The wheelbase was 8 ft 2 in., front track 4 ft 11.5 in. and rear track 4 ft 9 in. As usual, the works Coopers were painted dark green with prominent white stripes running from the nose to the cockpit.

Much of the development work was carried out by team manager Roy Salvadori, vastly experienced works Aston Martin and Cooper driver, at the wheel of a space-frame chassis (built in 1965 to take the never-completed Coventry-Climax flat-16 1500 cc engine) with the latest Maserati unit. The T81 was first shown to the public at the Racing Car Show in January 1966, the same month the team moved to new premises at Oyster Lane, Byfleet, and the new car was first raced at the *Daily Express* Trophy meeting at Silverstone in May. The works drivers were Jochen Rindt (in his second year with the team) and Richie Ginther (only available until the new Honda was raceworthy). John Surtees joined the team at the French Grand Prix following his disagreement with Ferrari at Le Mans. Chris Amon drove for the team only

22. *Although the cars were very bulky and the engines down on power the 1966 Cooper T81 showed considerable promise. Private owner Rob Walker raced this car through to the end of 1967 and his driver Jo Siffert is seen in the 1967 Monaco Grand Prix in which he retired because of engine problems.*

in the French race (he was a supernumerary once Surtees had joined the team) and the organizers of the Mexican Grand Prix paid for a drive in that race for local man Moises Solana. By the May Silverstone meeting T81s had been delivered to private owners Rob Walker (for Jo Siffert to drive), Guy Ligier (his car was painted French racing blue) and Jo Bonnier (red and white stripes).

In the early part of the year the cars were plagued by overheating and fuel vaporization problems, they were rather a handful on the tighter circuits and handled atrociously on their Dunlop tyres on oil-covered circuits – a problem solved by a switch to Firestone tyres at Monza in September. Jochen Rindt took a brilliant second place to Surtees's Ferrari on the rain-soaked Spa circuit, scene of the Belgian GP, Rindt took fourth place at Reims and Surtees and Rindt finished second and third in the German GP at the Nürburgring. For the Italian GP at Monza Maserati company produced an improved engine with the inlet ports inclined inwards so that the engine was more compact. Rindt drove a car fitted with one of these engines into fourth place, but it proved a poor race for Surtees. John Cooper was in charge of the mechanical preparation of the cars and refused to fill the fuel tanks until noon on race day. It was discovered that one of the bag-type rubber tanks was leaking and there was no time to change it before the race. Surtees retired with fuel everywhere and John Cooper was sacked from the team that his father had founded. Surtees finished third in the United States GP after colliding with Arundell's Lotus and rounded off the season with a fine win at Mexico City. Surtees took second place to Jack Brabham in the Drivers' Championship (with points scored using both Cooper and Ferrari cars) and Cooper were third in the Constructors' Championship.

23. Squat, square lines characterized the T86 Cooper-Maserati driven by Jochen Rindt in the 1967 British Grand Prix at Silverstone. The Cooper retired because of engine trouble.

T81 and T86 – 1967

Jochen Rindt stayed with the team in 1967 for the third year of his three-year contract, but Surtees left to drive for Honda and his place was taken by the young Mexican driver Pedro Rodriguez. For much of the year there was a strained atmosphere in the team, as Rindt, in any case a very difficult character, had an active dislike of Rodriguez. Fortunately Rodriguez was content to get on quietly with his racing, driving sensibly and conserving his car, while Rindt thrashed his car into the ground. There were few changes made to the cars for the start of the year, but a number of modifications appeared as the season progressed.

Because of a high level of attrition amongst other competitors and thanks to the Mexican's sensible driving, Rodriguez, despite the loss of third and fourth gears, won the South African GP at Kyalami from John Love's elderly, but fast, private 2.7-litre Coventry-Climax-engined Cooper, which had to stop to take on extra fuel. Siffert with the private Rob Walker-entered car took third places in the Race of Champions at Brands Hatch in March and the *Daily Express* Trophy at Silverstone in May. At the Monaco GP that month Cooper produced in practice a car fitted with a revised version of the Maserati engine. This had new cylinder heads with two inlet valves and one exhaust valve per cylinder and with the angle between the valves small enough to permit the use of one cam cover per bank of cylinders. Although the general layout of the engine was unchanged, it was much neater and more compact than the 24-valve unit. The sole Cooper finisher at Monaco was Rodriguez in fifth place.

Few successes came Cooper's way during the remainder of the 1967 season. At Spa Rindt took fourth place with the new T81B car of lighter construction, with a Hewland (instead of ZF) gearbox and welded magnesium wheels (first seen, but not used, at Monaco). Another new car appeared at the British GP at Silverstone in July 1967. This was the T86 with low, flat, square lines and fitted with the 36-valve engine. Rindt retired the T86, Rodriguez finished fifth with a T81 and Formula Two driver Alan Rees, entered in this one race, finished tenth with the team's spare car fitted with inboard rear brakes. By the German GP both entries were fitted with Hewland gearboxes, but again the team was out of the money. At the Canadian GP Dickie Attwood deputized for Rodriguez (badly injured in a Formula Two race at Enna), finishing tenth, whilst Rindt retired because of wet electrics. Rindt was fourth at Monza, and another newcomer to the team, Jacky Ickx, finished sixth.

At the United States GP at Watkins Glen the Cooper team entered for Rindt a T86 powered by a Maserati engine with 36 plugs to match its 36 valves, with the additional plugs inside the vee of the engine; Ickx drove a T81B with the usual 36-valve engine. Both cars blew up their engines – and after the race Rindt boasted that feeling that the 36-plug engine was about to go, he had deliberately booted it as hard as possible so that it would blow up spectacularly and never be used again! By this time relations between Rindt and the Cooper team were at a very low ebb and at the final race of the year Cooper entered only a T81B chassis with 36-plug engine for Rodriguez, who was just about fit enough to drive. Rodriguez took sixth place. In the Drivers' Championship Rodriguez was joint sixth with 15 points.

T86B – 1968

It was evident that Cooper desperately needed a new power unit for 1968. Roy Salvadori favoured the very successful Ford engine, but the other directors opposed this as they believed it would cause the team to lose its sponsorship from the British Motor Corporation. Salvadori left Cooper, John Cooper resumed responsibility for the Formula One cars and the team opted for the new 2999 cc (73.8 × 57.2 mm) V-12 BRM engine developing around 375 bhp at 10,500 rpm – no match for the 405/410 bhp of the Ford V-8.

For 1968 Cooper produced a lighter, more compact chassis, designated the T86B and mainly the work of Tony Robinson. There was a new monocoque structure, still incorporating three tubular steel bulkheads to which aluminium alloy sheeting was riveted and running to the rear of the engine. There were detail changes to the suspension and the wheels were of a welded type to Cooper's own design, as had been tried in 1967. In all four of the new cars were built, chassis numbers F1/1/68, F1/2/68 and F1/4/68 being raced with BRM engines and F1/3/68, which was used only for testing purposes with V-8 engines supplied by Autodelta and typed the T86C.

The new cars were not ready for the South African GP in January, so the old Cooper-Maseratis were raced one more time. Both cars, driven by Lodovico Scarfiotti (ex-Ferrari and to be a regular team driver) and Brian Redman (engaged on a race-to-race basis) retired with mechanical problems. For most of the year Cooper found themselves desperately short of drivers because Scarfiotti crashed fatally the weekend of the Belgian GP, practising with a Porsche 907 *Bergspyder* for the Rossfeld hill climb, and Redman crashed badly in the Belgian race after a front tubular wishbone had broken. Frank Gardner drove for the team at the *Daily Express* Trophy at Silverstone, Lucien Bianchi appeared for the team at a number of races, Johnny Servoz-Gavin and Vic Elford handled the cars at the French race (Elford remained with the team for the rest of the year) and Robin Widdows drove a works Cooper in the British GP.

This was no recipe for success; the team's best performances came early in the year with third and fourth places by Redman and Scarfiotti in the Spanish GP (there were only five finishers) and third and fourth places at Monaco by Bianchi and Scarfiotti (in this race the cars ran with short noses and tubular guards round the rear-mounted electric fuel pumps). Cooper pressed on with plans for 1969, but the poor results of 1968 had meant a loss of all sponsorship and Jonathan Sieff decided that the company could no longer afford to continue racing. The 1968 Formula One cars, together with a Formula 5000 Prototype, were sold at auction.

Cosworth

(United Kingdom)

The 1969 season saw a rash of four-wheel-drive projects, and probably the most interesting of these was the unraced Cosworth designed for Cosworth Engineering by Robin Herd. The basis of the design was a pair of sponsons which carried the fuel joined by a stressed steel floor with front and rear boxes carrying the suspension and differentials. There was a very smooth streamlined body with wedge-shaped nose and a small strutted wing above the tail. The power unit was the Cosworth DFV, but unique in that it was the only engine cast in magnesium to offset the weight of the four-wheel-drive system and turned round in the chassis so that the clutch was at the front. In front of the engine was a 6-speed gearbox with Cosworth casing containing Hewland gears. The power was taken to an angled bevel central differential to the right and with shafts running fore and aft. The rearward shaft ran to the back of the engine, from where a transfer box took the power to the rear differential in the centre of the car. The driver sat slightly to the left of the centre-line because of the fore and aft shafts. Disc brakes were mounted inboard front and rear.

The Cosworth was extensively tested by Mike Costin of Cosworth, Brian Redman and Trevor Taylor (the nominated driver) and, apparently, on one occasion by Jackie Stewart. It became apparent that with the power balanced front and rear there was too much power through the front wheels with excessive understeer and then available tyres could not cope with the power. The more power there was through the rear wheels, the better the Cosworth handled and the less sense there was in building a car other than with rear-wheel drive only. Although the Cosworth had been provisionally entered in the British GP at Silverstone, the entry was scratched and the Cosworth was never raced. It is now in the Donington Collection.

De Tomaso
(Italy)

By 1970 former Argentinian racing driver Alessandro de Tomaso was becoming well established as an automobile manufacturer with the V-8 Ford-powered Mangusta coupé in production and the Pantera under development. In 1969 GianPaolo Dallara had built a Formula Two car bearing the De Tomaso name and for 1970 he was authorized to go ahead with the construction of a Formula One car. The new car, confusingly typed the 308 but with the three examples constructed bearing chassis numbers 505/1, 2 and 3, was entered by Frank Williams Racing and driven by Piers Courage, who had performed well at the wheel of Williams's private Brabham in 1969.

The basis of the De Tomaso was a rather bulky aluminium alloy monocoque with magnesium bulkheads. Suspension front and rear was by double wishbones and outboard coil spring/damper units. Inevitably the De Tomaso was powered by the Cosworth DFV (although the team was plagued by a shortage of engines during the year) used in conjunction with the Hewland DG300 gearbox. In appearance the De Tomaso was neat and sleek, but it was on the heavy side and the track was widened early in the car's racing career. The wheelbase was 7 ft 11.25 in., front track 4 ft 10.5 in. and rear track 4 ft 9.25 in.

The De Tomaso made its debut in South Africa, where Courage was forced to retire after hitting a kerb and damaging the suspension. He non-started after crashing in practice at Jarama, but with a new and later chassis took a sound third place in the International Trophy at Silverstone (a non-Championship race) and was holding seventh position at Monaco when the steering began to tighten (he rejoined the race after the rack had been changed, but was too far behind to be classified). Engine failure caused Courage's retirement at Spa and then disaster struck in the Dutch GP. Courage was in seventh place when the De Tomaso mounted the bank, rolled and caught fire, and sadly died in the inferno.

With Courage's death, much of the spirit went out of the team and De Tomaso himself lost all interest. Williams struggled on to the end of the season after missing the French GP. Brian Redman non-started in the British race because of a hub problem and failed to qualify at Hockenheim. Because of Redman's commitments to the Golf-Porsche team, Tim Schenken took over for the remainder of the season, retiring in Austria and Italy with engine problems, running but unclassified in Canada and retiring with suspension problems in the United States. The De Tomaso entry was refused at the Mexican GP and the 308's

24. *Piers Courage and the Frank Williams-entered de Tomaso 505 in the pits at Zandvoort in 1970. This was the race in which poor Courage crashed with fatal results.*

career was at an end. In 1971 Frank Williams raced March cars and De Tomaso concentrated on developing the Pantera.

Eagle
(USA)

After an outstandingly successful racing career with Ferrari, BRM, Porsche and Brabham, Californian Dan Gurney launched his own breed of racing car for 1966, aimed at Indianapolis and Formula One and with finance from the Goodyear tyre company. The design was the work of Len Terry, so Lotus influence was conspicuous. The Formula One team was based at Rye in Sussex and was entered in the name of All-American Races (AAR).

1966

The Eagle was based on a full monocoque skinned in 18-guage aluminium with fully stressed front and rear scuttles. Front suspension was by unequal-length wishbones and coil spring/damper units, while at the rear there were upper wishbones, inclined coil spring/damper units and twin radius arms. Generally, Terry had followed closely the design of the Lotus 38, but the Eagle was lighter throughout. There were 15 in. six-spoke magnesium alloy wheels and Girling disc brakes mounted at the wheels.

For a power unit AAR turned to Weslake at Rye and contracted to buy the Aubrey Woods-designed 60-degree V-12 of 2997 cc (72.8 × 60 mm) with four overhead camshafts driven by a train of gears at the front, four valves per cylinder, the inlet ports in the centre of the vee, Lucas fuel injection and, initially, 364 bhp at 9500 rpm. Transmission was by a Hewland DG300 gearbox. At the start of the 1966 season the V-12 engine was not ready and so Gurney picked up four of the old Coventry-Climax FPF engines enlarged to 2.75 litres for Tasman racing, with power outputs varying from 190 bhp to 235 bhp and with appalling vibration.

The new car, 101, appeared at Spa in 1966 and Gurney finished seventh on this very fast circuit. A sound fifth place followed in the French GP at Reims and Gurney retired with engine trouble at Brands Hatch after holding second place; at this race the Eagle was much modified with better steering lock and elimination of anti-dive from the front suspension. More retirements because of engine trouble followed at Zandvoort and the Nürburgring, but a new car, 102, with V-12 engine appeared at Monza. Gurney retired early in the race with overheating oil, while Phil Hill non-started with the 4-cylinder car. At Watkins Glen Gurney retired his V-12 with lubrication problems but switched back to the Climax 2.75 litre for Mexico and finished fifth. The V-12 was driven by Bob Bondurant, but was eliminated by fuel-feed problems. The 4-cylinder car made one more appearance as a works car in the 1967 South African GP, where Gurney retired again. After that it was the V-12 all the way.

1967

Over the winter months a great deal of development work was carried out on the V-12 engine and power output was up to 410 bhp. As the season progressed, so Eagle succeeded in reducing the weight of the car, and during the year it showed considerable promise. There were now to be two regular entries, driven by Gurney and Richie Ginther.

At the start of the year Gurney scored a surprise and narrow win in the Race of Champions at Brands Hatch from Bandini's Ferrari, but Ginther retired because of brake problems. Ginther failed to qualify at Monaco, and then at Zandvoort withdrew from racing because he considered himself no longer competitive. In was at Zandvoort that Gurney drove the new AAR-104, a major attempt to lighten the Eagle, with magnesium-skin riveting and titanium suspension links and exhaust manifolds. The suspension modifications were later carried out on 105, the car driven in 1967 by Ginther, and other later changes were the adoption of certain magnesium engine castings.

Gurney retired at Zandvoort because of fuel metering problems. Then came Eagle's greatest Formula One success. In the Belgian GP

25. In 1967 Dan Gurney drove the Eagle to a fine victory in the Belgian Grand Prix at Spa.

at Spa the Californian scored a fine victory at 145.98 mph from Stewart's BRM H-16 and set a new lap record of 148.85 mph – but Clark had led with the Lotus 49 until forced to stop at the pits. For the French GP the Eagle team was joined by Bruce McLaren, who was waiting for his new V-12 BRM-powered car to be ready. Both Eagles retired in France, in the British GP and the German GP, – although Gurney had built up a 45-second lead at the Nürburgring with three laps to go when the Eagle suffered universal joint failure. In the Canadian GP Gurney was joined by Lodovico Scarfiotti, but again both Eagles retired, and it was the same story in the United States and Mexican races, where the sole entry was Gurney.

1968

For 1968 Eagle was hampered by financial problems and the team was convinced that the Weslake organization lacked the ability to assemble engines adequately for the stress and pressures of a full Formula One season. Initially Eagle arranged to build up engines themselves from parts supplied by Weslake. In South Africa at the beginning of the season the Eagles's V-12 proved uncompetitive and unreliable. As a result Eagle opened a new engine shop at Ashford in Kent and built and assembled their own engines. Here, in May, they were joined

26. The magnificent V-12 Gurney-Weslake engine of the Eagle.

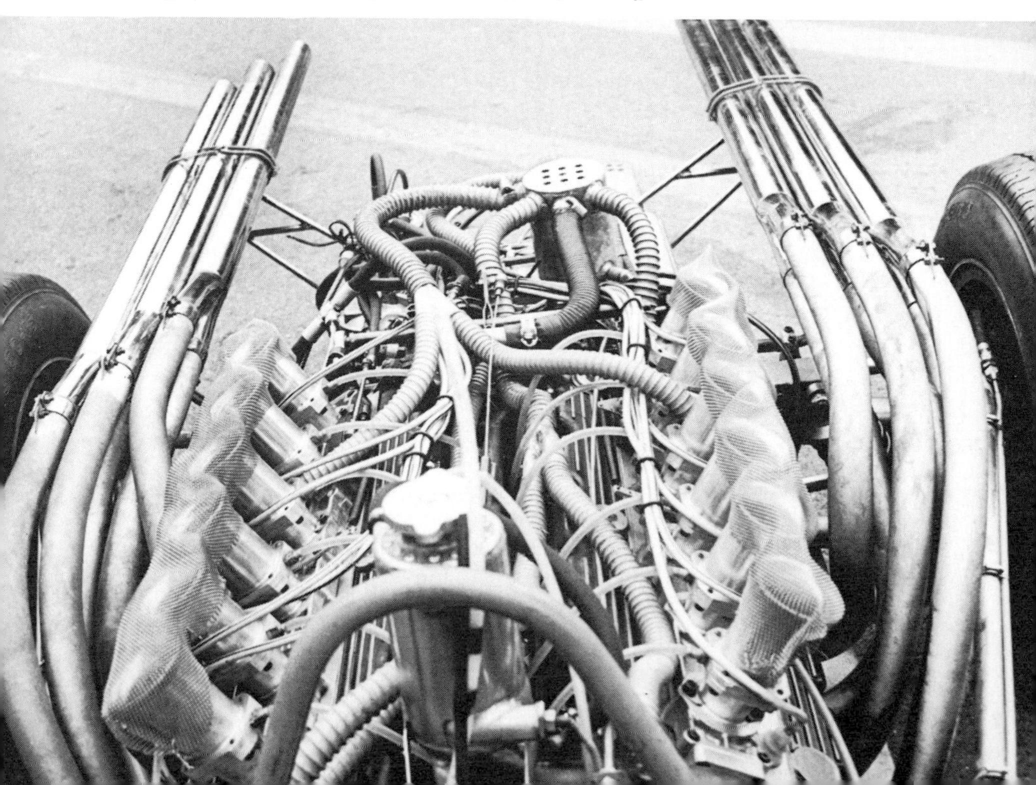

by Aubrey Woods, who had designed the V-12, but it was all too late. When one of the V-12 engines was tested on BRM's dynamometer at Folkingham, it was discovered to develop a mere 390 bhp. The financial situation was worsening and the team was forced to miss the Spanish GP. Gurney retired at Monaco and next appeared in the British race, where he again retired. After a ninth place at the Nürburgring and a seventh at Monza, Gurney abandoned the Eagle and drove a McLaren for the rest of the year. The 1969 Eagle, designed by Tony Southgate, a much smaller, slimmer car with magnesium skinning and outboard front suspension, was never raced. Henceforth Eagle restricted their activities to USAC racing. A V-12 Eagle can be seen in the Briggs Cunningham museum in California and the original 4-cylinder car, raced by Al Pease in the Canadian GP in 1967–69, is now in the Donington Collection.

Ensign

(United Kingdom)

N173 – 1973

Builder of Ensign Formula Three cars Morris Nunn was asked by wealthy Liechtenstein amateur driver Rikki von Opel to build him a Formula One car for 1973. Nunn devised the N173, a simple enough car with aluminium monocoque, front suspension by double wishbones and outboard coil spring/damper units and rear suspension by parallel lower links, single top links, twin radius rods and outboard coil spring/damper units. The power unit was the ubiquitous Cosworth DFV used with a Hewland FGA400 gearbox. In appearance, however, the Ensign was striking, with glassfibre body by Specialised Mouldings Ltd., side radiators, rear wing that flowed on as a continuous part of the body and a handsome green and pin-stripe finish. The Ensign made its debut in the French GP and von Opel both qualified and finished – in fifteenth place. Apart from a couple of races, he competed with the Ensign for the rest of the year, but only finished twice, 13th at Silverstone and in Canada, too far behind to be classified.

N173 and N174 – 1974

At the end of the year von Opel arranged to drive a Brabham, and although Nunn was stranded financially, he decided to stay in Formula One. A second car, the N174, with more conventional bodywork was built and Brian Redman drove this into eighth place in the International Trophy at Silverstone. At this point millionaire 'Teddy' Yip put up finance so that the car could run with Vern Schuppan at the wheel. He was entered five times, failed to qualify twice and his only finish was fifteenth place in Belgium. After this Mike Wilds was entered with the N173, now with modified bodywork, and without Yip finance, but he failed to qualify three times, and his only finish, fourteenth at Watkins Glen, was too far behind to be classified.

N173 and LNF75 – 1975

For 1975 Nunn arranged for the N173 to be driven by Roelof Wunderink, with sponsorship from the Dutch HB Bewaking alarm company. After a few poor performances, Wunderink was injured in a Formula 5000 race and the drive was taken over by Gijs van Lennep. He took tenth place in the Dutch GP, where the team produced the new LNF75 as a spare car. The LNF75 (also known as the N175) was designed by Dave Baldwin and featured rising-rate double wishbones with semi-inboard coil spring/damper units at the front, basically unchanged rear suspension and inboard brakes front and rear. The wheelbase was 8 ft 3 in., front track 4 ft 10 in. and rear track 5 ft 2 in. The new car was first driven by van Lennep in the French GP, and this Dutch driver finished sixth with the new car in the German GP, scoring Ensign's first Championship point. Chris Amon joined the team in Austria to drive the LNF75, while Wunderink handled the old N174, but neither here, nor at Monza, was any success gained. At the United States GP the sole Ensign entry was driven by Wunderink, again without success.

N174, LNF75 and LNF76 – 1976

As a result of disagreements between HB Bewaking and Nunn, the

27. The Ensign made its debut in the 1973 French Grand Prix at the Paul Ricard circuit where it was driven into fifteenth place by Rikky von Opel.

Dutch company retained LNF75 in 1976 and allowed Australian Larry Perkins to drive it under the name 'Boro'. Nunn soldiered on with N174 with Amon at the wheel. Amon drove the old car to fifth in the Race of Champions at Brands Hatch and managed to take a remarkable eighth place at Long Beach. Nunn managed to complete construction of a new LNF76 car designed by Dave Baldwin in time for Amon to drive at Zolder. The car was generally a development of LNF75, but it featured outboard front brakes and rear suspension incorporating inboard springs (the team reverted to outboard springs later in the year). The new Ensign seemed on the fragile side and Amon crashed badly twice, at Zolder when the rear suspension broke and in Sweden when the left-hand front wheel worked loose. Patrick Neve drove the car without success while Amon recovered; he returned for the British GP and withdrew from racing on the spot after witnessing Lauda's crash at the Nürburgring. After Hans Binder had driven in Austria, Jacky Ickx took the seat of the Ensign. He crashed very heavily in the United States GP, seemingly because of another structural failure, and LNF76 was destroyed.

N177 – 1977

For 1977 Nunn developed the new N177, very much a development of the previous year's car. Clay Regazzoni agreed to drive for Ensign, and from the British GP onwards a second car was entered by 'Teddy' Yip's Theodore team for Patrick Tambay. Although the year's results were dismal by most team's standards it proved the best year in Ensign's short history. Regazzoni finished sixth in the Argentine and fifth both in the Italian and United States GPs, while Tambay took

28. Chris Amon with the Ensign N176 in the 1976 Swedish Grand Prix at Anderstorp. He crashed when a steering arm broke.

sixth place in the German GP and fifth in Canada. Tambay had been holding a sure third place at Zandvoort when he ran out of fuel.

N177 – 1978

Nunn continued the struggle in 1978 with his now thoroughly outdated cars and a third chassis was completed. The cars were handled initially by Lamberto Leoni and Danny Ongais, but later Ickx and Derek Daly drove for the team. A fourth chassis was also completed for Val Musetti to drive in National events for David Price Racing. The only Ensign finish in the points was sixth place by Derek Daly in Canada.

N179 – 1979

For 1979 Nunn again received financial support from 'Teddy' Yip and produced the N179 with the radiator built into the scuttle ahead of the cockpit, a slightly longer wheelbase and suspension front and rear by upper rocking arms, lower wishbones and inboard coil spring/damper units. By Long Beach the car had been rebuilt with radiators in the side pods. Here Rebaque collided with the Ensign driven by Derek Daly, damage was extensive and the car returned too late to run in Spain, where Nunn fielded a N177 car. In all the Ensigns only qualified as starters at five races in 1979 and then failed altogether to finish in the first six.

N180 – 1980

Nunn had succeeded in obtaining sponsorship from Unipart and raced the N180 with Regazzoni at the wheel. The N180, designed by Ralph Bellamy and Nigel Bennett, was a close copy of the Williams FW07 riveted aluminium monocoque, with suspension by double wishbones and inboard springs front and rear and 8 ft 8 in. wheelbase. Clay Regazzoni was again the driver, but, apparently assured of fourth place, he crashed heavily at Long Beach, suffered severe injuries resulting in paralysis and never raced again. For the remainder of the season the Ensign was driven by Tiff Needell and Jan Lammers, but only finished twice – outside the points.

N180B – 1981

Nunn struggled on with a slightly modified version of the 1980 car driven by Marc Surer. Almost incredibly Surer finished fourth in the wet and set fastest lap in Brazil and took sixth place at Monaco. After the first six races the drive in the Ensign was bought by Chilean driver Eliseo Salazar, whose sole worthwhile performance was sixth place in the Dutch GP.

N180B and N181 – 1982

Initially the team ran the 1979–80 car slightly updated, with Roberto Guerreo at the wheel. The new N181 appeared at Long Beach. The changes were not significant and Guerrero, another great hopeful, achieved his best performance at Hockenheim, where he was eighth. In all he failed to qualify at five races. At the end of 1982 'Teddy' Yip acquired the Ensigns, merged them with the Shadow team which he had also bought and competed for another season with his own Theodore Racing team. Sadly, the Ensign name was not missed.

Ferrari

(Italy)

Tipo 312 – 1966

The earliest post-war Ferraris had featured a 60-degree V-12 engine, and for 1966, after an interval of 14 years, Maranello returned to this layout for a Formula One car. The new engine, with a capacity of 2989 cc (77 × 53.5 mm) was the work of Ing. Rocchi and it had much in common with the engine that powered the 1966 Tipo 330/P3 4-litre Sports Prototypes. There were chain-driven twin overhead camshafts per bank of cylinders, Lucas port-type fuel injection was fitted and the claimed power output was 360 bhp at 10,000 rpm. Transmission was by a 5-speed gearbox in unit with the final drive.

The chassis design of the 312 resembled that of the 1965 1500 cc cars and was based on a simple stressed skin monocoque formed by riveted aluminium wrapped round steel tubes and extending beneath the engine to provide mountings for the gearbox and suspension. At the front there were forged rocking arms, wide-based lower wishbones and inboard-mounted coil spring/damper units. The rear suspension consisted of lower wishbones and single upper transverse arms with twin radius rods on each side. The squarish, rather bulky body was distinguished by three slots on either side of the nose and the gold-painted Campagnolo spoked alloy wheels contrasted strongly with the bright red bodywork. The wheelbase was 7 ft 10.5 in., front track 4 ft 9 in. and rear track 4 ft 8.5 in.

At the beginning of the 1966 season only one of the new cars was ready and this was supplemented in early races by a 1965 chassis with a Dino V-6 2417 cc engine that had been built up for John Surtees to drive in the 1966 Tasman races. Because of Surtees's very bad crash with a CanAm Lola in practice for the 1965 Canadian GP this had never been raced. Surtees made a remarkably swift recovery from this near-fatal accident, and again led the Ferrari Formula One team in 1966, partnered by Italian driver Lorenzo Bandini.

Throughout 1966 the Ferrari was the most powerful car competing, and so long as Surtees was in the team, Maranello's prospects of success were high. Once Surtees had left the team after a disagreement with team manager Dragoni at the Le Mans 24 Hours race, Ferrari lacked driver quality and very little success came the team's way. Ferrari missed the South African GP and first competed at the non-Championship Syracuse race, where Surtees (V-12) and Bandini (V-6) cantered home in the first two places in the absence of serious opposition. Surtees was beaten into second place by Brabham at the International Trophy at Silverstone and retired at Monaco, where Bandini finished second with the V-6 behind Stewart's BRM. At the rain-soaked Spa race, Surtees drove magnificently, holding second place behind Rindt's Cooper-Maserati and powering through to win; Bandini finished third with the V-6 car.

By the French GP at Reims Surtees was out of the team and Mike Parkes had been brought in to back up Bandini. Because Parkes was so tall, he was provided with a car with lengthened cockpit and front section. Parkes finished second at Reims, Ferrari missed the British race and Bandini took sixth place at the Nürburgring, where a third entry, the V-6 car, had been made for Lodovico Scarfiotti. At the Italian GP Ferrari introduced a new V-12 engine featuring 36 valves – two inlet and one exhaust per cylinder – with the inlet ports between the camshafts and the exhaust ports on each side of the engine; power output was 370/380 bhp. The Ferraris were able to surge away from the opposition and Scarfiotti and Parkes took the first two places. A single V-12 for Bandini was entered in the United States GP and Bandini retired while leading. Ferrari missed the Mexican GP.

Tipo 312 – 1967

For 1967 Chris Amon joined Bandini in the Ferrari team. New cars were built (distinguishable by triangular air exits on the nose instead of slots), but the only important modification was the transfer of the exhausts to the vee of the engine. It was to prove a poor year for the team. Ferrari missed the South African GP and first competed in the Race of Champions at Brands Hatch, where Bandini took second place. Shortly afterwards Parkes drove his lengthened 1966 car to a win in the International Trophy at Silverstone. At Monaco Ferrari entered two modified cars with redesigned cockpit fairings for Amon and Bandini. Towards the end of the race Bandini lost control at the chicane, struck the barriers and overturned. Bandini was trapped in the car; no sooner had it been righted than it caught fire and the Italian suffered fatal burns. Amon's car punctured a tyre on the debris, but rejoined to finish third.

Shortly afterwards Parkes and Scarfiotti scored a dead heat for first place in the poorly supported Syracuse GP, but in major events the cars were becoming outclassed. After fourth, fifth and sixth places in the Dutch GP, Amon finished third in the Belgian GP at Spa. In this race Parkes crashed heavily and suffered injuries that put him out of racing until 1970. Scarfiotti decided to retire from racing (he returned in 1968) and so Amon was the sole Ferrari representative. He took third places at Silverstone and the Nürburgring and finished sixth in the Canadian GP at Mosport Park.

At Monza Ferrari produced a 48-valve version of the V-12 engine, very compact, with a single cam cover for each bank of camshafts, the inlet ports on the outsides of the banks of cylinders, the exhaust ports in the vee and a single plug per cylinder. Power output was 380/390 bhp. After a pit stop Amon finished seventh at Monza and the team gained no successes during the remainder of the year's races. Young Jonathan Williams had been entered in the Mexican GP and

29. Lorenzo Bandini with the Tipo 312 V-12 Ferrari in the 1967 Monaco Grand Prix. Sadly he crashed with fatal results in the closing stages of the race.

finished eighth, while Amon had run out of fuel and been classified ninth. In the non-Championship Spanish GP at Jarama only a single car was entered for Andrea de Adamich and he finished ninth after a stop to change a puntured tyre.

Tipo 312 – 1968

For 1968 Amon was joined in the team by de Adamich and European Formula Two Championship winner Jacky Ickx. De Adamich, however, crashed early in the season at Brands Hatch and put himself out of racing for the rest of the year. There were no substantial changes to the cars, but power output was now around 408 bhp. Not much in the way of success was gained by Ferrari during the year. Amon finished fourth in both the South African GP and the Race of Champions at Brands Hatch and he and Ickx were third and fourth in the International Trophy at Silverstone. The New Zealander was leading the Spanish GP when he retired with fuel pump failure. Ferrari missed the Monaco race and the V-12s next appeard at Spa fitted with small fixed aerofoils. Ickx, running in the race without the aerofoil, finished third. At Zandvoort Ickx and Amon were fourth and sixth. Then, in the rain-soaked French GP at Rouen, came Ferrari's best performance of the year; driving brilliantly in the wet Ickx pulled further and further away from Surtees's Honda to score Ferrari's only win of the year.

At Brands Hatch Amon and Ickx finished second and third behind the winning Rob Walker-entered Lotus of Jo Siffert. Ickx finished fourth in the German GP, Amon was second in the Gold Cup race at Oulton Park and in the Italian GP, where the Ferraris had larger hydraulically operated aerofoils and modified engines, Ickx finished third. When the throttles on his Ferrari jammed open in practice for the Canadian race, Ickx crashed and broke a leg. Derek Bell joined the team for the United States GP, but no successes were gained in the last three races of the year.

Tipo 312 – 1969

Ferrari devoted much of the 1969 season to the development of the new flat-12 cars and was content to enter a single V-12 for Amon at most races. The cars were now fitted with much modified engines with the inlet ports in the vee and the exhausts on the outside and with a claimed power output of 436 bhp at 11,000 rpm. Although no real success was gained, Amon turned in some stirring drives, leading in the Spanish race at Barcelona until the Ferrari ran its bearings and holding second place at Monaco until the final drive failed. He took a third in the Dutch GP, retired in the French race and at Silverstone, where a second car was entered for Pedro Rodriguez, both entries retired.

The team missed the German race, planning to concentrate on running the flat-12 at Monza. The car was not ready in time and Amon withdrew from the team. During the remaining four races of the year a V-12 was driven by Pedro Rodriguez. With this now thoroughly outdated car he finished sixth at Monza and fifth at Watkins Glen (where the car was entered in the name of the North American Racing Team).

Tipo 312B – 1970

Powering the 312B was a flat-12 2998.5 cc (79 × 52.6 mm) engine with twin overhead camshafts per bank of cylinders driven by a train of spur gears from the rear of the engine, a one-piece crankshaft running in four main bearings and inserted wet cylinder liners. The horizontally opposed design was chosen because it was lighter than a V-12 and because it permitted a lower centre of gravity. The layout was such that the inlet trumpets for the Lucas fuel injection were above the engine and the exhausts below. Ignition was by the Marelli 'Dinoplex' transistorized system and there were twin plugs per cylinder. Although the power output was little more than 420 bhp at the beginning of 1970, steady development work had boosted this to 460 bhp at 11,600 rpm by mid-season. Transmission was by a 5-speed gearbox in unit with the final drive.

In chassis design the 312B followed usual Ferrari practice and the monocoque structure was fabricated from a combination of small-diameter tubing and aluminium panelling, but with a backbone-type 'beam' extension to carry the engine. At the front the suspension was by upper rocking arms, inboard-mounted coil spring/damper units and wide-based lower wishbones, while at the rear there was a conventional double wishbone and coil spring layout. The front brakes were mounted outboard and had cooling ducts cast into the front suspension uprights while the rear brakes were mounted just inboard of the hub carriers. The rear aerofoil, which was mounted well forward, was fully adjustable, with both leading- and trailing-edge slots. In appearance the 312B was both graceful and aggressive and the traditional bright red paintwork was set off by a white aerofoil, nose fins and rear oil radiator ducts. The wheelbase was 7 ft 9.7 in., front track 5 ft 4 in. and rear track 5 ft 5.4 in.

At the end of 1969 Chris Amon left to drive for the new March team. Jacky Ickx, despite a successful 1969 season with Brabham, did not need much persuading to rejoin SEFAC Ferrari and although he was the sole 312B driver at races early in the season, later both Alfa Romeo sports car driver Ignazio Giunti and Swiss Formula Two driver Clay Regazzoni appeared for the team.

The 1970 season witnessed a battle between the new-found power of the Ferraris and the superior chassis of the new Lotus 72, aggressively and brilliantly driven by Jochen Rindt. In the early part of the season both marques suffered teething troubles, but there developed a magnificent battle that culminated in tragedy at Monza. Ickx was eliminated in the first three races of the year, but at Spa Giunti finished fourth and Ickx was eighth after a pit stop to sort out a fuel leak. At Zandvoort Ickx and Regazzoni finished third and fourth. Regazzoni finished in fourth place at Clermont-Ferrand, and in the German GP at Hockenheim Ickx finished second to Rindt. Ickx scored a brilliant victory in the Austrian GP with Regazzoni second and the scene was set for a magnificent duel between Ickx and Rindt on the very fast Monza circuit. Tragically Rindt crashed in practice with fatal results, and although Ickx led the Italian race, his car developed transmission problems and Regazzoni won the race for Ferrari. Subsequently Ickx and Regazzoni finished first and second in the Canadian and Mexican GPs and Ickx was also fourth at Watkins Glen. In the Drivers' Championship Ickx finished second with 40 points to posthumous winner Rindt with 45 points.

Tipo 312B and 312B2 – 1971

For the coming season Ferrari developed the 312B2, following the basic design of the 1970 cars, but there were so many detail changes that the two models had few components in common. A more pronounced wedge shape was adapted for the monocoque, which had a smaller frontal area, a heavier 16-gauge alloy skin (to comply with regulations that came into force for 1972) and fewer tubes. At the front the suspension geometry was revised, but at the rear there was a completely new layout with the coil spring/damper units mounted inboard almost horizontally across the back of the car and actuated by bell-crank upper wishbones, wide-based lower wishbones and single upper radius rods each side. The rear brakes were now mounted inboard on either side of the final drive unit. The dimensions were now wheelbase 7 ft 11.5 in., front track 4 ft 11.1 in. and rear track 5 ft 1 in. A number of changes had been made to the engine, including the fitting of roller main bearings, and it would now rev safely up to 12,800 rpm.

Regazzoni crashed the new car heavily during testing and for much of the year Ferrari relied on the original 312B. During the year Ferrari fielded cars for Ickx, Regazzoni and Mario Andretti, but the last-named drove only when his USAC commitments permitted. Andretti won the South African GP when Hulme's McLaren failed shortly before the finish and Regazzoni was third. The 312B2 made its debut in the Race of Champions at Brands Hatch driven by Regazzoni and he won thanks to the right choice of tyre; shortly afterwards Andretti won the non-Championship Questor GP in California with a 312B. At the Spanish GP the Ferrari team fielded 312Bs with the latest engines and Ickx finished second to Stewart (Tyrrell). Ickx was third at Monaco and shortly afterwards Ickx won the minor Jochen Rindt Memorial race at Hockenheim. Another victory for Ickx followed in the wet Dutch GP and Regazzoni took third place. As the season progressed the Ferraris proved less and less competitive. During the remainder of the year the only finishes in the points were third and fourth places by Regazzoni and Andretti at the Nürburgring and sixth place by Regazzoni at Watkins Glen.

Tipo 312B2 – 1972

Despite the failures of 1971 Ferrari relied on the existing design for the coming season, concentrating on development work, and there were few changes apart from wider front track and conventional wishbone and link rear suspension. During the year Ferrari scored only one outright victory, at the Nürburgring, where Ickx gave a virtuoso performance, taking pole position in practice and leading throughout; in addition Regazzoni finished second despite a last-lap collision with Stewart's Tyrrell. In the Argentine Ickx and Regazzoni finished third and fourth; Andretti was fourth in South Africa (where the cars were fitted with streamlined noses); Ickx and Regazzoni finished second and third in Spain and Ickx, who had been fastest in practice, had to settle for second place behind Beltoise's BRM in the torrentially wet Monaco GP. Regazzoni broke his wrist playing football and his place in the

30. Jacky Ickx was a stalwart of the Ferrari team between 1970 and 1973. He drove this 312B2 FLAT-12 car into second place in the 1972 Monaco Grand Prix.

team was taken by 'Nanni' Galli at the French GP. Here the Ferraris featured new rear suspension by single forward-facing radius rods, triangular lower wishbones and with new suspension. At the British GP Arturo Merzario was brought into the team and managed sixth place. There followed the brilliant interlude at the Nürburgring, but after that it was back to repeated failures and mediocrity. The only finishes in the points during the remainder of the season were fifth by Regazzoni in Canada and fifth and sixth places by Ickx and Andretti at Watkins Glen.

Tipo 312B2 and 312B3 – 1973

While development continued on a new car, the team ran the 312Bs in the early part of 1973, but the best performances were fourth by Ickx at Buenos Aires, fourth by Merzario and fifth by Ickx at Interlagos (the Brazilian GP) and a fourth by Merzario in South Africa.

The new Ferrari 312B3 made its race debut in the Spanish GP. Enzo Ferrari had for many years complained about industrial problems in Italy, but the fact that the monocoque of the 1973 312B3 was built in England gave some credibility to his claims. There was a full monocoque and, for the first time, it lacked any tubular framework to provide additional rigidity. The engine now served as a stressed member and the front bulkhead (which acted as a load carrier for the front suspension and located a forward tubular framework) and the centre and rear bulkheads were massive castings. The engine was bolted to the rear bulkhead and the rear suspension was bolted to the engine. At the front the suspension was mounted inboard, the front brakes

31. Ickx drove the new 312B3 in the 1973 Spanish Grand Prix on the Mountjuich Park circuit. This photograph was taken in practice. Ickx finished at the tail of the field.

were hub-mounted and the rear brakes were mounted inboard on either side of the final drive unit. The engine and transmission were unchanged. In appearance the 312B3 was long and wide, slightly larger than many of its rivals, with integral nose and front wing, the engine oil tank wrapped round the rear of the gearbox and, in orginal form, side water radiators ahead of the rear wheels. This radiator layout proved unsatisfactory during testing and by the time the 312B3 was first raced, it was fitted with a front-mounted radiator.

The new car proved a complete failure and after the first six races Ferrari withdrew to concentrate on a crash development programme. Mauro Forghieri returned to take control of the Grand Prix programme and in less than two months a much-revised version of the 312B3 was ready to race. There were new long, thin radiators mounted each side of the cockpit at a shallow angle, with the air entering from beneath and being expelled out of the top of the side sponsons, and the water passed from the engine to the top of the radiators through finned cooling tubes mounted within the sponsons. The oil tank was mounted on the right-hand side of the engine (it had previously formed part of the aerofoil mounting) and the oil radiator was mounted on the left-hand side of the engine. These changes shifted the weight distribution more towards the centre of the car.

The air intake for the engine was now mounted as a cold-air box above the roll-over bar behind the cockpit (previously there were twin ducts, one each side and surrounding the suspension radius rods). At the front a new chisel-shaped nose cowling with one-piece full-width aerofoil had been adopted and the rear aerofoil had been repositioned on a gearbox-mounted structure. In addition the suspension geometry had been redesigned to suit the new weight distribution. The wheelbase was 8 ft 2.4 in., front track 5 ft 4 in. and rear track 5 ft 3.2 in.

For Ferrari the remainder of 1973 was little more than a token effort preparatory for 1974 and there were no finishes in the first six during the remainder of the year.

Tipo 312B3 – 1974

There followed a season of brilliant success for the team; Mauro Forghieri remained in overall control of Ferrari engineering, while racing management was entrusted to 27-year-old Luca Montezemola (who had family connections with Fiat). The Ferrari drivers were Niki Lauda and Clay Regazzoni.

At the start of the season Lauda and Regazzoni took second and third places behind Hulme's McLaren in the Argentine, Lauda was in second place in the Brazilian GP when it was halted early because of heavy rain and he took second place in the Race of Champions at Brands Hatch. The Ferraris appeared in South Africa with revised rear suspension, but both entries retired because of loss of oil pressure.

In the Spanish GP at Jarama, Lauda played a waiting game, holding second place behind Peterson's JPS until the rain stopped, and as the track dried out went ahead to score his first win of the season with Regazzoni second. Another second place for Lauda followed in the Belgian GP at Nivelles, Regazzoni was fourth at Monaco, both cars retired in Sweden, but at the Dutch GP at Zandvoort the team recovered its form and Lauda and Regazzoni took the first two places. At Dijon, scene of the French GP, Lauda and Regazzoni had to settle for second and third places behind Peterson's JPS. At Brands Hatch Lauda led until a rear tyre developed a slow puncture; he stopped for a wheel-change just before the finish and the officials refused to allow him to rejoin the race to complete his final lap. The FIA Appeal court eventually awarded Lauda fifth place and two points in the World Championship. By then Lauda had blown his chances of winning the Championship by trying too hard and he failed to finish in any of the season's remaining races. Regazzoni, who had finished fourth at Brands Hatch, won the German GP, finished fifth in Austria and second in

32. Niki Lauda won the 1975 World Championship with the Ferrari 312T. He is on his way to victory in the French Grand Prix on the Paul Ricard circuit.

Canada. The World Championship went to Fittipaldi (JPS), but Regazzoni and Lauda took second and fourth places.

Tipo 312T – 1975

For 1975 Ferrari introduced the radically different 312T. To lower the centre of gravity and move the polar moment of inertia forwards (thereby improving the car's response to the driver and allowing it to be driven closer to the limit of adhesion) a completely new transmission layout was adopted; the gearbox was now mounted ahead of the final drive and with the gearbox shafts at right-angles to the centre-line of the car (hence the designation 312T or *Transversale*). The front suspension had been redesigned and featured longer rocking arms actuating the coil spring/damper units which now inclined inwards at the upper ends. There were completely new wheels and hubs which ran on very large-diameter ball races. The new monocoque chassis of the 312T tapered much more at the front and, engine apart, almost every component of the 312T was new. The wheelbase was 8 ft 3.1 in., front track 4 ft 11.5 in. and rear track 5 ft 0.2 in.

For the first two races of the year Ferrari entered the 312B3 cars. At Buenos Aires Regazzoni finished fourth and Lauda sixth. In the Brazilian race Regazzoni was again fourth and Lauda fifth. Lauda crashed his 312T heavily in practice for the South African race, but by intensive work it started the race and Lauda finished fifth. Shortly afterwards he won the International Trophy at Silverstone with the new car. Both Ferraris were pushed off the track in a first-lap mêlée at the Spanish GP, and although Regazzoni eventually rejoined the race, he was out of the picture when the race was stopped short because of Stommelen's crash.

By Monaco the Ferrari team was thoroughly sorted; Lauda won the race and followed this up with further wins at Zolder (where Regazzoni was fifth) and Anderstorp. Lauda and Regazzoni were beaten into second and third places at Zandvoort by Hunt (Hesketh) and Lauda was the winner in the French GP. The Ferraris were out of luck in the British GP. Lauda was third in Germany and the best that they could manage in Austria (another race, stopped short because of bad weather) was sixth by Lauda. Regazzoni won both the non-Championship Swiss GP at Dijon and the Italian race at Monza. Lauda was third at Monza and this meant that he had already clinched the World Championship, but he went on to win the final race of the year at Watkins Glen. At Watkins Glen Regazzoni was black-flagged for baulking second-place man Fittipaldi and in the ensuing argument Montezemola became involved in a scuffle in the pits with race officials. Lauda won the Championship with a total of 64½ points and Ferrari took the Constructors' Cup.

Tipo 312T2 – 1976

For 1976 Ferrari developed a revised car known as the Tipo 312T2 and which, engine and gearbox apart, was completely new. This latest car retained a monocoque of similar construction to that of the 1975 model, but of new design and with increased wheelbase of 8 ft 4.8 in., and track of 4 ft 11.5 in. (front) and 4 ft 9 in. (rear). At the front the familiar suspension layout incorporating upper rocking arms was retained, although the geometry was completely different. Ferrari also revealed a version of the 312T2 with de Dion rear axle, not seen since the Fifties, but, apart from one practice session, relied on the independent rear suspension all year.

Apart from Lauda's near-fatal crash at the Nürburgring, the season was marred by constant wrangles over the interpretation of the regulations and these were in reality all part of a constant battle for supremacy between Ferrari and McLaren. At the beginning of the year Lauda scored victories with the original 312T car at both Interlagos and Kyalami. The 312T2 first appeared (and retired) in the Race of Champions at Brands Hatch. In both this race and the International Trophy at Silverstone a 312T was entered by Scuderia Everest for Giancarlo Martini. Regazzoni and Lauda finished first and second at Long Beach.

Lauda with the 312T2 finished second on the road at Jarama, but was promoted initially to first place because Hunt's winning McLaren was fractionally wider than permitted – subsequently, however, Hunt was reinstated as the winner. At Zolder, Lauda was the winner with Regazzoni second and he won again at Monaco. Lauda finished third in the Swedish GP, both Ferraris retired in the French race and Lauda took second place at Brands Hatch, another race surrounded by a great deal of controversy and discussed in the McLaren section. At the Nürburgring Lauda crashed at the 120 mph Bergwerk corner, suffering terrible burns and severely corroded lungs from inhaling toxic fumes from the burning plastic cockpit section of the Ferrari. Initially Lauda's life hung in the balance and it seemed that he would never race again.

Ferrari missed the Austrian GP, but at Zandvoort Regazzoni brought the sole Ferrari entry across the line in second place. Almost miraculously Lauda was back at the wheel at Monza and drove a steady race to finish fourth. At this point Hunt was finally disqualified from the British race and Lauda promoted to winner, thereby increasing his lead in the World Championship. While the Ferraris failed in Canada and Lauda could not better third place in the United States GP, Hunt won both races and closed within three points of Lauda's Championship lead. The final race of the year was the Japanese GP run in torrential rain, and Lauda, making the difficult decision that conditions were too bad for racing, pulled out after two laps. Hunt finished third and took the Championship with 69 points to the 68 of Lauda.

Tipo 312T2 – 1977

Ferrari continued to rely on the 312T2 cars and Lauda was now joined in the team by Carlos Reutemann. For much of the year the Ferrari effort was overshadowed by the new 'ground effect' Lotus 78, but fortunately for Maranello the 78 was plagued by engine problems and there were sufficient pickings for Ferrari to ensure that Lauda won his second World Championship.

At the beginning of the year the cars were changed in detail only and Reutemann, after finishing third in the Argentine, scored a fine victory in the Brazilian GP. At Kyalami, Lauda's 312T2 was much altered, with modified bodywork, revised rear suspension pick-up points, new rear wing and repositioned water radiators. Lauda joined the winners in South Africa, he finished second in the United States GP (West) and at Monaco, Zolder and Silverstone; he won the German race at Hockenheim, finished second in Austria, won at Zandvoort and was second at Monza. A fourth place at Watkins Glen clinched the World Championship. At this point Lauda, who had become increasingly disenchanted with Ferrari and had signed for Brabham for 1978, informed the team that he would not be available for the last two races because of ill-health.

During the year Reutemann had performed well with a string of good placings: second in the Spanish GP, third at Monaco and Anderstorp and fourth at Hockenheim and the Österreichring. For the last two races of the year he was joined in the Ferrari team by French Canadian driver Gilles Villeneuve, and although both entries retired in the Canadian GP at Mosport Park, Reutemann took an excellent second place in the Japanese race on the Mount Fuji circuit. In Japan, Villeneuve was eliminated in an horrific accident when he drove over the back of Peterson's Tyrrell and the Ferrari catapaulted end over end; two spectators in a prohibited area were killed, but Villeneuve was unhurt.

Tipo 312T3 – 1978

For 1978 Ferrari switched to Michelin radial tyres from the familiar Goodyear cross-plys; during 1977 Goodyear tyre development had been concentrating more and more on the needs of the 'ground effect' Lotus 78s and the Ferraris were running on tyres with stiff side walls that proved, as the season progressed, more and more difficult to warm up to racing temperature. While Forghieri worked on a 312T specifically for use with Michelin tyres, the team relied on the existing cars in South America. Both Reutemann and Villeneuve stayed with the team. Both cars were out of the picture at Buenos Aires, but Reutemann drove a brilliant race in the oppressively hot Brazilian GP, taking the lead at the start and winning by a substantial margin.

Ferrari produced the 312T3 at Kyalami. The 312T3 featured completely new front suspension with tubular front rocker arms and much larger coil spring/damper units. At the rear there were transverse top links, radius arms and outboard coil spring/damper units. The aerodynamics were much revised with a distinctly square-cut flat body and engine cover. The wheelbase was unchanged, but the track was wider at 5 ft 3.67 in. (front) and 5 ft 1.4 in. (rear).

At Kyalami both drivers were out of the running because of tyre problems. The situation improved at the United States GP (West) at Long Beach, where Reutemann and Villeneuve were first and second fastest in practice. Villeneuve collided with Regazzoni's Shadow and put himself out early in the race, but Reutemann went on to score a fine victory. It was a temporary interlude in a depressing season, the tyre problems continued and the Ferraris were no match for the latest Lotus 79. Reutemann and Villeneuve finished third and fourth in the Belgian GP at Zolder and Reutemann won the British GP at Brands Hatch from Lauda's Brabham. Villeneuve finished third in Austria and Reutemann took third place at Monza. Then the Ferraris found their form again with Reutemann scoring a fine victory at Watkins Glen and Villeneuve winning the last race of the season at Montreal with Reutemann in third place. In the Drivers' Championship Reutemann took third place and Ferrari finished second in the Constructors' Cup.

Tipo 312T4 – 1979

For 1979 Ferrari signed up South African Jody Scheckter, who had enjoyed two good seasons with the Wolf team, and Gilles Villeneuve, the hero of so many young enthusiasts, stayed with the team. While work progressed on Ferrari's new 'ground effect' car, the team relied for the first two races on the 312T3s fitted with flexible skirts. Both cars were eliminated in the Argentine and they finished fifth (Villeneuve) and sixth (Scheckter) in Brazil.

The new 312T4 appeared at the South African race at Kyalami. Much of the work on the new car had been carried out in the Pininfarina wind tunnel and the result was a 'ground effect' car as distinctive in appearance as the 312T3. The 312T4 was 10 in. longer and the wheelbase had been lengthened slightly by less than six inches to 8 ft 10.4 in. The cockpit was situated almost centrally within the wheelbase with the fuel carried in a single cell behind the cockpit. The water radiator was in the left pod and the oil cooler in the right pod. At the front the suspension was basically similar to that of the 312T3, but at the rear the coil spring/damper units were inboard, running in channels within the castings behind the line of the rear axle line and actuated tubular rocker arms similar to these at the front. The body was even flatter and squarer than that of the 1978 cars.

The 312T4 soon proved the most effective and potent car racing in 1979 and throughout the year Scheckter and Villeneuve vied for success in the World Championship. Villeneuve and Scheckter took the first two places at Kyalami and these positions were repeated in the United States GP (West) at Long Beach. A minor success followed when Villeneuve won the Race of Champions at Brands Hatch with a 312T3 fitted with skirts. After a fourth place at Jarama because of tyre problems Scheckter won at both Zolder and Monaco. Villeneuve squeezed into second place between the turbocharged Renaults in the French GP at Dijon, but at Silverstone and Hockenheim the Ferraris were also-rans. Then the team looked up again with second place by Villeneuve in Austria and by Scheckter in Holland.

At Monza the Ferrari team produced the improved 312T4B with revised rear suspension, outboard-mounted rear brakes, twin calipers front and rear and a new exhaust system. In a magnificent race that delighted the home crowd, Scheckter and Villeneuve fought off Arnoux's Renault and Laffite's Ligier to take first and second places and ensure Scheckter's victory in the World Championship.

Now that Scheckter had the World Championship in the bag, Villeneuve felt free to battle it out with his team-mate for victory. The French Canadian led the Canadian GP until Jones forced his Williams into the lead and Villeneuve was beaten into second place by the nar-

33. 1980 proved a dreadful year for the Ferrari team, and the flat-12 312T/5 cars were completely outclassed. Here Jody Scheckter is on his way to eighth place at Zolder.

rowest of margins. Scheckter finished fourth. At the United States GP Villeneuve scored a magnificent victory in torrential rain, whilst Scheckter was eliminated by a burst tyre. The 1979 season had proved one of the most brilliant in Ferrari's long racing history.

Tipo 312T5 – 1980

Whilst Forghieri and the other Ferrari engineers were hard at work on the turbocharged cars to be raced in 1981, Maranello produced the 312T5 for 1980. These were rebuilds of the 1979 cars with modified monocoques that were slimmer at the front, new bodywork, revised suspension geometry and new aerofoils. The team also tried a number of cylinder head modifications with very wide angle valves to save overall engine width. Unfortunately these modifications resulted in such a level of unreliability that by Monaco they had been abandoned

Much of the lack of competitiveness of the Ferraris could be blamed on the Michelin tyres that were becoming more and more suited to the needs of the turbocharged Renaults and less to the needs of Ferrari. The Ferraris retired in the first three races of the year, Scheckter took fifth place at Long Beach, and Villeneuve was sixth in the Belgian GP and fifth at Monaco. The Ferraris did not run in the disputed Spanish GP and were out of the picture in the British race, and it was only by the most exuberant of press-on driving that Villeneuve finished sixth at Hockenheim and held fourth place in the Italian GP at Monza until rear tyre failure resulted in a bad crash. Scheckter, in his last season of racing, failed to qualify at the Canadian GP, while Villeneuve was fifth. In the final race of the year at Watkins Glen Villeneuve retired

34. By 1981 Ferrari had switched to turbocharged cars and Didier Pironi drove this 126C at Hockenheim. The engine blew up on the first lap.

after clipping the kerb and Scheckter finished 11th. It was one of the most disastrously unsuccessful years in Ferrari racing history.

Tipo 126CK – 1981

Ferrari's turbocharged Formula One contender was first revealed when Villeneuve drove in practice at the 1980 Italian GP at Imola and it was used exclusively by the team in 1981, a season that could be regarded as one of sustained development. The power unit was a 120-degree V-6 of 1496.43 cc (81 × 48.4 mm) with four overhead camshafts and, after unsuccessful tests with a Brown-Boveri system, an exhaust-driven KKK turbocharger. Initially power output was claimed to be 540 bhp at 11,500/12,000 rpm. The engine formed a fully stressed chassis member and the slim monocoque was constructed in the usual Ferrari manner of stressed alloy sheeting with a strong internal tubular frame structure. Transmission was by a strengthened version of the transverse gearbox in both 5- and 6-speed versions. Suspension front and rear was by upper rocking arms, lower wishbones and inboard-mounted coil spring/damper units. The cars were extensively developed and modified over the winter of 1980–81 and the cars were also tried with the Comprex turbocharger built by Brown-Boveri; although seen in practice in this form, they were never raced with the Swiss turbocharger.

Now that Scheckter had retired from racing, Villeneuve was partnered by French driver Didier Pironi. The year proved one of immense promise and with a fair measure of success. After disappointing performances at Long Beach and in South America, Villeneuve took pole position in practice at Imola and initially the Ferraris led the race with Pironi eventually taking fifth place. Then came a fourth place for Villeneuve and eighth for Pironi at Zolder. The first of the year's victories followes at Monaco, where Villeneuve was second fastest in practice and in the race squeezed past Jones's Williams to take the lead four laps from the finish. Three weeks later Villeneuve won again in the Spanish GP at Jarama. During the remainder of the season both Ferrari drivers battled hard and subsequently Pironi finished fifth at Dijon and Monza, while Villeneuve took third place on the Notre Dame circuit in Canada.

Tipo 126C2 – 1982

During 1981 Ferrari had been joined by former Hesketh, Fittipaldi and Wolf designer Harvey Postlethwaite whose brief was to design a completely new chassis for the 126. Postlethwaite produced a monocoque on the lines of the last of the Wolf designs with honeycomb sheeting and carbon fibre composite bulkheads. The result was a monocoque both stronger and lighter than the traditional Ferrari designs.

Although new in design, the suspension was similar in layout to that of the 1981 cars and the transmission was unchanged. The body was new and very much neater. The power unit was under constant development and was now pushing out around 580 bhp at 11,800 rpm.

Both of the 126C2s dropped out of contention at Kyalami. Pironi crashed heavily at the Paul Ricard circuit, writing off one of the cars, and badly bruised he struggled to finish eighth in Brazil, while Villeneuve spun into the guard rail. Villeneuve drove a car with a staggered double rear aerofoil into third place at Long Beach but was disqualified. At Imola, boycotted by the British teams, the Ferrari drivers battled with Arnoux (Renault) until the French car's engine failed. Villeneuve and Pironi now held first and second places and the team orders were for the drivers to hold their positions. On the last lap Pironi slipped into the lead and won the race. Villeneuve resolved never to speak to Pironi again. Thirteen days later Villeneuve was dead, killed during the final qualifying session at Zolder when, trying just too hard to beat Pironi's time, he clipped Mass's March, was launched into the sand at the side of the track and broke his neck as a result of the deceleration. It was a tragic blow for the Ferrari team.

Ferrari scratched from the Belgian race and ran a single car Pironi at Monaco. He almost won , but the engine cut because of an electrical fault on the last lap and he was classified second. At Detroit Ferrari produced a car with pullrod-operated double wishbone front suspension, but for the time being this was not raced. Pironi finished third at Detroit, and in the next race at Montreal he stalled his engine on the grid and was rammed by the Osella of Paletti. Paletti was killed and the race was stopped at the end of the first lap. Pironi drove the new car in the restarted race, but was ninth after a series of pit stops to sort out the fuel injection and ignition.

Shortly afterwards Pironi again crashed heavily at the Paul Ricard circuit, apparently because of a broken wishbone, and this chassis was a write-off. By the time that Patrick Tambay had joined the team at the Dutch GP, the cars were fitted with stronger wishbones, and the team was also experimenting with water injection. Pironi scored a fine win at Zandvoort (Tambay was eighth), and subsequently Pironi and Tambay were second and third in the British GP and third and fourth in the French GP at Paul Ricard, where they were outpaced by the Renaults.

In untimed practice for the German GP at Hockenheim in heavy rain Pironi's car ran into the back of Prost's Renault, launched itself over the right rear wheel, glanced off the guard rail and hit the grass at the side of the track. Pironi suffered two broken legs and has not raced again. Despite this terrible setback, Tambay won the German race and subsequently finished fourth in Austria after a pit stop to change a punctured tyre. Tambay suffered badly from the harsh ride of the Ferrari, typical of 'ground effect' cars of the period, and pains in his neck and right arm forced him to withdraw from the Swiss GP held at Dijon. For the last races of the year Mario Andretti joined the team. At Monza, Tambay and Andretti were second and third, but Tambay was forced to withdraw from the Las Vegas race because of a recurrence of his neck problems; Andretti was eliminated by rear suspension failure. Despite the problems of the year Ferrari won the Constructors' Cup with 74 points and Pironi had taken second place in the Drivers' Championship.

Tipo 126C2B and Tipo 126C3 – 1983

Ferrari modified the existing cars to comply with the 1983 flat-bottom rules, and from the Long Beach race onwards the cars were fitted with very large aerofoils and with extra winglets running forward on both sides. Tambay was now joined in the team by René Arnoux. Tambay finished a poor fifth in Brazil, Arnoux finished third at Long Beach (Tambay had led until he was shunted by Rosberg's Williams) and Tambay scored the first Ferrari win of the year at San Marino with Arnoux third. At Monaco Tambay was fourth and he finished second in the Belgian GP at Spa. Both cars were eliminated at Detroit and Arnoux won the Canadian GP.

By the British race Postlethwaite had ready the new Tipo 126C3 cars, quite similar in appearance to the earlier cars but changed in many respects, including a new monocoque constructed from carbon-composite reinforced with Kevlar and with the upper and lower mouldings bonded to form a single unit with the magnesium bulkheads integral. At Silverstone Tambay and Arnoux finished third and fifth, having led for the first quarter of the race. The problem was the decision to run with much smaller aerofoils, resulting in insufficient rear downforce and blistering of the rear tyres. Another problem was the use of water injection, which was protested by Tyrrell and resulted in another wrangle eventually decided in Ferrari's favour.

Arnoux scored a good win in the German GP at Hockenheim, finished second in Austria, won the Dutch GP and finished second at Monza. Arnoux was now only two points behind Prost (Renault) in the World Championship, but he spun off at Brands Hatch in the European GP and retired at Kyalami, the final round. Eventually he was third in the Championship behind Piquet and Prost. Ferrari, however, won the Constructors' Cup with 89 points to the 79 of Renault.

Tipo 126C4 – 1984

For 1984 Ferrari produced a team of cars (nine in all were built) that were basically similar to the C3s, but modified in detail, with lower weight and power output now around 680 bhp at 11,500 rpm. Despite his fine performances earlier in the 1983 season, Tambay was dropped from the team and replaced by Michele Alboreto. In 1984 the new turbocharged McLarens were overwhelmingly dominant and the Ferraris, so much to the fore the previous year, now found themselves scrapping with the Lotus 95Ts and the Renaults for the lower places.

After both entries had retired in the first two races of the year, Alboreto and Arnoux took first and third places in the Belgian GP at Zolder. It was to be the only win of the season, although Arnoux took second place at Imola, fourth at Dijon and Monaco, fifth at Montreal, second at Dallas, and sixth at Brands Hatch and Hockenheim, Alboreto was third in Austria, second at Monza and in the European GP on the rebuilt Nürburgring, and finished with fourth place in Portugal. In the Constructors' Cup Ferrari had at least achieved second place with 57½ points, but the winning McLaren team had amassed the incredible total of 143½ points.

Tipo 156/85 – 1985

Ferrari had been developing a new 4-cylinder turbocharged engine, but this was abandoned and the team continued to race further improved versions of the V-6 cars, with new low-mounted turbochargers much improved power output and much improved fuel consumption. There was a new moulded composite monocoque, and with constant suspension development and their long tails and low construction the Ferraris looked superb. However, it soon became evident that Ferrari, still unable to match the speed, reliability and fuel economy

35. Stefan Johansson has proved a steady and fast member of the Ferrari in 1985–86. He is seen in the 1985 Italian Grand Prix in which he finished in fifth place.

of the McLarens, had been trounced in the power race by BMW, Renault and Honda, and the Brabham, Lotus and Williams cars powered by these engines were significantly quicker. After the Brazilian race, Arnoux and Ferrari parted company and Alboreto was joined in the Ferrari team by Stefan Johannson. Mauro Forghieri was no longer responsible for the racing team and Harvey Postelthwaite was regularly seen at race meetings.

Alboreto's consistent performances early in the season put him in the lead in the Championship and he finished second in Brazil (Arnoux fourth), second in Portugal, second at Monaco, won in Canada (Johannson was second), third at Detroit (Johannson was again second), second in the British GP and won at the Nürburgring. When he finished third in Austria he dropped to level-pegging with Prost on 50 points. He rounded off the season with a fourth place in the Dutch GP and failed to score in the remaining five races. As a result he finished second in the Drivers' Championship with 53 points to the 73 of Prost. Other finishes in the points by Johannson were a sixth at Imola, fourth in France, fifth in Italy, fourth at Kyalami and fifth at Adelaide. Ferrari finished second in the Constructors' Cup with 82 points to the 90 of McLaren.

Tipo 186 – 1986

At the Fiorano test circuit in March the Ferrari team revealed their latest car, substantially redesigned so far as both engine and chassis were concerned. Although it was clear that a great deal of development and sorting would be needed, the Ferrari team gradually improved after a shaky start in Brazil, with Johannson finishing fourth at Imola and Johannson and Alboreto taking third and fourth places at Spa. There have been many times in Ferrari's history when the team has performed miserably and uncompetitively only to bounce back again to the forefront of racing. A resurgence of Ferrari success is inevitable.

Fittipaldi

(Brazil)

Formed by Wilson Fittipaldi, Emerson's elder brother who had enjoyed a mediocre career as a Fomula One driver, and sponsored by Copersucar, the Brazilian sugar-marketing corporation, the Fittipaldi was one of the sad also-rans of Formula One. It lasted longer than many of this class of competitor, but when the team finally disappeared it was mourned by no one.

FD01 – 1975

Designed by mechanic Richard Divila – hence the designation – the FD01 featured a simple monocoque with front suspension by double wishbones and outboard coil spring/damper units and rear suspension by parallel lower and single upper links, twin radius rods and coil spring/damper units. The wheelbase was 7 ft 11 in., front track 4 ft 11 in. and rear track 5 ft 1 in. Inevitably the Fittipaldi was powered by the Cosworth DFV engine and it used the Hewland TL200 gearbox. In appearance the FD01 was delightfully sleek with full-width nose-mounted wing above one radiator and another radiator at the rear. Wilson started from the back of the grid in the Argentine, crashed heavily when the car went out of control on the straight and the Fittipaldi was badly damaged by fire. A second chassis with twin rear radiators and stronger rear suspension (apparently suspension failure was the cause of the crash) appeared in Brazil. It was an appalling season for the new team; Fittipaldi failed to qualify twice and his best finish was tenth place at Watkins Glen.

FD04 – 1976

For 1976 Emerson Fittipaldi, previously with McLaren, was persuaded to lead the team with Ingo Hoffman as number two. The team raced improved FD04, again designed by Divila, with shapely side pods housing the radiators, shapely chisel nose with wide aerofoil, lengthened wheelbase of 8 ft 5 in. and the Hewland FGA400 gearbox. All the money pumped into the team by Copersucar proved a complete waste and the best performances of the season were sixth places by

36. Yet another unsuccessful Formula One contender was the Fittipaldi. This is Emerson Fittipaldi with the FD04 in the 1976 Brazilian Grand Prix.

Emerson at Long Beach, Monaco and Brands Hatch. Hoffman finished 11th with an FD01 in Brazil and failed to qualify at the other three races in which he entered.

FD04 and F5 – 1977

In the early part of the season the team continued to rely on the 1976 cars. Although Hoffman was entered in the Argentinian and Brazilian GPs, for the rest of the year only a single car was fielded for Emerson Fittipaldi. He finished fourth in the Argentine and Brazil (Hoffman was seventh at Interlagos), fifth at Long Beach, but failed to finish in the points elsewhere with the FD04. At Dijon the team ran the new F5 designed by Dave Baldwin. The F5, apparently a straight derivative of the LNF75 that Baldwin had designed for Ensign in 1975, featured double wishbones with inboard springs at the front, parallel lower links, single upper links, twin radius rods and outboard springs at the back and 8 ft 11 in. wheelbase. Unfortunately Baldwin quit the team just before the French GP and the design was not properly developed. During the remainder of the year Fittipaldi failed to finish in the points, not qualifying at Hockenheim and Monza, and the team missed the last race of the season in Japan.

F5A – 1978

For 1978 the team relied on the existing design, updated as a 'wing car' by Giacomo Caliri and at long last Emerson began to achieve some competitive performances. He finished second in Brazil, sixth in Sweden, fourth in Germany and Austria, fifth in Holland and fifth at Watkins Glen. It was all quite encouraging!

F5A and F6A – 1979

After finishing sixth with the F5A in the Argentine, Fittipaldi appeared at the Brazilian GP with the new Ralph Bellamy-designed F6. This superb-looking car with slim nose, heavy rearward podding, suspension front and rear by upper rocking arms, lower wishbones and with inboard springs and 9 ft 1 in. wheelbase proved a complete flop. Fittipaldi opted for the older car for the race, raced the F6 in South Africa and reverted to the F5A at Long Beach; Emerson appeared with the new car in modified F6A form at Hockenheim and used it for the remainder of the season. Fittipaldi failed to finish in the points with the F6A in 1979 and Alex Ribeiro did not qualify with a second car entered in the Canadian and United States GPs.

F7 and F8 – 1980

Fittipaldi took over the Wolf team and, with management by Peter Warr and new sponsorship from Skol Brasil, raced the Wolf team cars (see Wolf) in the early part of the year. The drivers were Emerson and Keke Rosberg. Rosberg finished third in the Argentine, Fittipaldi third at Long Beach, Fittipaldi sixth at Monaco and fifth in Spain. At Brands Hatch, Fittipaldi appeared with the first of the new F8 cars, designed by Harvey Postlethwaite on the lines of his successful honeycomb monocoque Wolfs with mainly aerodynamic changes that included a conspicuously short nose and long side pods. By the German race there was a second of these cars for Rosberg, but during the remainder of the year the only finish in the points was a fifth by Rosberg at Monza.

F8C – 1981

At the end of the year Fittipaldi retired from racing, but Rosberg stayed with the team and was joined by Chico Serra. Postlethwaite had left to join Ferrari and the slightly modified 8C car was developed by Gary Thomas. Fittipaldi no longer had a major sponsor and they were plagued by engine and tyre problems throughout the year. It proved a terrible time for the team, Rosberg failing to qualify five times during the year and Serra nine times; there was not a single finish in the Championship points.

F8D and F9 – 1982

For one more season the Fittipaldi team struggled on, entering a single car for Serra. Initially Serra raced a sightly modified car, typed the 8D, failing to qualify three times and finishing sixth in Belgium. At the French GP the team produced the F9 designed by Richard Divila and Tim Wright, but again Serra failed to qualify. Serra again failed to qualify at Las Vegas at the end of the year and there were no more finishes in the points. Unable to raise further sponsorship, the team disappeared from the race tracks.

Hesketh

(United Kingdom)

All in all, it was good fun while it lasted, but it did not last very long. Funded, without sponsorship, by Lord Alexander Fermor-Hesketh, exuberant, enthusiastic, decidedly overweight and somewhat feckless, the Hesketh team entered Formula One and Formula Two Surtees cars for James Hunt in 1972 and a Formula One March in 1973, the latter year culminating in a second place and fastest lap for Hunt at Watkins Glen. From this the Hesketh Grand Prix programme developed.

308 – 1974

Hesketh Racing decided to build their own car for 1974, designed by Harvey Postlethwaite, featuring a monocoque with flat top and curved sides, nose-mounted radiator, front suspension by double wishbones and outboard coil spring/damper units and rear suspension by parallel lower links, single upper links, twin radius rods and outboard coil spring/damper units. The new car, typed the 308, was yet another user of the Cosworth DFV engine and Hewland FGA400 gearbox. The wheelbase was 8 ft 4 in., front track 4 ft 10 in. and rear track 5 ft 2 in. 'Bubbles' Horsley remained as team manager and James Hunt was again the driver. In the first part of the season the team continued to run the March, although Hunt had tested the 308 at Interlagos, and the Hesketh made its race debut at Brands Hatch in the Race of Champions, where Hunt was fastest in practice but withdrew from the race because of handling problems. The first Grand Prix outing was in South Africa, where Hunt again retired, but during the year he finished third in Sweden, third in Austria, fourth in Canada and third in the United States. In addition, early in the year, Hunt was fastest in practice and won the International Trophy at Silverstone, a success that had raised the hopes of the Hesketh team a little too high. During the year developments had included new bodywork, side radiators and rubber-controlled front suspension.

308B and 308C – 1975

Hunt remained with the team for 1975, racing the Hesketh in so-called 308B form, sometimes with rubber-controlled suspension but otherwise largely unchanged until a completely new car was ready mid-season. Hunt finished second in the Argentine, sixth in Brazil, and

37. James Hunt with the Hesketh 308 in the 1975 French Grand Prix at the Paul Ricard circuit. He took a fine second place to Lauda's Ferrari.

scored a surprise but well-deserved victory at Zandvoort after making an early decision as rain eased to change on to 'slick' tyres and finishing just under a second ahead of Lauda's Ferrari. By this time Hesketh had sold one car to Harry Stiller to run for Alan Jones and rented a second car to Torsten Palm. A second place followed in the French GP and a fourth at Silverstone, and by the German GP the first of the 308s had been sold to German privateer Harald Ertl, who finished eighth at the Nürburgring. Another second for Hunt followed in Austria, and now Brett Lunger was renting Hesketh drives.

At the non-Championship Swiss GP at Dijon the Hesketh team produced the 308C, with new, shallow monocoque, in-line side radiators, rubber springing front and rear, slightly shorter wheelbase and narrower track and a lack of rigidity in the monocoque that marred the handling qualities, During the remainder of the year Hunt finished fifth at Monza and fourth at Watkins Glen.

308D – 1976

Hesketh abandoned Formula One at the end of 1975; Hunt went off to drive for McLaren, while the 308C cars were sold to Walter Wolf. Horsley carried on at the premises at Towcester, preparing and rebuilding Ford DFV engines and renting out both the old 308B and the marginally improved 308D to drivers willing to pay. Harald Ertl raced under the Hesketh Racing banner, while from the Belgian GP onwards Guy Edwards appeared with a car sponsored by *Penthouse* and Rizla and with a lurid painting of a female model on the nose. Edwards was involved in Lauda's crash at the Nürburgring, his place was taken at Zandvoort by Stommelen, but he reappeared at Monza. Alex Ribeiro drove the Rizla car at Watkins Glen, but this did not run in Japan. No finish in the Championship points was gained during the year.

308E – 1977

The team built five new 308E cars for 1977, distinguished by a smooth, tapering profile. Drivers during the year included Harald Ertl, who gave up in mid-season, Rupert Keegan, who crashed in the Canadian GP, Hector Rebaque and Ian Ashley, who suffered an horrific accident in practice in Canada when his car launched itself over the barriers. Once again success was not obtained.

308E – 1978

Horsley struggled on into 1978, not winding the team down until May. In the meanwhile Eddie Cheever had driven in South Africa, Divina Galica and Derek Daly had both spun and crashed in the International Trophy at Silverstone and Daly had failed to qualify at Long Beach, Monaco and Zolder.

Hill
(United Kingdom)

Up until the end of 1972 Graham Hill had always driven cars entered by others, but for 1973 he formed his own team, Embassy Racing Team, named after its cigarette sponsor. He raced a Shadow DN1 in 1973, a team of Lola 370 cars in 1974 and then for 1975 went ahead with cars built and raced under his own name.

GH1 – 1975

Originally known as the Lola 371, but subsequently given the designation GH1, Graham Hill's new car incorporated many Lola design features and was the work of former Lola employee Andy Smallman. The monocoque closely resembled the Lola and featured inward-sloping sides to give a roughly triangular shape; construction was by TC Prototypes, the company run by John Thompson. At the front, suspension was by double wishbones and outboard coil spring/damper units, while at the rear there were parallel lower links, single upper links, twin radius rods and outboard coil spring/damper units. The Ford DFV engine was used in conjunction with the Hewland FGA400 gearbox. The wheelbase was 8 ft 6 in., front track 5 ft 4 in. and rear track 5 ft 5 in.

Initially the cars were driven by Rolf Stommelen and Graham Hill himself, but after Hill failed to qualify in Spain, he was entered only once more, at Monaco, where he again failed to qualify. At the Spanish

38. Immense driver promise that was never fulfilled – Tony Brise with the Hill GH1 in the 1975 German Grand Prix at the Nürburgring.

GP Stommelen led the race until an experimental carbon-fibre rear wing post collapsed and the Hill launched itself over Pace's Brabham and killed four spectators. François Migault had driven the other Hill in Spain and only the one car was entered at Monaco, but from Zolder onwards the Hill team was joined by promising newcomer Tony Brise. Vern Schuppan drove a Hill in Sweden, where Brise finished sixth. Alan Jones was in the team at Zandvoort onwards, finishing fifth at the Nürburgring, and Stommelen again took his place in the team in Austria. There were no other finishes in the points during the year.

In November the team tested the new Smallman-designed GH2 at the Paul Ricard circuit and it was flying back from that test session that Britain's most popular racing driver crashed with fatal results for himself, Brise and other members of the team. The GH2 is in the National Motor Museum at Beaulieu.

Honda
(Japan)

Honda first entered Formula One racing in 1964 with the unconventional RA271, featuring a transversly mounted 60-degree V-12 engine and 6-speed gearbox. During 1964 the RA271 was driven at three races by American Ronnie Bucknum. For 1965 Honda developed the improved RA272 and fielded two cars for Richie Ginther and Bucknum. As the season progressed so the Hondas improved in power and reliability and Richie Ginther won the last race of the 1500 cc Formula, the Mexican GP. By this time Honda was well advanced with development of new cars for the 3000 cc Formula, and the drivers were again Ginther and Bucknum.

RA273 – 1966

The heart of the new Honda was a 90-degree V-12 engine (much bulkier than an engine with the more usual 60-degree layout) of 2992 cc 78 × 52.2 mm) with the drive taken from the centre of the crankshaft; there were twin overhead camshafts per bank of cylinders, four valves per cylinder and a tortuous exhaust system emerging from the centre of the vee. Roller bearings were used throughout – a legacy of Honda motor-cycle racing practice – and the resultant friction loss was more than offset by the greater bulk of the engine resulting from this design feature. Honda eventually claimed 420 bhp at 10,200 rpm, but this proved very much on the optimistic side, and the 1966 figure was probably around 380 bhp. With all the power and torque at the top end of the rev range, the 5-speed gearbox proved inadequate.

No serious attempt had been made to keep weight down and the chassis was as bulky as the power train. The chassis was a conventional full-length aluminium monocoque with equally conventional suspension: at the front by lower wishbones, upper rocking arms and coil spring/damper units and at the rear by lower wishbones, transverse links, twin radius rods each side and coil spring/damper units. The wheelbase was 8 ft 2.8 in., front track 4 ft 8.25 in. and rear track 4 ft 7 in. The RA273 ran on Halibrand magnesium wheels and Goodyear tyres. The front bodywork was painted white with a red stripe each side and HONDA on each side of the cockpit. There was no bodywork over the rear of the car and the RA273 weighed 740 kg empty.

Ginther first appeared with the new Honda, F-101, at the 1966 Italian GP. He was fourth fastest in practice with this deafeningly noisy car and was holding second place in the race when a rear tyre deflated at the Curva Grande and the Honda disappeared into the trees. By the United States GP at Watkins Glen, Honda had ready two new cars for Ginther and Bucknum, F-102 and F-103, and the former had the track front and rear increased by a massive 7.75 in. Ginther finished well down the field at Watkins Glen in eighth place, but at the last race of the season at Mexico City he took fourth place and set fastest lap.

RA273 and RA300 – 1967

For 1967 Honda ran a single entry driven by John Surtees, who ran his own semi-works team, Honda Racing, from premises in Slough with a crew of experienced British and specialist Japanese. Honda claimed 412 bhp in 1967, but in the later part of the year power output was around 385 bhp. Engines with elektron castings (said to weigh 90 lb less) were used at Monaco and Zandvoort, but were plagued by expansion and pressurization problems. A new two-shaft lightweight gearbox (the original was a hefty three-shaft design) worked well but did nothing to help Surtees cope with all that top-end power that could only be exploited on the fastest circuits. When the engine speed dropped the low-pressure injection system permitted fuel to become overheated in the fuel lines and resulted in persistent misfiring. Surtees' best performances were a third at Kyalami and a fourth at the Nürburgring. It became only too obvious that the logistics of communicating with a research base in Japan inhibited development and Honda were too involved in their production car development to devote enough time and facilities to the Formula One programme.

During 1967 Surtees agreed with Honda that the team at Slough should build an interim chassis. This was based on the Lola Indianapolis T190 monocoque and was a result of the close liaison between Surtees and Eric Broadley, whose cars Surtees raced in sports/racing and Prototype events. The new monocoque terminated at the rear bulkhead, to which was attached a multi-tubular frame supporting the engine, gearbox and rear suspension mountings. Although there were many Lola components and the nose cone came from the existing Lola body mould, from that point backwards the design was new. The new Honda was 228 lb lighter than its predecessor and featured a much simpler tankage system of three tanks. The RA300 first appeared at Monza, where Surtees scored a very narrow win from Jack Brabham's Brabham. Stronger wishbones were fitted to the RA300 for the United States GP, but Surtees was plagued by fuel injection trouble again. He finished fourth in Mexico. Only one RA300 was built.

RA301 and RA302 – 1968

For 1968 Honda finally produced their own much improved car typed the RA301, lower and flatter than the earlier works car, with outboard suspension and much modified engine. Now the V-12 unit featured the inlet ports in the vee, valve gear similar to that of Honda's Formula Two engine, with torsion bar valve springs and low-level outside exhausts. Unfortunately the RA301 was still heavier than the car built at Slough and the handling and roadholding were less than satisfactory. The new car, F-801, ran without success early in the

39. David Hobbs in the pits at Monza in 1968 with the RA301 Honda. Honda withdrew from racing at the end of the 1968 season.

40. The air-cooled V-8 RA302 Honda with Schlesser at the wheel at the 1968 French Grand Prix at Rouen. Schlesser crashed with fatal results.

season, although at Spa, where the Honda was raced with a rear aerofoil for the first time, Surtees took the lead and stayed in front until the rear suspension collapsed. Later in the year Surtees finished second at Rouen and third at Watkins Glen. A second RA301, chassis F-802 with the monocoque skinned in lighter magnesium, appeared at Monza; it was driven by David Hobbs, but retired with valve trouble. F-802 was used by Surtees in practice in Canada and the United States, and in the last race of the year, at Mexico City, was driven into fifth place by Joakim Bonnier.

During 1968 Honda revealed the remarkable RA302 with heavily finned air-cooled 120-degree V-8 2987 cc (88 × 61.4 mm) engine with four valves per cylinder driven from the rear of the crankshaft and of remarkably light construction. The initial power output was 380 bhp at 9000 rpm. Honda used a very low-weight monocoque skinned in magnesium, a front bulkhead mounted the front suspension and the engine was suspended from a boom extending from the rear bulkhead and was bolted to the rear bulkhead. A new 5-speed gearbox was attached to the back of the engine. The suspension was similar to that of the 1967 V-12 Hondas. The RA302 had a wheelbase of 7 ft 8 in., front track 4 ft 11 in., rear track 4 ft 9 in. and was said to be right on the minimum weight limit of 500 kg. Overall the car looked compact and highly competitive with potential for adequate development.

Although Surtees had briefly tested the RA302 at Silverstone, there was no immediate plan to race the car. However Mr. Soichiro Honda was in Europe on business at the time of the French GP and it was decided to run the RA302 with French driver Jo Schlesser at the wheel. The car ran very raggedly and Schlesser lost control on the third lap of the race when the engine cut out, mounted a bank, somersaulted and crashed; in the resulting fire poor Schlesser was killed. By the Italian GP the Honda team had ready a second RA302, F-802, which Hobbs drove before the start of official practice and Surtees used for a few laps in practice.

For Honda the end had come and the team withdrew from Formula One racing at the end of the 1968 season.

Kauhsen

(West Germany)

WK – 1979

Willi Kauhsen had earned a fine reputation as a sports car driver and entrant, but his team's appearance in Formula One was expensive, brief and disastrous. The Kauhsen was a Lotus-inspired, advanced 'wing car' designed by Klaus Kapitza, a Ford Cologne engineer, working in conjunction with the Aachen Technical School. It was Cosworth-powered and used a Hewland gearbox. It has been claimed that there were three prototypes that were abandoned and that the two cars that Kauhsen brought to the Spanish GP, chassis numbers 004 and 005, were really the fourth and fifth to be built. OO4 had extra side tanks, whilst 005 had only a single fuel cell behind the cockpit. Otherwise the cars were identical, low and flat with the rear aerofoil mounted on endplates. At Jarama the cars were driven by Gianfranco Brancatelli, but he was around five seconds slower than the speed needed to qualify. Another blow for Kauhsen at Jarama was a fine of $30,000 imposed by FISA, the governing body of the sport, because the Kauhsen team had failed to join the Championship in the correct manner at the start of the season. The team tried once more at Zolder, where Brancatelli was nine seconds slower than the slowest qualifier, and then decided not to race again.

Kojima

(Japan)

KE007 – 1976

Designed by Masao Ono and built by Matsuhisa Kojima's Kojima Engineering Company, the KE007 represented a simple, conventional approach to the construction of a Formula One car with aluminium riveted monocoque, front suspension by double wishbones and outboard coil spring/dampers and rear suspension by parallel lower links, single upper links, twin radius rods and outboard coil spring/damper units. The engine was the ubiquitous Cosworth DFV used in conjunction with a Hewland FGA400 gearbox. There were side radiators, outboard front brakes and inboard rear brakes. The wheelbase was 8 ft 10 in., front track 4 ft 7 in. and rear track 4 ft 9 in. The one exceptional feature of the Kojima was the sleek, black bodywork with Ferrari-type ducting round the cockpit. Masahiro Hasemi drove the Kojima at the 1976 Japanese GP and was tenth fastest in practice before crashing heavily. The car was rebuilt overnight and Hasemi finished eleventh and last after two pit stops. At his last pit stop he had fitted qualifying tyres and went on to set fastest lap of the race.

KE009 – 1977

For the following year's Japanese GP, the Kojima company built two improved cars, designated the KE009 and driven by Noritake Takahara and Kazuyoshi Hoshino. Hoshino finished the race in 11th place, two laps in arrears, while on the second lap Takahara crashed into Binder's Surtees, which was trying to avoid a wheel shed by Andretti, who had collided with Laffite! The Kojimas were not raced again.

41. Masahiro Hasemi with the Kojima KE007 in the 1976 Japanese Grand Prix. He crashed heavily, but the car was rebuilt in time to start the race.

LEC

(United Kingdom)

CRP1 – 1977

Designed by Mike Pilbeam and sponsored by Charles Purley of the LEC Refrigeration company, the LEC CRP1 represented an uncomplicated, conventional Formula One car of its period built round the Cosworth DFV engine and Hewland FGA400 gearbox. There was an aluminium riveted monocoque of angular form, with side radiators, front suspension by double wishbones and inboard coil spring/damper units and rear suspension by parallel lower links, single upper links, twin radius rods and outboard coil spring/damper units. The wheelbase was 8 ft 10.5 in., front track 4 ft 8 in. and rear track 5 ft 0 in.

The LEC was driven by David Purley, who had previously raced March Formula One cars. Purley drove the car on its debut in the the Race of Champions at Brands Hatch, finishing sixth, failed to qualify in Spain, finished at the tail of the field in Belgium and Sweden and crashed at Dijon. At Silverstone, during practice for the British GP, Purley had an horrific crash at Becketts when the LEC sliced through the marker cones and straight on into the outside bank at around 110 mph. The cause was jammed throttles, seemingly because extinguisher powder had been left in the system after a previous incident, and the result for Purley was multiple injuries. David Purley eventually made a full recovery only to lose his life recently at the controls of a Pitts aerobatic aircraft. In 1979 he had reappeared with a further example of the LEC in minor races.

42. The LEC CRP1 was a promising venture that came effectively to an end when David Purley crashed badly at Silverstone. Here Purley is seen in the 1977 French Grand Prix at Dijon.

Ligier
(France)

Never a dominant marque, the Ligier, run by construction company boss Guy Ligier, has achieved a rare consistency that has meant that in most years the cars have finished in the Championship points and in all have won a total of eight Championship Grands Prix. Automobiles Ligier was formed at Vichy in 1969 and Ligier adopted a 'JS' series of numbering in memory of his great friend Jo Schlesser, who was killed at the wheel of the air-cooled Honda at Rouen in 1968. The first Ligiers were intended for Sports Car racing and it was not until 1976 that a Formula One car was first raced.

JS5 – 1976

The JS5 was designed by Michel Beaujon and, as arrangements had been made to use the Matra V-12 engine, Ligier was able to use the services of Gérard Ducarouge to assist with design and development. Beaujon designed a very conventional monocoque with front suspension by double wishbones and inboard-mounted coil spring/damper units and rear suspension by parallel lower links, single upper links, twin radius rods and outboard coil spring/damper units. The Matra MS73 engine, claimed to develop 520 bhp at 12,000 rpm, was used with the Hewland TL200 gearbox. The wheelbase was 8 ft 7 in., front track 5 ft 0.5 in. and rear track 5 ft 3 in. Gitanes cigarettes sponsored the team, it was managed by Ducarouge and the driver was Jacques Laffite.

For a team in its first year it proved very successful, Laffite finishing fourth in the team's third race at Long Beach. At Jarama a change in the regulations had compelled Ligier to abandon the enormous airbox which had led to the Ligier being nicknamed the 'teapot' and the wing was further forward. Laffite finished third at Zolder and, fourth in Sweden, and in Austria the team raced the new JS5 with many less curves than the original and with this Laffite finished second behind Watson's Penske. Laffite was fastest in practice at Monza and finished third. There were no other successes that year.

JS7 – 1977

Few changes were made to the monocoque of the Ligier, but the JS7 had the Matra MS76 engine, which was lower, the weight distribution was altered, the bodywork was more rounded and there was a full-width front wing. After problems during the first few races of 1977,

Laffite came through to win the Swedish GP after Andretti's Lotus had run out of fuel. There followed a sixth place in the British GP at Silverstone, a second at Zandvoort and a fifth place in the last race of the season in Japan.

JS7 and JS9 – 1978

Ligier were running into problems, partly because Matra were losing interest in further development of the V-12 engine and partly because SEITA, the state-owned company that made Gitanes, was facing restrictions over cigarette advertising and was very late in confirming its continued support. Initially, therefore, Ligier relied on the JS7, updated by use of the lighter FGA400 Hewland gearbox that permitted quicker changes and by long rear stablizing fins. Laffite finished fifth at Kyalami and Long Beach. At Monaco the team raced the JS9 with longer wheelbase, but the gearbox broke, and at Zolder he drove an interim JS7/9 car into fifth place. Subsequently, with the JS9, Laffite finished third in Spain and Germany. He raced the second of the JS9 cars with revised suspension geometry into fifth place in Austria and

43. The late Patrick Depailler with the Ligier JS11 in the 1979 Monaco Grand Prix. He was classified fifth despite the engine blowing up two laps from the finish. Ligier started 1979 strongly with three wins, but faded as the year progressed.

fourth at Monza. The results would have been better if Matra had continued engine development and in fact they withdrew from racing at the end of the year.

JS11 – 1979

For 1979 Ligier switched to Cosworth power and Ducarouge and Beaujon designed a 'ground effect' car with aerodynamics developed by Charles Deutsch's SERA concern, featuring deep side pods and pronounced flip-ups ahead of the rear wheels so that the rotation of the wheels acted as extractors. The JS11s had a long 9 ft 2 in. wheelbase and front and rear suspension by upper rocking arms, lower wishbones and inboard springs. For the first time Ligier entered two cars for Laffite and Patrick Depailler. Initially the Ligiers were the pace-setters and it looked as though they would dominate the year's racing. Laffite won in both the Argentine and Brazil and Depailler took second place in the Brazilian race, both Ligiers crashed in South Africa, Depailler finished fifth at Long Beach and won in Spain, Laffite finished second in Belgium and Depailler was fifth at Monaco. The Monaco race was Depailler's last of the year because he broke both legs in a hang-gliding accident. Gitanes were determined that he should be replaced by a French-speaking driver and so, against Ligier's wishes, Belgian Jacky Ickx was brought into the team. Ickx had not handled a Formula One car for a couple of years and he simply could not get to grips with the Ligier. This, coupled with chassis and aerodynamic problems later in the year, destroyed Ligier's chances of winning the World Championship. Laffite was in third place in the British race when he retired with engine trouble and Ickx finished sixth. Laffite finished third at Hockenheim, the Österreichring and Zandvoort (where Ickx was fifth), but nothing else was gained during the remainder of the year. Laffite finished fourth in the World Championship and Ligier took third place in the Constructors' Cup.

JS11/15 – 1980

For the coming year the existing design was updated with redesigned wing and skirt systems and modified suspension. The drivers were Laffite and Didier Pironi, who tended to race against each other, rather than with each other, as had Laffite and Depailler during the early part of 1979. Throughout the year the team never quite managed to get its act together and the results fell far short of the team's potential. In the second race of the year, in Brazil, Pironi finished fourth. At Kyalami the team introduced a high-speed circuit 'kit' with smaller side pods and rear wings, and this was used at all the faster circuits during the year. In South Africa Laffite and Pironi finished second and third, Pironi was sixth at Long Beach and his best performance of the year was at Zolder, where he was second fastest in practice and led throughout the race. Pironi was fastest in practice at Monaco and led until his Ligier jumped out of gear and he hit the barriers. Laffite finished second to Reutemann's Williams. Pironi and Laffite finished second and third in the French race and tyre problems prevented victory at Brands Hatch, but Laffite came through to score a fine win in the German GP at Hockenheim. Laffite was fourth in Austria, third in Holland, Pironi fifth at Monza and third in both Canada and the United States. Laffite and Pironi were fourth and fifth in the Drivers' Championship and Ligier took second place in the Constructors' Cup. The year's results had been dominated by Williams, but it could so easily have been very different.

JS17 – 1981

For the 1981 season Ligier returned to Matra power, using the latest MS81 engine, and ran as Talbot-Ligiers. Beaujon and Ducarouge designed the completely new JS17, a straightforward design with 9 ft 1 in. wheelbase and front and rear suspension by upper rocking arms, lower wishbones and inboard coil spring/damper units. The drivers were Laffite and Jean-Pierre Jabouille. Jabouille had injured himself in a crash with a Renault late in 1980 and for the first two races his place was taken by Jean-Pierre Jarier. For much of the year the Ligier team was plagued by Matra engines giving far less power than promised and by the difficulties of devising a satisfactory lowering suspension, adopted by all the teams following the ban on sliding skirts. Nothing much was gained in the early part of the season, although Laffite was sixth in Brazil, third at Monaco, second in Spain (after which Jabouille's place was taken by Patrick Tambay) and third at Silverstone (by when Ducarouge had left the team) and Hockenheim. In Austria the Ligier team sprang a surprise. With the Matra engine really on song, the right choice of tyres and everything else working

44. *Jacques Laffite scored a fine, but unexpected win in the rain-soaked 1981 Canadian Grand Prix with the Matra-powered Ligier JS17. Here he leads Prost's Renault.*

well, Laffite came through to win the race from Arnoux's Renault. Another victory for Laffite followed in Canada and he finished sixth at Las Vegas, after holding second place before a stop for tyres. In the Drivers' Championship Laffite finished third with 43 points.

JS17 and JS19 – 1982

At the start of the 1982 season Talbot-Ligier continued to race the JS17s and the drivers were Laffite and Eddie Cheever. Apart from a third place by Cheever at Zolder, nothing was gained in the early part of the year and at Monaco the team revealed the JS19. As well as pull-rod-operated double wishbone suspension and shorter 8 ft 10 in. wheelbase, the new car featured full-length side pods and skirts. The rule book was consulted and it was determined that the side pods could be no longer than the wheelbase, so the rear portions of the skirts were removed and the Ligiers lost a good proportion of their downforce. Both cars retired in the race. The same decision was reached at Detroit, the JS19 entered being scratched and the team running the old JS17s; Cheever drove a fine race to finish second with Laffite sixth. The JS19s reappeared with abbreviated side pods in Holland, revised side pods and suspension appeared at Hockenheim and in Austria Laffite managed third place, Ligier's best performance of the year. Cheever also took sixth place at Monza and third at Las Vegas.

JS19 and JS21 – 1983

Matra withdrew from racing again at the end of the 1982 and Ligier rebuilt the JS19s to take Cosworth engines. The JS21 was built from scratch to take the Cosworth and to comply with the new flat-bottom rule. Racing was increasingly dominated by the turbocharged cars and the Ligier drivers Jean-Pierre Jarier and Raoul Boesel had minimal chances of success. For the first time in Ligier history the cars failed to score Championship points at any race.

45. De Cesaris finished fourth with the turbocharged Renault-powered Ligier JS25 in the 1985 Monaco Grand Prix.

JS23 – 1984

Renault agreed to supply turbocharged engines to Ligier in 1984, and to take these engines, used with the Ligier/Hewland gearbox, Michel Beaujon and Claude Galopin designed a new carbon-composite monocoque with a 9 ft 3 in. wheelbase and raced at the end of the year with push-rod operated wishbone suspension (in which form it was known as the JS23B). The drivers were Andrea de Cesaris and François Hesnault (a newcomer to Formula One). The Ligiers were simply not competitive and the only finish in the points was a fifth in South Africa by de Cesaris.

JS25 – 1985

Ligier were already developing the JS25 when the team was joined by Gérard Larrousse, sacked by Renault, and Michel Tétu, Renault chassis designer. Jacques Laffite returned to the team he had driven for over so many seasons and de Cesaris remained with Ligier. Laffite's steady driving and the development work carried out by Larrousse and Tétu resulted in a good run of places, with Laffite sixth in Brazil and Monaco, third in Britain and Germany and second in Australia. De Cesaris' career has always been marred by his wild crashes, and after rolling and flipping his car in Austria in spectacular fashion he was dropped from the team. His replacement, Philippe Streiff, finished third in Australia despite ramming Laffite in his efforts to gain second place from his team-mate. Earlier in the year de Cesaris had finished fourth at Monaco. It looked as though Ligier were on the way back.

JS27 – 1986

Laffite remained with Ligier and was joined by ex-Ferrari man René Arnoux to drive the latest JS27 cars. Laffite and Arnoux finished third and fourth in Brazil, Arnoux and Laffite were fifth and sixth at Monaco, Laffite was fifth at Spa, Arnoux sixth in Canada and Laffite second at Detroit. It was coming right for the team once more.

Lola

(United Kingdom)

Over a period stretching back to 1959, Eric Broadley's Lola Cars has built many successful single-seaters, but there have been only three designs for Formula One bearing the Lola name. The first of these was the Coventry-Climax-powered Mk4 design built for Bowmaker Racing in 1962. In 1974 came the T370 built for Graham Hill's Embassy Racing Team.

T370 – 1974

This was a conventional straightforward design, rather on the heavy side, with front suspension by double wishbones and outboard coil spring/damper units and, at the rear, parallel lower links, single upper links, twin radius rods and outboard springs. The Ford DVF engine was used with the Hewland FGA400 gearbox. The wheelbase was 8 ft 6 in., and front and rear track 5 ft 4 in. It was a neatly constructed car, well finished and with its appearance dominated by a very large and very tall air-box.

Graham Hill drove throughout the year. Guy Edwards was in the team until he broke a wrist, and his place was taken in the British GP by Peter Gethin and thereafter by Rolf Stommelen. Although the Lolas showed a good level of reliability, they were slow and the only finish in the points was sixth place by Hill in Sweden. The team raced the cars in the first three races of 1975 until the new Hill GH1 was ready, but no success was gained.

THL1 – 1985–86

Initially with heavy sponsorship from the American Beatrice Foods group and American Lola concessionaire Carl Haas, new cars bearing the Lola name (originally known as the Beatrice-Lola) were raced by Teddy Mayer's FORCE team from late 1985 onwards. The new car was designed by Neil Oatley, an ex-Williams engineer, and there was little connection with Lola apart from the name. The new car, with push-rod double wishbone suspension front and rear, initially the Hart 415T turbocharged engine and Hewland-based 6-speed gearbox, was driven by Australian ex-World Champion Alan Jones. It appeared at

46. Promising newcomer – the Lola TH1 with Alan Jones at the wheel in the 1985 Grand Prix of Europe at Brands Hatch.

Monza, missed the Belgian race, non-started in South Africa because the driver was unwell and failed to finish in any of its three starts.

By 1986 the team had lost its Beatrice backing because of a major change of policy by the American company and a second Lola was driven by Patrick Tambay. By the third race of the season at Imola the team was able to run a car for Jones with the long-awaited Cosworth-designed Ford V-6 turbocharged engine and by Monaco the team was able to field a second Ford-powered car for Tambay. Not surprisingly, in the highly competitive Formula One of 1986, no finishes in the points were gained in the early part of the year and the team had a long, hard development programme ahead of it.

Lotus

(United Kingdom)

33 and 43 – 1966

Although plans were well advanced for the development of a new engine to power Lotus Grand Prix cars, at the start of the new Formula in 1966 the team was forced to rely on the old 1500 cc models with enlarged engines and on the H-16 engines supplied by BRM. For the first races in 1966 Team Lotus used only the 33 model, an improved version of the original 1962 25 monocoque car that had first appeared in 1964, one example of which was powered by the Coventry-Climax twin-cam V-8 engine increased in capacity from 1.5 to 2-litres by the use of a longer-stroke crankshaft and developing around 250 bhp. Later in the year Team Lotus also raced a 33 powered by a 2-litre BRM engine, which necessitated the transfer of the gear-change to the left of the cockpit.

At the Belgian GP the team introduced the new 43 powered by the BRM H-16 engine. Just as the Lotus 43 inspired the later and brilliantly successful 49 model, so it itself was inspired by the earlier 39, which had been designed to take the 1.5-litre flat-16 Coventry-Climax engine and which had been used during the first months of 1966 for Tasman racing powered by the 4-cylinder Climax FPF engine. The 43 consisted of a monocoque forward structure to which the H-16 engine (stressed to carry the rear suspension without any chassis structure) was bolted; the rear suspension was located at points on the cylinder heads and gearbox bell housing. Compared with BRMs own H-16 car, the Lotus 43 had a smaller frontal area and was aerodynamically smoother and more efficient. Apart from its persistent lack of reliability, the BRM engine was also very heavy and Team Lotus regarded it purely as a stop-gap until their own engine became available. The 43 had a wheelbase of 8 ft 0 in., and front and rear track were both 5 ft 0 in.

Throughout 1966 Team Lotus was plagued by mechanical problems and little success was achieved. Jim Clark took pole position at Monaco with the Climax-powered 33 and was in third place when eliminated by a broken suspension upright. He was forced to pull out of the French race after he was struck in the face by a bird during practice (Rodriguez took his place in the race) and it was not until the British GP at Brands Hatch that he finished, in fourth position. Team-mate Peter Arundell had been classified eighth with the 2-litre BRM-powered car at both the Nürburgring and Monza. At Monza Clark had driven the H-16 Lotus 43 for the first time, but retired with transmission failure; he finished third with the Climax-powered 33 in the Gold Cup race at Oulton Park and rounded off the year with a surprise win with the H-16 car in the United States GP at Watkins Glen, a win largely attributable to the retirement of much of the opposition. Arundell finished sixth in this race with the Climax-powered 33.

49 – 1967

It had been an appalling year for Team Lotus, but great things were to come. For 1967 Graham Hill rejoined Lotus after seven years with BRM. After racing the 43s in South Africa, the team relied on the old 2-litre cars in the early part of the season, with Hill finishing fourth with a BRM-powered car in the International Trophy at Silverstone and second at Monaco. The Dutch GP at Zandvoort was marked by the debut of the new Lotus 49, which won on its first outing (in itself an unusual feat), and the new car was powered by the Cosworth-designed Ford DFV engine, which was to dominate Grand Prix racing until the end of the 1982 season.

Although the Ford engine was produced specifically for Lotus as a direct result of a deal between Colin Chapman and Ford, the direct advantages to Lotus were limited to the free loan of five engines in 1967 and the exclusive use of the engine that year only. The DFV was a compact and highly efficient four overhead camshaft 2993 cc (85.67 × 64.8 mm) unit initially developing 405 bhp at 9000 rpm and was admirably matched by a chassis design derived from that of the 1966 43 model. A basically similar monocoque was used (but lighter and slimmer, primarily because the Ford engine was so much smaller than the BRM H-16) constructed from 18 swg aluminium sheet, with the engine an integral stressed member and mild-steel bulkheads. The fuel load was contained in 15-gallon rubber bag fuel tanks mounted in the sides of the monocoque and a similar 10-gallon tank mounted behind the driver's seat. The engine was attached to the rear bulkhead at four points (by lugs on each cam-box and studs projecting from a bracing below the auxiliary drive belt). Transmission was by a German-made ZF 5DS 12 5-speed gearbox.

A tubular sub-frame to locate the front suspension was bolted to the front bulkhead. At the front the suspension consisted of upper rocking wishbones, leading link/trailing arm lower wishbones, inboard-mounted coil spring/damper units and an anti-roll bar. The rear suspension was attatched to the engine by means of triangulated sub-frames, and comprised single upper links, lower wishbones, twin radius arms, outboard coil spring/damper units and an anti-roll bar. The thick, ventilated disc brakes were mounted slightly inboard of the wheels and Lotus 15 in. cast magnesium wheels were fitted. The body was the ultimate in simplicity, side-panels and a long nose-cone, and the 49s were finished in the usual Lotus green and yellow colours.

Clark won the Dutch race by a margin of 30 seconds after Hill had retired because of broken timing gear teeth. The 49s failed in their next two races at Spa (Clark was sixth after two pit stops for plug changes) and in the French GP, but Clark won again in the British GP at Silverstone. Failures followed again at the Nürburgring and Mosport (in Canada, Hill was fourth after spinning, stalling and push-starting his car); at Monza the 49s dominated the race, but not the results, for Hill was eliminated by engine failure whilst leading, and Clark also led, only to finish third when he ran low on fuel. Lotus finished the year in fine style, with Clark and Hill taking the first two places at Watkins Glen, and Clark won at Mexico City. Clark and Hill also took the first two places in the non-Championship Spanish GP at Jarama.

47. The sensation of the 1967 season was the appearance of the Ford-powered Lotus 49. Here Jim Clark is seen in the Belgian Grand Prix which he led during the opening laps.

49 and 49B – 1968

In the South African GP the 49s ran in the traditional Team Lotus green and yellow colours for the last time and Clark and Hill took the first two places. The team had now secured sponsorship from John Player and from now on until the end of 1971 ran in the red, white and gold colours of Player's Gold Leaf cigarettes. In April Jim Clark was killed at the wheel of a Lotus 48 Formula Two car at Hockenheim. Despite this terrible blow Lotus carried on racing and entered a single car for Hill in the International Trophy at Silverstone (where he retired) and the Spanish GP, which he won after the retirement of Amon's Ferrari.

Present, but unraced at Jarama, had been a new and improved version of the Formula One car known as the 49B. The wheelbase had been increased by angling the upper rocking arms forwards; the rear suspension was carried on a much stonger sub-frame, and the Hewland DG300 gearbox which absorbed suspension loads through its casing was fitted (so that suspension loads were no longer carried by the cylinder heads); the rear suspension featured longer and lower radius rods; and externally the car was modified by a new nose fitted with adjustable fins and an upward-sweeping glass-fibre engine cover attached both at the front and to the gearbox.

By Monaco the team had been joined by Jack Oliver and in this race Hill drove the new 49B to victory. The 49Bs were out of the picture at both Spa and Zandvoort. At Rouen the Lotus team followed the fashion set by Brabham and Ferrari and the 49Bs were fitted with high rear aerofoils. In practice the aerofoil of Oliver's car lost its traction

48. The last Grand Prix win by a private entrant was in the 1968 British Grand Prix in which Jo Siffert drove Rob Walker's Lotus 49 to victory.

in the slipstream of Attwood's BRM and crashed into a wall at around 140 mph. Oliver was unhurt, but the car was wrecked. Only Hill started the race and he retired. Both the works cars retired in the British GP, but the race was won by Jo Siffert at the wheel of Rob Walker's new 49B, the last Grand Prix win ever by a private entry. In the rain-soaked German GP Hill finished second after spinning and push-starting his car and Oliver took third place in the Gold Cup race at Oulton Park. During the remainder of the year Lotus achieved some fine results. Although the 49Bs retired at Monza, Hill finished fourth in Canada despite broken engine mounts; he took second place at Watkins Glen and won the Mexican race. With 48 points to the 36 of Jackie Stewart (Matra), Hill clinched his fourth Drivers' Championship. Mario Andretti had been entered by the team at Monza, where he was not allowed to start because he had competed in the United States the previous day at Watkins Glen, and Bill Brack drove for the team in Canada.

49B – 1969

At the end of 1968 Jack Oliver left the team and was replaced by young Austrian driver Jochen Rindt. For much of 1969 Hill and Rindt fought a bitter duel between themselves instead of working together as a team, thereby making it all the easier for Stewart with his Ford-powered Matra to clinch the World Championship; and Chapman became increasingly – and mistakenly – preoccupied with the development of the 63 four-wheel-drive car, and at one stage in the season proposed selling off the 49s!

In South Africa cars were entered for Hill, Rindt and Andretti, but of the works cars only Hill's finished, in second place, with Siffert fourth with the Rob Walker entry. The race was won by Stewart with the Matra and they were to prove the dominant combination during the year. Hill finished second in the Race of Champions at Brands Hatch, Rindt second in the International Trophy at Silverstone and in Spain the 49Bs of both Hill and Rindt were eliminated by crashes following the collapse of the very high rear wings. At Monaco a ban was placed on the use of high aerofoils and the Lotus entries were hastily fitted with upswept tail panels. Hill drove a fine race to score his fifth win at Monaco, Siffert was third with the Walker entry and Attwood (deputizing for Rindt, injured in Spain) finished fourth.

During the remainder of the year very little success came the way of Team Lotus. Hill and Rindt battled for the lead at Zandvoort until both drivers ran into problems, Hill was a poor sixth at Clermont-Ferrand and at Silverstone Rindt finished fourth after fighting a bitter duel with Stewart and two pit stops. Hill finished fourth in the German GP. At Monza Rindt carried on the fight with Stewart, beaten into second place by four-fifths of a second, he was third in Canada and scored his first ever Championship race victory at Watkins Glen.

For Hill the United States GP was a disaster. He was in fifth place when a rear tyre started to deflate, spun off and push-started his car. He rejoined the race with his safety harness undone (this could only be done up by the mechanics) and he indicated to the pits that he would stop at the end of the next lap; on that final lap the tyre deflated completely, the Lotus rolled off the track and Hill was flung out of the cockpit and suffered severe leg injuries. Only a single 49B for Rindt was entered in the Mexican GP and he retired because of a broken front rocker arm.

49C – 1970

By the end of the 1969 season Chapman had given up all hope of turning the 63 into a raceworthy proposition and work was well advanced on the car that was to bring Jochen Rindt a posthumous World Championship. In the meantime the team had to make do with the 49, now in its fourth season of racing, but in an improved form, the 49C, with modified front suspension and new hubs to permit the fitting of 13 in. wheels; the result of these modifications was a reduction in unsprung weight, thereby improving the stability and lightening the steering.

John Miles (who had driven the 63 in 1969) now partnered Rindt in the Lotus team and Hill, who had made a remarkable recovery from his accident, now drove a Lotus for Rob Walker. Miles finished fifth in South Africa with Hill sixth, and Rindt took second place in the Race of Champions. The new 72 appeared at the Spanish GP, but was far from right, and Rindt reappeared at Monaco with the 49C fitted with a three-tier rear aerofoil of the type first tried on the 72. The Austrian drove an inspired race and scored a surprise victory when Jack Brabham hit the barrier at the last corner on the last lap. From the Dutch GP onwards Rindt and Miles drove 72s, but at three races Lotus still entered the 49C, for Emerson Fittipaldi in the British GP (he was eighth), and in 1971 for Wilson Fittipaldi in the non-Championship Argentine GP (ninth) and Tony Trimmer in the Spring Cup at Oulton Park (sixth).

56B – 1971

During 1968 the gas-turbine Lotus 56 with Canadian Pratt & Whitney engines had been raced in USAC events, including Indianapolis, by Andy Granatelli's STP team. From this development programme there had eventually emerged a version of the Pratt & Whitney engine, with single axial compressor stage and single centrifugal stage feeding an annular combustion chamber, that complied with the equivalency formula for Formula One cars. The engines were installed in a 56 chassis that had not been raced. The 56 featured four-wheel drive, a wedge-shaped 'bathtub'-type monocoque and suspension front and rear by double wishbones and inboard-mounted coil spring/damper units. The monocoque was reworked in lighter alloy and later featured large bulges either side to accommodate extra fuel, which eventually totalled 62 gallons.

Chapman had hoped that the 56B would be ready to run at Monza in 1970, but in fact it did not appear until the following year. Fittipaldi drove the 56B in the Race of Champions at Brands Hatch, but retired because of rear suspension damaged through bottoming, Wisell retired with suspension failure at Oulton Park and in the International Trophy at Silverstone Fittipaldi retired in the first heat because of suspension failure but finished third in the second heat. Dave Walker drove the 56B in the Dutch GP, but through an error of judgement crashed into the fencing. In the British GP the gas turbine was handled by Wisell, but it lost its power, and at the finish he was too far behind to be classified. Because of possible repercussions from Rindt's death at Monza in 1970 that could have led to the cars being impounded, the 56B only, painted gold and black and entered in the name of 'World Wide Racing', was driven by Fittipaldi and finished eighth. A week later Fittipaldi drove the 56B into second place in a Formula 5000 race at Hockenheim. The car had been purely an experimental prototype and here the experiment ended.

49. Too heavy and too unwieldy, but a fascinating experiment – the Pratt & Whitney gas turbine-powered Lotus 56B seen here with Emerson Fittipaldi at the wheel at the 1971 Race of Champions.

63 – 1969

During the late sixties the very promising performances of four-wheel drive cars at Indianapolis had encouraged the development of four-wheel drive in Formula One and, Cosworth apart, cars were built by McLaren, Matra and Lotus. Of these Lotus was the most serious contender and Chapman was convinced of the future of four-wheel drive. The new 63 featured a bathtub monocoque similar to that of the 56 Indianapolis car with as much weight as possible concentrated within the wheelbase, fuel cells in pontoon side-boxes and, of necessity, the driver's seat well to the front with the driver's feet below the front axle tube. The Cosworth engine was reversed in the chassis, but quite well forward, so that the clutch assembly was at the front with drive through a Lotus-Hewland gearbox; the fore and aft drive-shafts, running in enclosed tubes, were to the left (as on Lotus Indianapolis cars) and drove offset ZF final drives on each axle. Suspension front and rear was by fabricated rocker arms operating inboard coil spring/damper units. The large ventilated Girling disc brakes were mounted inboard front and rear. In appearance the 63 looked sleek and purposeful with a long, pointed nose and wedge-shaped profile.

Although the 63 was intended to eventually replace the 49, it was driven initially by John Miles, who had no previous Formula One experience, and therefore no preconceived ideas, and Mario Andretti, a great four-wheel drive enthusiast on the basis of his Indianapolis experience. Miles drove the 63 on its debut in the French GP, but retired on the second lap because of fuel pump failure, and he struggled across the line in ninth place in the British GP after the gearbox had jammed in third. Andretti crashed at the Nürburgring, Rindt finished second in the Gold Cup race at Oulton Park and Miles retired with camshaft failure in the Italian GP. Two more failures followed: at Watkins Glen Andretti retired after a first lap accident and in Mexico Miles retired because of a misfiring engine. During the latter part of the year the 63 (of which two were built) ran with by far the greater proportion of torque to the rear wheels, thus negating the idea behind the design, and the cars were plagued by chronic understeer and heavy steering. At the end of the year the project was abondoned.

72 – 1970

The new 72, conceived by Chapman and designed in detail by Maurice Phillipe, represented a major step forward in racing practice. Wedge shaped to achieve the maximum air penetration, the 72's monocoque, fabricated from multi-curvature panels formed over steel bulkheads, tapered towards the front; because of the basic wedge shape, a conventional front-mounted radiator could not be accommodated, so there were twin side-mounted radiators, and the flush-riveted 18-

guage outer skin of the monocoque flowed smoothly outwards towards the radiator ducts. The 20-guage Alclad inner panels of the monocoque sloped inwards sharply at the base of the cockpit to provide adequate fuel capacity. Other conspicuous external features of the 72 were the very low, flat nose with wide fins and a three-tier rear wing.

Under the skin the design of the 72 was even more revolutionary. The familiar coil spring suspension had been completely abandoned in favour of a new compound torsion bar layout. The torsion bars consisted of an outer tubular component with a solid bar passing through the tube and joined to it at the inner end; the tubular section was rigidly mounted to the chassis, while the inner bar protruded outwards and was attached to the linkage retaining the wheel. The result was a progressive suspension system which permitted, by Grand Prix standards, very soft springing, without any loss in handling qualities. Front and rear the suspension was located by upper and lower wishbones fabricated from nickel-chrome-molybdenum sheet. To give anti-dive at the front the wishbones were mounted at a very steep angle, with the front mountings lower than the rear mountings; at the rear the front mountings were higher to prevent anti-squat. Another unusual feature of the car was the inboard mounting of both the front and rear brakes; there were solid brake discs and the brakes were operated through drive-shafts. The wheelbase was 8 ft 4 in., front and rear track 4 ft 9 in. and the height a mere 2 ft 11 in. The Ford DFV engine was retained and transmission was by the Hewland FG300 gearbox (although the heavier DG300 was fitted orginally).

At the start of the season the 72 was far from right and after failures in Spain and in the International Trophy at Silverstone, Team Lotus relied on the 49Cs at Monaco and Rindt also drove a 49C at Spa. At Spa the 72 that should have been driven by Rindt (it was taken over by Soler-Roig, who failed to qualify) featured modified suspension

50. Another interesting experiment was the four-wheel-drive Lotus 63 raced with some success in 1969. John Miles drove this 63 on its actual race debut in the French Grand Prix at Clermont-Ferrand, but retired because of fuel pump failure.

eliminating anti-dive and anti-squat. By Zandvoort a stiffer rear frame had been adopted and in this form the car later became known as the 72C.

Rindt was fastest in practice at Zandvoort and won the race. He followed this up with victories in the French race at Clermont-Ferrand and at Brands Hatch (despite a lengthy augument at the British race as to whether the height of Rindt's rear aerofoil exceeded that permitted). Rindt's fourth successive win followed in the German GP at Hockenheim, he retired in Austria where Ickx (Ferrari) was the winner and then disaster struck at Monza. In practice Rindt's 72 left the road at the Parabolica curve, hit the Armco on the outside of the circuit and the very low nose of the 72 passed under the barrier; Rindt suffered terrible injuries to which he succumbed almost immediately. The other Lotus entries for Miles and Emerson Fittipaldi, together with Rob Walker's new 72 to be driven by Hill were withdrawn. Lotus missed the Canadian GP and entered two 72s for Fittipaldi and Swedish driver Reine Wisell at Watkins Glen. Fittipaldi took the lead, while Rodriguez' BRM made an unscheduled refuelling stop, and went on to win with Wisell third. The Lotus team was out of the picture at the last race of the year in Mexico. Jochen Rindt was posthumous World Champion.

72C and 72D – 1971

Fittipaldi and Wisell remained with the team in 1971, but it proved

51. The 72 was probably the most successful Lotus Formula One design. Jochen Rindt drove this car to the 72's first race victory in the 1970 Dutch Grand Prix at Zandvoort.

a season of only limited success. Nothing was gained in the early part of the year and by Monaco the team had produced the revised 72D car; the latest low-profile tyres had been causing problems and to cure these the rear suspension was modified to incorporate additional lower radius rods, parallel lower links (instead of the wishbones), new upper links and an upper cross-member and tubular sub-frame bolted under the gearbox casing (in place of the original rectangular structure which-carried the rear suspension). At Monaco Fittipaldi drove the 72D into fifth place.

Shortly afterwards Fittipaldi was injured in a road accident and his place at the Rindt Memorial race at Hockenheim was taken by Formula Three driver Dave Walker and at Zandvoort by South African Dave Charlton (Walker crashed during practice and Charlton non-started). Fittipaldi was back in the team by the British race, but the only successes during the remainder of the year were a third by Fittipaldi at Silverstone, second in Austria and second in the Rothmans-sponsored race at Brands Hatch in October.

72D – 1972

It was all change at Team Lotus at the end of 1971. Henceforth the 72Ds were known as 'John Player Specials' and entered by 'John Player Team Lotus' in very smart black and gold colours. Although Fittipaldi remained team leader, Wisell was replaced by Dave Walker. Apart from air-boxes of revised design, new aerofoils, a revised oil tank arrangement and suspension refinements, the 72Ds were unchanged, but careful development was paying off and the cars were again competitive.

The JPS team failed in the Argentine, but Fittipaldi finished second in South Africa, won the Race of Champions at Brands Hatch and the International Trophy at Silverstone. Fittipaldi's first Championship race win of the season came in the Spanish GP, JPS failed at Monaco, but Fittipaldi won on the Nivelles circuit in Belgium and finished second in France. During this period he also took second place in the Gold Cup race at Oulton Park and won the Gran Premio Republica Italiana at Vallelunga, both of course non-Championship races. Another win for Fittipaldi followed in the British GP, he was well down the field at the Nürburgring because of gearbox trouble and won the Austrian GP, the Formule Libre Rothmans 50,000 race at Brands Hatch and the Italian GP at Monza (still, because of the Rindt accident, only a single car was entered in the name of World Wide Racing). Although the JPS team failed in the last two races of the year, Fittipaldi had the World Championship in the bag with 61 points to the 45 of Stewart (Tyrrell). Wisell had replaced Walker in Canada and drove a third JPS entry at Watkins Glen.

72D – 1973

Colin Chapman was struggling with new Formula One developments, but meanwhile the team battled on with the 72D and the very strong driver combination of Fittipaldi and Ronnie Peterson. Peterson, after three years with March and second place in the 1971 Championship, was probably the world's fastest driver, but had yet to win a Grand Prix.

The season started brilliantly with wins by Fittipaldi in both the Argentine and Brazilian GPs, and he followed these successes up with a third place in South Africa. There were only two non-Championship races in 1974. By the Race of Champions the 72Ds had been modified to comply with the new deformable structure regulations. They featured a wider front track (tried in practice only), modified rear suspension to improve traction and new cast rear suspension uprights. Both JPS entries retired at Brands Hatch, but Peterson finished second shortly afterwards in the International Trophy at Silverstone.

Fittipaldi, despite a deflating rear tyre, won the Spanish GP after Peterson's leading car had dropped out with transmission problems. At the Belgian GP at Zolder Peterson crashed both his race car and spare during race-morning practice and he crashed again in the race proper. In Belgium Fittipaldi finished third, Fittipaldi and Peterson finished second and third at Monaco behind Stewart's Tyrrell and Peterson finished second in Sweden after a rear tyre punctured. Peterson won the French GP after Fittipaldi had collided with Scheckter's McLaren and Peterson finished second in the British race, but the JPS entries were out of the picture at both Zandvoort and Hockenheim. By the Austrian GP the team had regained its form; Peterson was the winner, and he and Fittipaldi took the first two places at Monza. Fittipaldi took another second place in Canada and Peterson was the winner at Watkins Glen. In the Drivers' Championship Fittipaldi took second place with 55 points and Peterson was third with 52 points, whilst JPS won the Constructors' Cup.

72D – 1974

The real hope for the 1974 season was the 76, but this proved a failure, and for much of the season Peterson, now partnered by Jacky Ickx, drove the ageing 72Ds. Fittipaldi had left to drive for McLaren. It was mainly due to Peterson's insistence that the team relied on the 72Ds and abandoned the struggle with the 76, and he achieved a reasonable measure of success. Ickx, however, seemed unable to get to grips with the 72D and his only successes of the year were a third place in the Brazilian GP, a win in the Race of Champions, fifth in the French GP, third in the British race and fifth in the German GP.

Peterson loved high-speed circuits and his press-on driving coupled with the very good straight-line performance of the 72D brought the team a fair measure of success. At Monaco Peterson fought his way to victory from Scheckter's Tyrrell, he scored another victory in the French GP at Dijon, finished fourth at the Nürburgring and won the Italian GP at Monza at a record 135.41 mph. Peterson rounded off the season with a third place in Canada. He finished fifth in the Drivers' Championship, and JPS/Lotus were a poor fourth in the Constructors' Cup.

72D – 1975

Despite three Grand Prix victories in 1974, Chapman's team had lost much of the splendour and aura of past years and was rapidly sinking into mediocrity. The team's complete failure throughout 1975 was to shatter what little remained of the Lotus image. Both Peterson and Ickx remained with the team, and although work was progressing on a new car, for the whole of the year the two unhappy and disillusioned drivers were obliged to rely on what was now uncompetitive machinery – and their morale sunk accordingly.

During this very poor season the best performances were third and fourth by Peterson and Ickx in the the Race of Champions, Ickx was classified second in the Spanish GP, brought to a premature end follow-

52. Four years later Lotus were still racing the same model and Ronnie Peterson won the 1974 Italian Grand Prix with this car.

ing Stommelen's bad accident, and Peterson took fourth place at Monaco. By the French GP on the Paul Ricard circuit the 72Ds had the wheelbase lengthened by five inches by inserting a new oil tank the engine and the rear bulkhead. Neither driver finished in the first six and the confidence of Ickx, eliminated for the second time in 1975 by drive-shaft failure, was completely shattered. The Belgian driver was 'rested' for the remainder of the year.

Chapman now concentrated on one well-prepared car for Peterson and tried out different drivers in the team's other entries. These included John Watson, Brian Henton and Jim Crawford. All that was gained was a fifth place by Peterson in the Austrian GP, stopped prematurely because of bad weather conditions, fourth in the non-Championship Swiss GP at Dijon and fifth at Watkins Glen.

Despite the misfortunes of 1974–75, the 72 had won a total of 20 World Championship Grands Prix and the Constructors' Cup in three seasons. It was a magnificent design that had simply been raced for far too long.

76–1974

The Lotus 76 – or John Player Special Mk. I as the team insisted

53. Not a successful design – the Lotus 76 seen here with Ronnie Peterson at the wheel in the 1974 International Trophy at Silverstone; Peterson retired because of tyre and engine problems.

that it should be called – was an attempt to capitalize on the qualities of the 72, but with lower weight. There was a new and updated monocoque 'tub' constructed in 16-gauge alloy sheet, slightly wedge shaped and very shallow and eliminating the separate front sub-frame of the 72. Torsion bar springing was retained front and rear, with fabricated double wishbones at the front, and at the rear a system of twin parallel upper links, single lower links and twin radius rods. The most novel feature of the 76 was an electronic clutch and four pedals. The pedal on the extreme left was used for starting from rest and thereafter the clutch was actuated by a gear-knob button. There were two linked brake pedals so that the driver was able to use the left foot for braking, enabling him to balance the car smoothly into corners. The transmission incorporated the usual Hewland FG400 5-speed gearbox. The 76 had a wheelbase was 8 ft 5 in., front track 4 ft 10 in. and rear track 5 ft 2 in. (the track was the same as the then current version of the 72).

JPS raced the new car only in the early part of the season. In South Africa Ickx's car lacked the electronic clutch mechanism, whilst on Peterson's car the pedals had been rearranged so that the left-foot brake was to the left of the clutch. On the first lap Peterson's throttles jammed, he collided with Ickx and both JPS entries were eliminated. In the next three races, the International Trophy at Silverstone and the Spanish and Belgian GPs, the 76s were raced with conventional clutch and braking arrangements and it was said that the electronic clutch was undergoing further development. No success had been achieved so far, the drivers were unhappy with the handling of the 76 and as a result of Peterson's pressure the team reverted to the 72Ds at Monaco. Although taken to races as spare cars, the 76s were not raced again until the Nürburgring. After Peterson had crashed in practice when a wheel broke, he drove to fourth place in the race a car that combined the monocoque of the 76 with the engine and rear suspension of a 72. Ickx drove a 76 with 72 rear end in both Austria and Italy and Tim Schenken drove the 76 at Watkins Glen. Rather than attempt to develop the 76, it was abandoned so that the team could press on with a completely new design for 1976.

77 – 1976

Chapman was only too well aware that Lotus/JPS Formula One development had not kept pace with the evolution of the sport, both in terms of the technical developments of other teams and the circuit changes. The Type 77, otherwise known as the John Player Special Mk. II, was in effect an interim experimental car that was to prove the basis for the following year's very successful Type 78. The slim monocoque, designed by Geoff Aldridge, incorporated a structural inboard brake system in which the callipers also acted as pick-ups for the suspension wishbones and links. At the front suspension was by double wishbones and outboard coil spring/damper units, whilst at the rear there were single lower links, parallel upper links, twin radius rods and outboard coil spring/damper units. As usual the engine was the Cosworth DFV and transmission was by a Hewland FG400 gearbox. The 77 had many shortcomings, especially the aerodynamics, which one commentator described as dreadful. However, Chapman had set up a research development group to exploit the basic versatility of the 77, experimenting with variations of wheelbase, track geometry and weight distribution; as the season progressed, the lessons learned would be incorporated in the team cars.

In Brazil the 77s driven by Peterson and Mario Andretti collided and were eliminated. Peterson, weary of Lotus failures, left the team to drive once more for March, while Andretti had been engaged for the one race only. For the next few races Lotus engaged Bob Evans and Gunnar Nilsson. It was not until Spain in May that any signs of success were seen; Andretti had joined the team on a regular basis and Nilsson finished third on the Jarama circuit. By this time the 77s were fitted with outboard front brakes incorporating Ralt suspension uprights, the work of freelance designer Len Terry. Now designer Tony Southgate joined the team from Shadow and further improvements were seen. Andretti finished fifth in the French GP on the Paul Ricard circuit, Nilsson was fifth at the Nürburgring and third in Austria and Andretti was third at Zandvoort and third in Canada; in the Japanese GP on the Mount Fuji circuit the vast improvements made to the cars showed when Andretti was fastest in practice and took the lead as the circuit dried out to score the team's only win of the season.

78 – 1977

In developing and building the Type 78 (also known as the John

54. Gradual development turned the Lotus 77 into a race-winning car and Andretti drove this 77 to victory in 1976 in the rain-swept and misty Japanese Grand Prix.

Player Special Mk. III), Lotus relied heavily on the lessons learned with the 1976 cars and introduced one important new factor. The monocoque was slim and shapely, like the 77, but there were broad flat panniers between front and rear wheels, there was a fully stressed tank section to the rear of the cockpit and a structural scuttle panel. Cellite (two thin dural sheets sandwiching aluminium honeycomb) was used extensively in the front bulkhead and side skins. At the front suspension was by swept-back rocker arms, wide based fabricated lower wishbones and inboard-mounted coil spring/damper units. The rear suspension geometry remained unchanged, but there were fabricated lower wishbones. Apart from the first car, the wheelbase was 8 ft 11 in., front track 5 ft 7 in. and rear track 5 ft 3 in. The most important aspect of the new car was the adoption of the broad panniers which housed the water radiators; these, together with a bristle skirt had been developed by aerodynamicist Peter Wright to provide an inverted wing section creating an airflow whereby the car would be sucked down on to the road. Thus the first ground-effect car had arrived in Formula One. The 78 was also fitted with three fuel cells in line behind the cockpit concentrated around the centre of gravity. By varying the order

55. At the wheel of the Lotus 79 Mario Andretti won the 1978 World Championship. He is seen here in the Swedish Grand Prix in which he retired with engine trouble.

and extent to which the fuel cells could be drained, the driver could adjust the trim of the car.

During the year Andretti was plagued by failures of the Cosworth engines, both Cosworth development engines and DFVs rebuilt by Nicholson-McLaren Engines, and no satisfactory explanation was found. In practice for the first race, the Argentine GP, Andretti's on-board fire extinguisher exploded and wrecked the front of the car, so he took over Nilsson's 78 to finish fifth. Nilsson finished fifth in Brazil and it was not until Long Beach that the team found its form; here Andretti won a race-long battle with Scheckter when the South African's right front tyre started to deflate, and this was the first of four Championship race wins during the year. A second victory followed in Spain, where Nilsson was fifth, and Andretti was fifth at Monaco. Through over-exuberance Andretti triggered off a first-lap collision with Watson (Brabham) at Zolder, he finished sixth in Sweden, having led for 68 laps until his car ran low on fuel, won at Dijon when Watson's Brabham ran low on fuel on the last lap and won again at Monza; he also took second place at Watkins Glen. In addition Nilsson won in Belgium and finished third in the British GP. Andretti took third place in the Drivers' Championship with 47 points and the team was second in the Constructors' Cup with 62 points to the 95 of Ferrari. Lotus had made a remarkable comeback and much of it was attributable to the close working relationship between Chapman and Andretti.

78 and 79 – 1978

Although the existing 78 cars were raced in the early part of the 1978 season, they were soon replaced by the new 79. Now that both Southgate and Bellamy had left Lotus, Chapman took a very active role in the development of the new car. There was a very slender monocoque constructed from sheet aluminium, a fabricated stressed-panel bulkhead and the fuel carried in a single tank behind the driver. The single water radiator was on the right-hand side and the oil cooler on the left. At the front the suspension was no longer swept back and the coil spring/damper units were mounted well inboard. At the rear the coil spring/damper units were now inboard. There was a new and lighter gearbox, the result of a long development study, designed by Lotus and built in Germany by Getrag. The 79 had been designed to exploit 'ground effect' to the full, with the side pods as wide as possible, rigid skirts, the rear wing supported by the endplates, the driving position well to the front and enclosed engine bay.

Andretti was joined in the team by Ronnie Peterson and it was to prove a brilliantly successful but also tragic year for JPS. At the start of the year Andretti was fastest in practice for the Argentine GP, led throughout and Peterson took fifth place. Andretti finished fourth in Brazil and Peterson won the South African GP. Another success followed at Long Beach, where Andretti took second place. The 79 had first appeared at the International Trophy, and, driven by Andretti, it made its Grand Prix debut at Zolder. Andretti won the race and Peterson finished second with a 78. By this stage the Lotus-Getrag gearbox had been abandoned in favour of the familiar Hewland. In Spain both drivers had 79s and Andretti and Peterson again took the first two places. A third for Peterson followed in Sweden, Andretti and Peterson were again first and second in the French GP, Andretti won at Hockenheim, Peterson in Austria and then Andretti and Peterson took the first two places in Holland. It must be remembered that after the controversial Brabham 'fan car' had been banned following the Swedish GP, Lotus were the only team to exploit ground effects to the full in 1978. Disaster struck at Monza, where Peterson at the wheel of a 78 after he had crashed his 79 in practice was involved in a first-lap multiple accident, suffered badly broken legs and died as the result of complications causing blood clots. Andretti won the restarted race on the road, was penalized a minute for jumping the start and dropped to sixth place. A second car for Jean-Pierre Jarier was entered in the last two races of the year, but neither he nor Andretti finished in the points. Andretti won the Drivers' Championship with 64 points (poor Peterson had finished second with 51 points) and Lotus won the Constructors' Cup with 89 points to the 58 scored by Ferrari.

79 and 80 – 1979

Andretti was joined in the team by Carlos Reutemann and Lotus was now sponsored by Martini, with the result that the cars were painted green with Martini stripes. For most of the season the team raced the 79s, in the latter part of the season with shorter rear bodywork, revised suspension geometry and outboard rear brakes. The team did, however, produce the new 80 with honeycomb aluminium monocoque, the side pods curving inside the rear wheels, curved sliding skirts and a completely new rear end with a new casting for the gearbox and oil tank. The 80 was raced only three times during the year and its best performance was third place and fastest lap by Andretti in the Spanish GP.

So Lotus struggled with the 79, losing out because other teams had made vast strides in the development of ground-effect cars, proving no match in the early part of the season for the Ligiers and overwhelmed in the latter part by the latest Williams entries. Lotus performances can be summarized as follows: second and fifth by Reutemann and Andretti in the Argentine GP, third by Reutemann in the Brazilian GP, fourth and fifth by Andretti and Reutemann in the South African

GP, fourth by Andretti at Long Beach, second by Reutemann in Spain, fourth by Reutemann in Belgium, third by Reutemann at Monaco and fifth by Andretti at Monza. In the early part of the season, consistent placing in the points, but, latterly, almost complete disappearance from the results tables as other teams grew in strength and reliability.

81 – 1980

Once again it seemed that the Lotus team had lost its sense of direction and development, and the new car, the 81, proved little more successful than its immediate predecessor. The 81, with aluminium monocoque, was developed from the 79, featured similar suspension and dimensions, but incorporated aerodynamic changes that Chapman hoped would solve the problems of 1979. The team was now sponsored by Essex Petroleum and Carlos Reutemann was partnered by former Shadow driver Elio de Angelis. It proved a season of failure and in the early part of the year the best performances were a second by de Angelis in Brazil after a very steady and mature drive and a third by de Angelis in Spain, but there were no other finishes in the points. At Hockenheim Lotus had produced the improved 81B with new monocoque and this was raced by newcomer to the team Nigel Mansell in the Austrian and Dutch GPs and crashed by him in practice for the Italian GP at Imola. During the latter part of the season the only finishes in the points were sixth by de Angelis in the Austrian GP, fourth by de Angelis at Imola and sixth by Andretti at Watkins Glen.

81, 87 and 88 – 1981

Lotus continued to race the 81s in the early part of the year, but had also produced two new designs. Chapman had pinned a great deal of optimism on the 88 – but probably not much real hope. In essence the 88 was a twin-chassis design, the main chassis consisting of the bodywork, side pods, wings and radiators, with, riding within that structure, a secondary chassis consisting of the monocoque, engine, transmission and suspension. The outer chassis was suspended on coil spring/damper units couple to the wheel uprights. The aim was to maximize the benefits of ground effect by the primary chassis absorbing the aerodynamic loads and minimize the enervating strain of ground effect on the driver. It was a typically ingenious Lotus concept following the ban on sliding skirts. The 88 was driven by de Angelis in practice at Long Beach and in Brazil, but was eventually banned completely.

Early in the year, driving the 81, de Angelis finished third at Kyalami, fifth in Brazil, sixth in the Argentine, the team withdrew from the San Marino GP because of the ban on the 88 and at Zolder Mansell finished third and de Angelis fifth. By the Monaco GP the team had ready the 87, a simpler carbon monocoque variant of the 88 without the illegal

56. Elio de Angelis was a consistent and reliable driver for Lotus, but not always as fast as expected. He drove this 87 into fifth place at Zandvoort in 1981. He is followed by Rebaque (Brabham) and Patrese (Arrows).

complications. In Spain, de Angelis and Mansell finished fifth and sixth, de Angelis was sixth at Dijon and at the British race the team was proposing to run modified 88B cars, which the RAC had indicated they would accept; FISA, the governing body, ruled that the cars were illegal and the mechanics rushed to convert Mansell's car to 87 specification, whilst a spare 87 for de Angelis was brought from the team's Hethel headquarters. Mansell failed to qualify and de Angelis was black-flagged for passing Laffite's Ligier while the yellow flag was out and withdrew from the race. During the remainder of the season de Angelis finished fifth at Zandvoort, fourth at Monza and sixth in Canada, whilst Mansell was fourth in the last race of the year at Las Vegas. Lotus had also competed in the non-Championship South African GP in February and here de Angelis had finished third with an 81.

91 – 1982

Although Lotus, once more with Player sponsorship, raced the 87 in the first of the 1982 Championship series, by the Brazilian race two months later the new 91 was ready. Like the old 77, the 91 featured variable wheelbase and front track, it retained suspension front and rear by upper rocker arms, lower wishbones and inboard springs, and in appearance it was distinguished by a far forward cockpit, long down-swept engine cover and stubby nose. Engine and transmission were unchanged.

It was to prove another mediocre year for the team, with third place by Mansell in Brazil, fifth by de Angelis at Long Beach, Lotus missed the San Marino race, de Angelis was fourth in Belgium, Mansell and de Angelis were fourth and fifth at Monaco, de Angelis was fourth at Montreal and Brands Hatch and then scored an unexpected but well-driven victory in Austria. It was the 150th win by the Ford-Cosworth DFV engine. During the remainder of the season de Angelis finished sixth in the Swiss GP at Dijon, but otherwise the team was out of the points. Lotus still had a long way to go to recover their form of yesteryear.

93T and 94T – 1983

Before his tragic death from a heart attack Chapman had arranged a deal with Renault to use their turbocharged engines in 1983. Peter Warr was now solely in charge of the team. During the early part of the year Lotus raced Cosworth-powered 92s, the previous year's cars modified to comply with the new 'flat bottom' rule. The first 93T with turbocharged Renault engine appeared at round one of the Championship in Brazil. De Angelis drove it in practice, but the engine broke on the warm-up lap; the Italian switched to the team's spare 92, started from the pit lane, but was disqualified. De Angelis raced a single 93T during the first eight rounds of the Championship, whilst Mansell was at the wheel of a Cosworth-powered car, but the only finish in the points was sixth place by Mansell at Detroit. In June Gérard Ducarouge, sacked by Alfa Romeo, joined the team and while he worked on a new and more functional project, Lotus was able to field an additional 93T for Mansell at Silverstone. In the British race Mansell finished fourth. By the German race Ducarouge had ready the new 94T, based on the 91 monocoque, much lighter, with improved weight distribution and handling. During the remainder of the year Mansell finished fifth in Austria, de Angelis fifth at Monza and Mansell third in the European GP at Brands Hatch. There was a long way to go, but most of the motor racing world had immense confience in Ducarouge's ability and there seemed little doubt that Lotus was well on the way out of the wilderness.

95T – 1984

For the 1984 season Ducarouge produced the 95T, only four exam-

57. Ayrton Senna with the turbocharged Renault-powered Lotus 97T in the 1985 Detroit Grand Prix.

ples of which were built. The 95T, with pull rod-operated double wishbone suspension and inboard springs front and rear and different aerodynamics for fast and slow circuits, was a thoroughly tested and reliable car and appeared the best-handling chassis to be raced that year. In a year dominated by the McLaren-TAGs, the 95Ts performed consistently and came very close to winning three races. As it was the team had to settle for a third by de Angelis in Brazil and Imola, a third by Mansell at Dijon, sixth by de Angelis at Monaco, fourth by de Angelis in Canada, third by de Angelis at Detroit and Dallas, fourth by de Angelis at Brands Hatch, fourth by Mansell at Hockenheim, third and fourth places by Mansell and de Angelis at Zandvoort and fifth place by de Angelis in the Estoril race, a new addition to the Championship series. Mansell also finished fifth at Zolder.

97T – 1985

Ducarouge was following a policy of steady development, and the 97T of which again only four examples were built, was basically an improved version of the 1984 car with aerodynamic changes. The wheelbase was 8 ft 11 in., front track 5 ft 10.9 in. and rear track 5 ft 3.7 in. Young Brazilian Ayrton Senna had joined the team and Nigel Mansell had left to drive for Williams. It was a year of ever-improving performances, with outright wins by Senna in Portugal and Belgium, together with second in Austria and at Brands Hatch, third in Holland and Italy. De Angelis finished first at Imola, third in Brazil and at Monaco, fourth in Portugal, fifth at Montreal, Detroit, Paul Ricard, Austria, Zandvoort and Brands Hatch and sixth at Monza. It was the best season that Team Lotus had enjoyed for many years, Senna had displayed his tremendous potential and he and de Angelis were fourth and fifth in the Drivers' Championship.

98T – 1986

Steady development work had resulted in the 98T, but there had been major changes at Lotus. De Angelis had left to drive for Brabham, and Lotus, turning their backs on the notion of an experienced teammate for Senna, signed up Formula Three driver Johnny Dumfries. Senna started the season with second place in Brazil, won the Spanish GP, retired at Imola, finished third at Monaco, second at Spa, finished fifth in Canada and won at Detroit. Grand Prix racing was now more competitive than ever and Lotus was back at the front.

Lyncar
(United Kingdom)

006 – 1974–75

Designed by Martin Slater and one of a series of single-seaters built by him under this name, the 006 was commissioned by John Nicholson of Nicholson McLaren Engines, who had previously raced a Formula Atlantic Lyncar. The 006 was a very conventional design with aluminium riveted monocoque, front suspension by double wishbones and coil springs and rear suspension by lower wishbones, single upper links, twin radius rods and outboard coil spring/damper units. The engine was the usual Cosworth DFV with transmission by the Hewland FG400. The Lyncar had a wheelbase of 8 ft 2 in., front track of 4 ft 9 in. and rear track of 4 ft 11 in.

With sponsorship from the Pinch (Plant) company, Nicholson first entered the Lyncar at the Race of Champions in 1974 finishing unclassified, but still running. He was classified sixth in the International Trophy at Silverstone, but failed to qualify at the British GP at Brands Hatch. In 1975 Nicholson raced the Lyncar again, retiring in the Race of Champions and finishing 13th in Silverstone's International Trophy. He qualified as slowest starter in the British GP, was one of many drivers to go off in the heavy rain that caused the race to be stopped and was classified 17th. From this point on Nicholson concentrated his spare time efforts on power-boat racing.

58. John Nicholson with the Lyncar on his way to sixth place in the 1974 International Trophy at Silverstone.

Maki
(Japan)

F-101 – 1974

This simple Cosworth DFV-powered car with unconventional bodywork was designed by Kenji Mimura and Masao Ono (the latter was also responsible for the design of the Kojima). It featured double wishbones and outboard coil spring/damper units at the front and parallel lower links, single upper links, twin radius rods and outboard coil spring/damper units at the back. The wheelbase was 8 ft 4 in., front track 4 ft 8.7 in. and rear track 5 ft 3.4 in. It appeared in 1974 with Howden Ganley at the wheel. He failed to qualify at the British GP, and during practice at the Nürburgring lost control at speed when the suspension broke, collided with the guard-rail and the complete front of the car was torn off. By any standards the construction looked flimsy in the extreme.

F-101 – 1975

A second chassis was built for 1975. After two no-shows, the Maki appeared at Zandvoort and Silverstone driven by Hiroshi Fushida, but failed to qualify. Tony Trimmer tried in vain to qualify the Maki at the Österreichring and Monza, but drove the Maki into 13th place in the non-Championship Swiss GP at Dijon.

F102A – 1976

Trimmer appeared with what was claimed to be a new Maki at the Japanese GP, but failed to qualify.

59. Howden Ganley with the Maki F101 in practice for the 1974 British Grand Prix at Brands Hatch.

March
(United Kingdom)

March Engineering was formed on 1 October, 1969, by Formula Two driver Max Mosley, former Winkelmann Racing team manager Alan Rees, Graham Coaker and designer Robin Herd. Initially it looked as though March would seize a position at the forefront of Formula One, but although the team enjoyed two excellent first seasons, as the years passed its efforts became concentrated with great success on other categories of single-seater racing.

701 – 1970

Herd's first March Formula One car featured a riveted aluminium-alloy monocoque with the front bulkhead formed by a magnesium casting, front suspension by double wishbones and coil spring/damper units and rear suspension by reversed lower wishbones, single upper links, twin radius rods and coil spring/damper units. The Cosworth DFV engine was used with the Hewland DG300 gearbox. The wheelbase was 7 ft 11 in. and front and rear track was 4 ft 11 in. The March was distinguished by bodywork of distinctly squarish lines and wing-shaped glass-fibre supplementary fuel tanks bolted to the sides of the monocoque.

Lacking any cars until his own new design was ready, Ken Tyrrell bought three cars to be raced by Stewart and Servoz-Gavin, STP-

51. The 72 was probably the most successful Lotus Formula One design. Jochen Rindt drove this car to the 72's second race victory in the 1970 Dutch Grand Prix at Zandvoort.

sponsored works cars were driven by Chris Amon and Jo Siffert and, at some races, Mario Andretti, and another car was sold to Colin Crabbe's Antique Automobiles team for Ronnie Peterson to drive. In a year dominated by the Lotus 72 and the Ferrari 312B, the 701s scored a fair measure of success. Stewart finished third in South Africa, won in Spain (Andretti was third and Servoz-Gavin fifth), was second at Zandvoort and second at Monza; by the last race of the year at Watkins Glen Stewart was at the wheel of the new Tyrrell 001. The works cars had a thoroughly miserable year. Andretti's car was wrecked in Austria and never seen again, Amon managed second at Spa and Clermont-Ferrand, fifth at Brands Hatch, third in Canada and fifth at Watkins Glen, while Siffert never managed to finish in the first six.

711 – 1971

For 1971 Herd produced an advanced and futuristic-looking car with aluminium-alloy monocoque, double wishbone front suspension with inboard coil spring/damper units and rear suspension by upper trailing arms with short adjustable top links, lower wishbones, adjustable track rods and outboard coil spring/damper units. Originally there were inboard front brakes, but these were abandoned after a breakage at the Race of Champions on the private 711 driven by Pescarolo for Frank Williams. The bodywork was much influenced by the design ideas of Frank Costin and incorporated a prominent nose-mounted aerofoil and the side radiators enclosed in streamlined nacelles – but the latter feature was abandoned after overheating at Kyalami.

While Ronnie Peterson drove the Cosworth-powered works cars, Autodelta sponsorship allowed a second Alfa Romeo-powered car to be driven by Andrea de Adamich and 'Nanni' Galli, but this car achieved no success. Peterson also drove an Alfa Romeo-powered car in two non-Championship races and the French GP. Apart from the Frank Williams entry, other 711s appeared for Mike Beuttler entered by Clarke Mordaunt Racing, John Love and Gene Mason for Skip Barber. In the early part of the year Alex Soler-Roig paid his way with a works car and Niki Lauda drove a sponsored works car in Austria.

Although Peterson failed to win a single Grand Prix, on the strength of second places at Monaco, Silverstone, Monza and Mosport, together with a third at Zandvoort and fourth place at Watkins Glen, he took second place in the Drivers' Championship.

721, 721X and 721G – 1972

March started the season with the 721, a logical development of the 1971 car and said to incorporate fifty modifications. A large one-piece glass-fibre engine cover incorporating the roll-over bar and air-box, together with a flatter nose with side fences were the most obvious changes. One of these cars was sold to Frank Williams for Pescarolo to drive, but the works drivers Peterson and Niki Lauda contested only the Argentine and South African races with these cars, Peterson finishing sixth at Buenos Aires and fifth at Kyalami, together with second in the non-Championship Brazilian GP.

At the Race of Champions March produced the 721X with inboard rear suspension and a gearbox based on Alfa Romeo components that was mounted ahead of the rear axle and final drive. In theory this should have vastly improved the weight distribution of the March, but, mainly because of the Goodyear tyres used by March, it resulted in appalling handling. The works drivers handled the 721X cars only in Spain, Monaco and Belgium and, Peterson only, in the Gold Cup race at Oulton Park, where the 721X was fitted with 721 rear suspension and a Hewland gearbox.

In Spain the Clarke Mordaunt team had fielded the 721G car for Beuttler (who in fact failed to qualify) and this incorporated the March Formula Two chassis, modified to take the 3-litre DFV engine and with fuel capacity increased to 42 gallons by the addition of side tanks. 721G chassis were hastily built for Peterson and Lauda and during the rest of the season Peterson finished fifth at Clermont-Ferrand, third at the Nürburgring and fourth at Watkins Glen.

Another March variant raced in 1972 was the Eifelland, a 721 fitted with special bodywork designed by Luigi Colani. The original wide nose-section caused overheating and had to be abandoned, and as the season progressed the car reverted more and more closely to standard trim. Rolf Stommelen struggled on until after the German GP, when his entrant, Eifelland Caravans, withdrew from racing. The car later passed to car dealers Hexagon of Highgate and John Watson drove it on his Formula One debut into sixth place in the John Player race at Brands Hatch in October.

61. In 1972 Rolf Stommelen drove the Eifelland, a March 721 with special bodywork. It achieved no success. Here Stommelen is seen in the Spanish Grand Prix.

731 – 1973

After 1972 March took only very limited interest in Formula One. Rees had left to set up the Shadow team and Herd and Moseley concentrated increasingly on Formula Two and Three cars. The new 731 was derived from the 721G, but featured tank-protecting side pods (to conform with the new deformable structure rules) and narrower rear track. A works car was driven by Jean-Pierre Jarier and then by Roger Williamson. Williamson was eliminated in the British GP as a result of Scheckter's accident and, sadly, crashed with fatal results at Zandvoort. March did not race again in Formula One that year, but private cars were driven throughout 1973 by James Hunt (for Hesketh), Mike Beuttler and David Purley. Hunt finished sixth in France, fourth in Britain, third in Holland and was narrowly beaten into second place at Watkins Glen.

741 – 1974

In 1974 March continued to race cars based on Formula Two monocoques with the 741, of which two examples were built. They were simple, straightforward cars with front suspension by double wish-

62. The unsuccessful March 721X with gearbox ahead of the rear axle line driven by Peterson in the rain-soaked 1972 Monaco Grand Prix.

bones and outboard springs, rear suspension by parallel lower links, single upper links, twin radius rods and outboard springs and with 8 ft 2 in. wheelbase and 4 ft 10 in. track front and rear. Hans-Joachim Stuck drove for the team all season; Howden Ganley drove in the first two races, but then his place was taken by Vittorio Brambilla with sponsorship from Beta Tools. It was a low-budget operation and the only successes gained during the year were fifth by Stuck at Kyalami and fourth in Spain, whilst Brambilla took sixth place in Austria.

741 and 751 – 1975

Brambilla remained with the team, racing initially a 741, but by the Spanish race March was fielding two 751s for Brambilla and Lella Lombardi. The latest cars were updated and featured a slightly longer wheelbase and narrower track. By the British GP March had supplied a third 751 to Roger Penske for Mark Donohue to drive. In Spain Brambilla finished fifth and Lombardi sixth in a race stopped short following Stommelen's accident. Brambilla led the Swedish GP until a universal joint failed and in the British GP, stopped after many of the entries had crashed in a rain storm, Donohue and Brambilla were classified fifth and sixth. In practice in Austria Donohue crashed as the result of tyre failure and sustained injuries which proved fatal. It was another race stopped short because of the weather and when the flag came down after 29 laps Brambilla was leading.

761 – 1976

For 1976 March produced the 761, with longer 9 ft 1 in. wheelbase, 4 ft 8 in. front track and 4 ft 10 in. rear track, and Brambilla stayed with the team. Ronnie Peterson switched from Lotus back to March after the Brazilian GP, the first race of the season. It was a year of considerable success for such a very low budget and Peterson finished sixth in Austria and scored a brilliant victory at Monza. Brambilla finished sixth in Holland, while Stuck, entered by the Jägermeister team, was fourth in Brazil and Monaco and fifth at Watkins Glen.

63. Peterson drove this March 761 to victory in the 1976 Italian Grand Prix.

761B and 771 – 1977

For 1977 March produced the improved 761B and the 771, which featured a nose-mounted radiator. Because the company was under pressure from BMW to concentrate its efforts on Formula Two, a separate Formula One team run by Max Mosley with Rothmans sponsorship entered cars for Ian Scheckter and Alex Ribeiro, but they never finished in the first six. A number of cars were sold to private teams, Herd played with a car with two front wheels and four rear wheels (reversing the layout of the Tyrrell P34s) and the newly formed Williams Grand Prix Engineering entered a 761 for Patrick Neve.

At the end of this unsuccessful year March sold its membership of the Formula One Constuctor's Association to Hans Gunther Schmid's ATS team. March returned to Formula One in 1981, but the cars bore the name RAM and are discussed under that heading.

Martini

(France)

Tico Martini had started his involvement in motor racing in the Channel Islands with a remarkable hill-climb 'special' of kart ancestry. Later he set up business at the French Magny-Cours circuit, building initially Formula Three and later Formula Two cars that were to win the European Formula Two Championship. By the time that he had decided to dabble in Formula One, his numbering system had reached 23 and the MK in the type number stood for 'Martini-Knight' (the

64. When Martini entered Formula One, the team underestimated what was involved and withdrew in mid-season. Here René Arnoux is at the wheel at Kyalami.

latter the name of the family that ran the racing drivers' school at Magny-Cours.

MK23 – 1978

Martini devised a simple monocoque car with front suspension by upper rocking arms, lower wishbones and inboard springs and with rear suspension by parallel lower links, single upper links, twin radius rods and outboard springs. The Cosworth DFV engine was used with the Hewland FGA400 6-speed gearbox. The wheelbase was 8 ft 9 in., front and rear track 5 ft 3 in. It was a neat and attractive car, but Martini had simply underrated the problems of competing in Formula One.

René Arnoux drove the Martini, failing to qualify on the car's debut at Kyalami, non-starting in the International Trophy at Silverstone because of loss of oil pressure and failing to pre-qualify at Monaco. The Martini finished ninth in Belgium, 14th in the French GP, failed to pre-qualify at Hockenheim, took ninth place at the Österreichring and retired at Zandvoort when the wing failed. By this time the team had absorbed the realities of Formula One and withdrew.

Matra
(France)

When Matra entered motor racing, it was part of a long-term plan to establish the company, mainly engaged in the military hardware field, as a serious automobile manufacturer. In 1964 Matra took over the hard-pressed René Bonnet company, which built Renault-powered cars for sports car racing and road use. A year later Matra produced a Formula Three car, Formula Two chassis for Ken Tyrrell followed in 1966 and the same year Matra became involved in sports car racing with BRM-powered coupés. By 1967 development was well under way with a new V-12 engine for Formula One, but apart from racing their own V-12 cars, Matra supplied chassis to Tyrrell to race with Cosworth DFV engines.

MS9, MS10 and MS11 – 1968

The prototype Formula One car was a direct derivative of the successful MS7 Formula Two chassis. The monocoque featured structurally incorporated fuel tanks, the DFV engine was attached directly to the rear bulkhead and there was a small unstressed space-frame attached to a bulkhead round the Hewland DG300 gearbox on which the rear suspension was mounted; the purpose of this frame was to keep all components in position when the engine was removed. Front suspension was by upper rocking arms, lower wishbones and inboard-mounted coil spring/damper units. The rear suspension consisted of upper wishbones, reversed bottom triangles, twin radius rods and coil spring/damper units. The wheelbase was 8 ft 11 in., front track 4 ft 8 in. and rear track 4 ft 10 in.

Jackie Stewart drove the MS9 at Kyalami, but retired when a con-rod went through the block, By the Race of Champions at Brands Hatch the definitive MS10 was ready and the only real difference was the increase in fuel capacity from 120 litres to 190 litres. The Matra suffered handling problems at Brands Hatch, Stewart missed the Spanish GP because he had injured his wrist in a Formula Two race (Beltoise drove in his place and finished fifth) and at Monaco Servoz-Gavin drove the MS10, but retired after clouting the barriers.

Matra's own MS11 car had appeared in practice in Spain, and at Monaco it retired after Beltoise had bent the suspension on a kerb. The V-12 engine with a capacity of 2985 cc (79.7 × 50 mm) featured twin overhead camshafts per bank of cylinders driven by a train of straight-cut gears driven from the front of the crankshaft, four valves per cylinder, Lucas fuel injection and an initial power output of about 400 bhp (subsequently increased to 420 bhp at 9000 rpm). The chassis was similar to that of the Ford-powered cars, but the original rear extensions of the Formula Two monocoque were retained, there was no supplementary tubular structure and the engine was unstressed.

By the Belgium GP Stewart was back at the wheel of the MS10 and was leading when the Matra appeared to run out of fuel (in fact the

65. Jackie Stewart led the 1968 Belgian Grand Prix with his Matra MS10 until he ran into fuel pick-up problems on the penultimate lap; he was classified fourth.

pumps were failing to pick up the last four gallons) and after a pit stop he finished fourth with Beltoise seventh. In the rain-soaked Dutch GP Stewart scored a fine victory with Beltoise second, he was third in the French GP at Rouen and, slowed by pain from his wrist, finished sixth at Brands Hatch. A fortnight later he scored a brilliant victory at the Nürburgring on a near-flooded track. At the Italian GP Tyrrell fielded two MS10s, and although Stewart's engine broke, Servoz-Gavin came through to take a fine second place. Stewart finished sixth in Canada after a pit stop to change a cracked wishbone (here Matra entered two of the V-12s for the first time, the second car being driven by Pescarolo), he scored another win at Watkins Glen, but was out of the picture in Mexico when dislodged tank sealant clogged the fuel pump. In the Drivers' Championship Stewart finished second with 36 points to the 48 of Graham Hill.

MS80 and MS84 – 1969

Although Stewart drove the MS10 twice in 1969, at Kyalami and in the International Trophy at Silverstone (winning both races), Matra's efforts were concentrated on the new MS80, a new Ford-

66. The installation of the DFV engine in the Matra MS10 chassis.

powered car, while the V-12 was left unraced. The MS80 featured a completely new monocoque retaining the structural fuel tanks (which meant that the MS80 could not be raced in 1970, when rubber bag fuel tanks became mandatory). The monocoque widened at the waist to lower the polar moment of inertia by bringing the weight of the fuel as close to the centre of gravity as possible. Fuel capacity was increased to 210 litres. At the front the suspension was now outboard (because of cooling problems on the MS10) and consisted of double wishbones and coil springs. There was also a new rear suspension layout with upper wishbones, two lower parallel links and coil spring/damper units. At the rear a large aerofoil was mounted on the suspension uprights. The wheelbase was 8 ft 10.5 in., and front and rear track 5 ft 3 in. The MS80s were raced by Tyrrell's Matra International Team and for one year Beltoise drove for the British team.

Matra also built an experimental four-wheel drive car typed the MS84 with tubular space-frame chassis (easy to modify as development progressed), suspension as on the MS80 and a transmission system designed and built by Harry Ferguson Research. The engine was reversed in the chassis so that the clutch faced forwards; in a single casing behind the cockpit were the 5-speed Hewland gearbox, the central differential and control unit and the stepped take-off drive. From the Ferguson unit enclosed drive-shafts ran fore and aft on the left-hand side of the car to the offset differential housings with power transmitted to the wheel hubs by very short universally jointed drive-shafts. The MS84 first appeared in practice at Zandvoort and was raced by Beltoise at Silverstone (ninth) and by Servoz-Gavin in Canada (sixth), United States (seventh) and Mexico (eighth). It suffered the same problems as the other four-wheel drive projects and was abandoned by Matra at the end of the year.

With the MS80 Stewart enjoyed a brilliantly successful season that was to bring him his first Drivers' World Championship. He won the

67. Jean-Pierre Beltoise with the works V-12 Matra MS11 in the 1968 Dutch Grand Prix; he finished second behind Stewart's Ford-powered car.

Spanish GP at Barcelona (Beltoise third), the Dutch GP, the French GP (Beltoise was second), the British GP, was second at the Nürburgring, won at Monza (Beltoise was third), Beltoise finished fourth in Canada and he was fourth at Mexico City (with Beltoise fifth). He had accumulated 63 points to the 37 of second-place man Ickx.

MS120 – 1970

Matra had tried to persuade Tyrrell to race V-12 cars in 1970, but he preferred to stay with Ford power, so Matra Sports fielded the MS120 cars with Simca sponsorship as Matra-Simcas driven by Beltoise and Pescarolo. The V-12 engine had been revised so that the inlet ports were in the centre of the vee, it was much more compact and claimed power output was 420 bhp. In most respects the MS120 chassis was similar to that of the MS80, but had been redesigned to take rubber bag fuel tanks to comply with the lastest regulations.

Despite the MS120s' fine, rather angular looks and the superb sound of the V-12 engines, very little success came the team's way. Beltoise finished fourth in South Africa, Pescarolo took third place at Monaco, Beltoise and Pescarolo finished third and sixth in Belgium (Pescarolo had stopped because of loss of fuel pressure), Beltoise finished fifth at Zandvoort, Pescarolo was fifth in France and Pescarolo was sixth at Hockenheim. It was sixth again for Beltoise in Austria, third at Monza and fifth for Beltoise at Mexico City.

MS120B – 1971

For 1971 Matra signed up Chris Amon as joint number one driver

68. Jackie Stewart and the Matra MS80 were the winning combination in 1969 – but not at Monaco where the MS80 was eliminated by drive-shaft failure.

with Beltoise. The MS120B was only a very slightly modified version of the 1970 car, but with a great deal of development work carried out on the engine that had resulted in new camshafts, modifications to the inlet porting, improved exhaust system and improved lubrication. Power was never in excess of 450 bhp (and usually more like 430 bhp), the engines were supposed to rev to 12,000 rpm (but this usually resulted in valve spring trouble) and they were far from reliable. Apart from a win by Amon in the non-Championship Argentine GP, no outright victories were gained, but Amon finished fifth at Kyalami, third at Barcelona, fifth at the Paul Ricard circuit and sixth at Monza. Beltoise, whose licence was suspended following the accident that had resulted in the death of Ignazio Giunti in the Buenos Aires 1000 Km Sports Car race at the beginning of the year, finished sixth at Barcelona.

MS120C and MS120D – 1972

During 1972 Matra were content to enter a single car for Chris Amon, initially the MS120C, which featured new front suspension wishbones and revised geometry. Amon failed to start in the Argentine because of transmission problems just before the off, but he finished sixth at Monaco with an old MS120B after four pit stops caused by a misting visor and he was sixth again in Belgium. At the French GP Matra produced the MS120D with completely new monocoque of more bulbous shape. Here Amon went superbly until a tyre punctured, and after a pit stop he fought his way back through the field to finish third. There followed a fourth place in the British GP, fifth in Austria and sixth in Canada.

69. Two years later Chris Amon is seen at the same corner at Monaco with the works V-12 Matra MS120B; this Matra was also eliminated by drive-shaft failure.

In 1972 the Matra team had won at Le Mans and it seemed a good point at which to cut their Formula One losses and concentrate on sports car racing. Subsequently, in 1975 (with Shadow) and in 1976 and 1981 (with Ligier) Matra returned to Formula One purely as a supplier of engines.

McLaren

(United Kingdom)

New Zealand driver Bruce McLaren had been a works Cooper driver since 1958, but in 1964 he had bought Roger Penske's very fast Zerex-Climax sports/racing car and from this he had developed a line of successful Group Seven competition sports cars. With the introduction of the 3-litre Grand Prix Formula, he became the second driver to race a Formula One car bearing his own name.

M2B – 1966

Designed by Robin Herd, the new Formula One car featured a monocoque constructed from Malite (balsa wood compressed between two thin sheets of aluminium), conventional suspension and powered by the four overhead camshaft Ford Indianapolis engine reduced in capacity from 4.2 litres to 2995 cc (95.66 × 52.07 mm). With Hilborn-Travers fuel injection the power output was claimed to be 303 bhp at 8750 rpm and a ZF 5-speed gearbox was used. The wheelbase was 8 ft 0 in., front track 4 ft 10 in. and rear track 4 ft 10.75 in.

Development of the Ford engine was slow, it was plagued by bearing failure, power was developed over a very narrow rev range and it was too heavy. After running the M2B with Ford power at Monaco, McLaren switched to the Italian V-8 2996 cc Serenissima engine for the Belgian GP, but non-started because of loss of oil pressure, and subsequently used the M2B with this engine to take sixth place in the British GP. McLaren reappeared with the Ford engine at the end of the season, but gained no success and this unsuccessful design was abandoned.

M4A and M5A – 1967

Although a new car was under development, at several races in 1967 McLaren drove one of his M4A Formula Two cars fitted with a BRM 2-litre V-8 engine and 5-speed Hewland gearbox. He finished fifth in the Spring Cup race at Oulton Park, fifth in the International Trophy at Silverstone, fourth at Monaco and went off the road at Zandvoort. Shortly afterwards the car was destroyed during testing at Goodwood, when a fuel pipe broke and it caught fire. In the next three races McLaren drove for the Eagle team.

At the Canadian GP McLaren brought out the M5A, developed from the Formula Two car, with new full aluminium monocoque and powered by the BRM V-12 engine. Although no success was gained in 1967 the new car displayed good performance and handling. It appeared once as a works car in 1968, at Kyalami, where it was driven into fifth place by Denis Hulme, and then it was sold to Joakim Bonnier.

M7A – 1968

For 1968 the McLaren team developed the improved M7A with full aluminium-sheet monocoque, the Ford DFV engine acting as a stressed member, Hewland DG300 gearbox, front suspension by lower wishbones, upper rocking arms and outboard-mounted coil spring/damper units and rear suspension by double wishbones and coil springs. The wheelbase was 7 ft 11 in., front track 4 ft 9 in. and rear track 4 ft 5.4 in. Denis Hulme now joined Bruce McLaren in the team and the cars were painted a new and very attractive shade of orange. Although the team was not able during the year to match the overall performance of the Lotus 49 or the Matra MS10 driven by Jackie Stewart, McLaren enjoyed substantial success.

McLaren and Hulme started the season with first and third places in the Race of Champions at Brands Hatch and Hulme and McLaren were first and second in the International Trophy at Silverstone. At the Spanish GP, where the team tried aluminium pannier fuel tanks mounted on tubular outriggers, Hulme finished second to Hill's Lotus.

70. Bruce McLaren with the 2-litre BRM-powered M4A McLaren which he drove into fourth place at Monaco in 1967.

Hulme was fifth and last at Monaco after a pit stop to change a drive-shaft, and McLaren won the Belgian GP after Stewart's Matra had run into fuel pick-up problems. At the French GP, where the McLarens appeared with rear aerofoils, Hulme finished fifth, Hulme was fourth in the British GP and he scored a convincing victory at Monza. Another victory for Hulme followed in Canada with McLaren second, McLaren was sixth at Watkins Glen and the *patron* was second at Mexico City. Hulme finished third in the Drivers' Championship and McLaren were third in the Constructors' Cup.

M7A, M7C and M9A – 1969

Throughout the year Hulme drove the M7A, but the team also produced two variants of the basic design. At Kyalami and the Race of Champions Bruce McLaren drove the M7A/B with pannier fuel tanks blended into the monocoque. McLaren was fifth in South Africa, but he was not happy with the handling of the car and it was sold to Antique Automobiles and driven for them by Vic Elford until he wrote it off at the Nürburgring. McLaren now drove the M7C based on the team's Formula 5000 M10A monocoque (which extended round the back of the cockpit) with M7A running gear.

Hulme took third place in South Africa and in the Race of Champions, McLaren finished second in the Spanish GP and third in the British and German GPs, while Hulme won the Mexican GP at the end of the season. McLaren had failed to keep pace with the developments of their rivals, notably Matra.

McLaren were another team to experiment with four-wheel drive, and their M9A ran in the British GP driven by Derek Bell. The M9A,

71. Two years later in 1969 Bruce McLaren drove this M7C into fifth place at Monaco.

designed by Jo Marquart, featured a riveted light alloy monocoque with inboard coil spring/damper units and inboard brakes. The Ford engine was reversed in the chassis and the drive to the front and rear wheels was taken out to the left side of the car through a two-shaft 5-speed McLaren gearbox incorporating Hewland gears. The central differential incorporated quick-change torque-split ratios that could be changed in a matter of minutes. The drive was taken front and rear through differentials with Hewland/ZF anti-spin locks. At Silverstone Bell retired early in the race when a rear suspension upright broke and the M9A, like all other four-wheel drive projects, was abandoned.

M14A and M14D – 1970

The M14A was generally similar to the M7C, but with many detail changes, including increased fuel capacity, which necessitated a narrower cockpit. McLaren had entered into an arrangement with Autodelta to field a third car with an Alfa Romeo engine, initially an old M7A, later a variant of the M14A known as the M14D, for Andrea de Adamich. During the year the Alfa Romeo-powered cars achieved no success. Hulme took second place in the South African GP, third in the Race of Champions and McLaren was second in the Spanish GP, while Hulme finished fourth at Monaco. In June Bruce McLaren was killed in a testing accident with a CanAm car at Goodwood, Hulme suffered badly burnt hands in an accident at Indianapolis and, after missing the Belgium GP, the McLaren team returned to Zandvoort with cars for Dan Gurney and Peter Gethin. Gurney withdrew from the team after two races in favour of Gethin, and Hulme was back

72. *Another interesting McLaren variant was this M7A with side fuel tanks. It was sold by the works to Antique Automobiles and Vic Elford drove it into tenth and last place for the new owners in the 1969 Dutch Grand Prix.*

in the team after missing only one race. During the remainder of the year Hulme finished fourth in the French GP, third in the British and German races, fourth at Monza and third at Mexico City, while Gethin was sixth in Canada.

M19A – 1971

For 1971 ex-Brabham designer Ralph Bellamy produced the M19A with low, wide monocoque (imitating the style of the Matra MS80), new rising-rate suspension and hub carriers, suspension uprights, steering and wheels from the M14A. By the end of the year the rising-rate suspension had been abandoned and the conventional M14A suspension substituted. In addition the cars were plagued by aerodynamic problems during the year. In the first race of the year, the South African GP, Hulme led until a few laps from the finish, but this was very much a flash in the pan. Successes were limited to a third place by Hulme in the non-Championship Questor GP, a fifth by Hulme in Spain and a fourth at Monaco. By the Austrian GP Peter Gethin had left to drive for BRM and his place was taken by Jack Oliver. By the Canadian GP the second M19A had been sold to Roger Penske for Mark Donohue

73. Derek Bell in practice for the 1969 British Grand Prix with the four-wheel-drive McLaren M9A.

to drive and Donohue achieved McLaren's best result of the season by finishing third, ahead of Hulme in fourth place.

M19A and M19C – 1972

The McLaren team was revitalized for 1972 and with sponsorship from Yardley (which meant adequate financing) enjoyed a season of solid success from drivers Hulme and Peter Revson. Hulme started the season with second place in the Argentine GP, he won the South African GP (with Revson third), finished third in the Race of Champions and was fourth in the International Trophy at Silverstone. At Monaco Hulme drove the improved M19C with a lighter, fabricated front chassis bulkhead and other modifications to lighten the car. He finished at the tail of the field at Monaco (where he was partnered by Brian Redman because of Revson's Indianapolis commitments), won the Gold Cup race at Oulton Park with a M19A, finished third in the Belgian GP, Revson was third in the British GP, and Redman (again deputizing for Revson) took fifth place at the Nürburgring. At the Austrian race there was a second M19C for Revson to drive and Hulme and he took second and third places. Redman was also second in the Rothmans Formule Libre race at Brands Hatch at the end of August. At Monza Hulme and Revson were third and fourth, in Canada Revson was second and Hulme third and Hulme was again third in the last race of the year at Watkins Glen. It was a most satisfactory year for the team.

M19C and M23 – 1973

At the beginning of 1973 Hulme and Revson continued to race the M19C cars in slightly modified form, with Hulme finishing fifth in the Argentine and third in Brazil. At Kyalami Hulme appeared at the wheel of the new Gordon Coppuck-designed M23. The M23 was low and aerodynamic, with wedge-shaped nose, complete engine and gearbox cover, the driver seated well to the front of the car and the radiators enclosed within the monocoque structure. The M23 had been specifically designed to comply with the deformable structure regulations and the monocoque had inner and outer skins of 16-gauge aluminium with foam injected between. At the front there was a rising-rate suspension with tubular upper and lower wishbones; upper links extended inboard to operate separate rockers through push-rods and the rockers operated the inboard-mounted coil spring/damper units. At the rear the suspension consisted of lower reversed wishbones, single upper adjustable links, twin radius rods and outboard coil spring/damper units. The wheelbase was 8 ft 8 in., front track 5 ft 4.2 in. and rear track 5 ft 5 in.

Hulme finished fifth at Kyalami, while Revson was second with one of the familiar M19C cars. At this race Jody Scheckter, South African

74. Denis Hulm with the McLaren M19C in the 1972 French Grand Prix at Clermont-Ferrand. He finished seventh.

newcomer, drove Hulme's usual M19C. Hulme finished second in the Race of Champions and by the International Trophy at Silverstone a second M23 was ready for Revson. Revson finished fourth at Silverstone, Revson was fourth in Spain and fifth at Monaco, but substantial success eluded the team until the Swedish race, where Hulme fought his way through the field to take the lead and victory when Peterson's Lotus suffered a puncture on the last lap. Scheckter drove for the team in the French GP, where he was pushed off by Fittipaldi, and at Silverstone, where he spun across the track and triggered off a multi-car accident that resulted in the race being stopped and later restarted. When the race was resumed Revson came out the winner with Hulme in third place. Jacky Ickx drove the team's spare M23 at the Nürburgring and finished third. Revson finished third in the Italian GP and scored the team's final win of the year in Canada.

M23 – 1974

For 1974 Emerson Fittipaldi joined Denis Hulme to race in Marlboro's distinctive red and white colours, while a third M23 was fielded under the Yardley banner for the popular British driver Mike Hailwood. Unfortunately the Yardley entry seemed doomed to failure and Hailwood achieved only a third in South Africa and fourths in the Race of Champions and at Zandvoort before bringing his racing career to an end with a bad crash at the Nürburgring. For the remainder of 1974 the Yardley entry was driven without success by David Hobbs and Jochen Mass.

At the beginning of the year Hulme won the Argentine GP with the M23 (now with slightly longer wheelbase), but only after Pace's Brabham had gone on to seven cylinders shortly before the finish. However, most of the team's success in 1974 was gaind by Emerson Fittipaldi, who won the Brazilian GP, the non-Championship President Medici GP also held in Brazil, took third place in Spain, won in Belgium (with Hulme sixth), finished fifth at Monaco, fourth in Sweden, third at Zandvoort and second at Brands Hatch. Hulme was second in the Austrian race, but Emerson bounced back to take second place at Monza and win the Canadian GP (Hulme was sixth). Fittipaldi won the Drivers' Championship with 55 points to the 52 of Regazzoni (Ferrari) and McLaren also won the Constructors' Cup.

M23 – 1975

The M23 entered its third season of racing in 1975 with minor modifications that included simpler rising-rate front suspension, narrower rear track and modified nose and air-box. Denis Hulme had retired from racing and Fittipaldi was now partnered in the McLaren team by young German driver Jochen Mass. 1975 was a Ferrari year, but

Fittipaldi enjoyed a good measure of success, scoring McLaren's second successive win in the Argentine GP, finishing second in Brazil (with Mass third), second in the International Trophy at Silverstone, and in the Spanish GP, boycotted by Fittipaldi on safety grounds, Mass was leading when the race was stopped after Stommelen's crash. Fittipaldi and Mass were second and sixth at Monaco, Fittipaldi was fourth in the French GP and was leading the British GP when it was brought to an end in bad weather. Mass finished fourth in Austria, another race stopped short because of the weather, and third in the non-Championship Swiss GP at Dijon, while Fittipaldi took second places at both Monza and Watkins Glen. In the Drivers' Championship Fittipaldi finished second with 45 points.

M23 and M26 – 1976

Emerson Fittipaldi left to drive for his brother Wilson's new Copersucar-financed team and his place was taken by James Hunt. Although the team produced a new car during the year, the M23 was still proving so successful that it was raced until the end of the season. Hunt and Mass were second and third to Lauda's Ferrari at Kyalami

75. In the 1974 Italian Grand Prix, Emerson Fittipaldi finished second with this McLaren M23. He won the 1974 World Championship.

and Hunt won both the Race of Champions and the International Trophy at Silverstone. At the Spanish race Hunt was winner on the road, but was disqualified because the rear track of his M23 was 1.7 cm wider than permitted and then reinstated as winner, with a fine substituted for disqualification. Two retirements and a fifth at Monaco followed, but Hunt was soon back on form again, winning the French GP and finishing first on the road at Brands Hatch. This was another race restarted after a multi-car accident initiated by Regazzoni, and Hunt was disqualified on appeal by Ferrari because his car was too badly damaged to have completed the first lap and was not runnning when the race stopped.

Immediately after the British race McLaren announced the M26, basically a much improved version of the M23 with the alloy monocoque having top and bottom honeycomb structures which gave greatly increased strength. There was an additinal monocoque structure at the front to protect the drivers feet. Mass drove the M26 in both the Dutch and Italian GPs.

Another victory for Hunt followed in the German GP, the race marred by Lauda's bad crash. Hunt finished fourth in Austria, won at Zandvoort and retired after colliding with Pryce's Shadow at Monza (there had been ructions in practice over the fuel used by McLaren and Penske, who forfeited their only practice times in the dry and started from the back of the grid). Hunt won both the Canadian and United States GP. In Japan he finished third in a race from which Lauda withdrew because of the terrible weather conditions, and the result was that Hunt won the World Championship by the margin of a single point.

M23 and M26 – 1977

McLaren continued to rely on the M23 cars in the early part of 1977 and Hunt finished second in Brazil and fourth in South Africa with Mass fifth. In Spain, Hunt raced the M26 without success, the M23s were used at Monaco, where Mass was fourth, and he reappeared with the M26 at Zolder. As the season progressed, handling problems with the new car were cured and although Mass finished second with an M23 in Sweden, it was not until the French race that the M26 showed any real form. Hunt was third at Dijon and won the British GP (with Mass fourth), Mass was sixth in Austria and fourth at Monza, but Hunt was fastest in practice and won at Watkins Glen, and won again in Japan. Hunt was fifth in the Drivers' Championship with 40 points.

M26 – 1978

For 1978 Hunt was joined in the McLaren team by Patrick Tambay and an M26 was sold to the Chesterfield team for Brett Lunger to drive (he had raced an M23 for this team in 1977). Already the McLaren's star was fading, the wing-cars became increasingly dominant and success during the year was very limited. Hunt finished fourth in the Argentine, and finished sixth in Spain after leading early in the race and stopping for fresh tyres, Tambay took fourth place in Sweden, Hunt was third in France and Tambay sixth at Brands Hatch, fifth at Monza and sixth at Watkins Glen. All rather mediocre compared with McLaren performances of the preceeding few years.

M28 and M29 – 1979

Gordon Coppuck produced the new M28 for 1979, based on a Nomex honeycomb monocoque, with very large underwing area and very large overall dimensions. The wheelbase was 9 ft 5 in., front track 5 ft 10 in. and rear track 5 ft 4 in. Suspension was inboard front and rear with rocker arms and lower wishbones at the front and upper and lower wishbones at the rear. The cars proved slow and heavy and lacked sufficient grip. Tambay was now joined in the team by John Watson, and although Watson finished third in the Argentine, little other success was gained. In Spain Watson drove the shorter M28B and with this car finished sixth in Belgium. At Monaco Watson was at the wheel of the M28C with new inboard front suspension and revised bodywork, and with this he finished fourth. By the British Grand Prix the team had developed the M29, very imitative of the Williams FW07, with much shorter 8 ft 10 in. wheelbase, slim monocoque, narrower track and outboard front brakes. Watson finished fourth at Silverstone, fifth at Hockenheim and sixth in both Canada and the United States.

M29 and M30 – 1980

In the early part of 1980 McLaren raced the M29C with improved weight distribution and Watson was now partnered in the team by Alain Prost. Prost finished sixth in the Argentine and fifth in Brazil, Watson was fourth at Long Beach and Prost was sixth in the British GP. At Zandvoort, McLaren produced the new M30 with stiffened monocoque, slightly shorter wheelbase and widened track, the suspension inboard and the brakes outboard front and rear. Prost finished sixth at Zandvoort, Watson was fourth in Canada in the M29C and Prost crashed the M30 heavily in practice at Watkins Glen, possibly the result of suspension failure. It had been a thoroughly miserable year. Clearly the McLaren team had lost its edge and its sense of direction.

MP4/1 – 1981

There was a complete revitalization of McLaren for 1981 following the formation of McLaren International in September 1980. This merged the interests of Teddy Mayer and Tyler Alexander of Team McLaren and Ron Dennis, Creighton Brown and John Barnard of Project 4. John Watson was partnered by young Italian Andrea de Cesaris, whose career with the team was marked by a series of crashes that has continued ever since and, despite his considerable talent, has made him virtually unemployable. Watson finished fifth with an M29 in the South African GP and after this race the team switched to the modified M29F cars. By the San Marino GP at Imola, Barnard had ready the first of the MP4 cars with the monocoque constructed from moulded carbon-fibre, a material combining low weight, high stiffness and far greater strength in a crash than most critics had expected.

Although Watson was out of the running at Imola, where de Cesaris took sixth place with the M29F, the new car soon found its form, and Watson finised third in Spain, second in France, won the British GP, was sixth at Hockenheim and the Österreichring and second in Canada.

MP4/1B – 1982

Barnard's development programme had concentrated on weight reduction, improving stiffness and suspension development, and the results of this work were seen in the basically similar MP4/1B cars raced in 1982 by Niki Lauda and Watson. Throughout the year the McLarens displayed that they were the best of the Ford-powered runners, along with the Williams, and very substantial success was gained. Lauda finished fourth in South Africa (with Watson sixth), Watson

76. John Watson drove this McLaren MP4/1 into third place in the 1981 Spanish Grand Prix. Here he leads Laffite's Ligier JS17.

second in Brazil and then on the slow Long Beach circuit Lauda scored the first McLaren win of the year with Watson in sixth place. McLaren, along with the other FOCA teams, missed the San Marino GP at Imola, but in Belgium Watson was the winner with Lauda third (on the road but disqualified because his car was underweight at the finish) and the Irishman won again at Detroit. In Canada Watson took third place, Lauda was fourth at Zandvoort and Lauda scored another win at Brands Hatch. A fifth place followed for Lauda in Austria, he was third in the Swiss GP and Watson finished fourth at Monza and second at Las Vegas. Although Rosberg (Williams) won the Drivers' Championship with 44 points, Watson and Pironi (Ferrari) finished equal second with 39 points and McLaren were second in the Constructors' Cup with 69 points to the 74 of Ferrari.

MP4/1C and MP4/1E – 1983

In the early part of the year McLaren International ran the MP4/1C cars, 1982 models modified to comply with the latest 'flat bottom' rules. The designation MP4/1D was applied to the test hack with the new turbocharged Porsche-designed and developed TAG engine and the first turbocharged cars to be raced were designated MP4/1E. The TAG PO1 is an 80-degree V-6 of 1499 cc (82 × 47.3 mm) with twin gear-driven camshafts per bank of cylinders, four valves per cylinder and a single KKK turbocharger for each bank of cylinders. Power output is speculative, but in race boost form it is now around 750 bhp at 12,000 rpm.

With the Ford-powered cars Lauda finished second in Brazil (after Rosberg's disqualification), Watson and Lauda took first and second places at Long Beach, Watson was fifth at Imola, third at Detroit and sixth in Canada, Lauda was sixth in the British race, Watson fifth at Hockenheim (here Lauda was fifth on the road, but disqualified) and Lauda sixth in Austria. The first of the turbocharged cars was driven by Lauda at Zandvoort, but retired with brake problems, while Watson finished third with his Ford-powered MP4/1C. By Monza both drivers had the turbocharged MP4/1Es, but the cars were too new for any success to be gained in 1983.

MP4/2 – 1984

Barnard had now designed a new carbon-fibre monocoque around the shorter TAG engine to take a larger fuel tank – the 220-litre fuel consumption limit prevented the use of smaller tanks and refuelling stops – and although the design concept of the earlier cars had been retained, in almost every respect the chassis was new. Lauda was joined in the team by Alain Prost and they enjoyed a season of unparalleled success, substantially attributable to the detailed design, development

77. The turbocharged McLaren MP4s of Prost and Lauda in the 1985 South African Grand Prix. This was one race that McLaren did not win and Prost, 1985 World Champion, finished third.

and planning and careful preparation of McLaren International. Of the year's 16 Championship races, the McLaren won 12. Prost was the winner at Rio de Janeiro, Imola, Monaco (stopped short and so only scoring half-points), Hockenheim, Zandvoort, the new shortened Nürburgring (scene of the European GP) and Estoril. In addition he was second at Kyalami, third at Montreal and fifth at Detroit. Niki Lauda won at Kyalami, Dijon, Brands Hatch, the Österreichring and Monza, but he also finished second at Montreal, Hockenheim, Zandvoort and Estoril. While Lauda pipped Prost for the World Championship with 72 points to Prost's 71½, McLaren had won the Constructors' Cup with the phenomenal total of 143½ points to the 57½ of Ferrari.

MP4/2B – 1985

For 1985 the improved MP4/2Bs featured new rear suspension with push-rod-operated rockers, completely new bodywork, new hubs and new front suspension uprights. Despite the strength of the Lotus and Williams oppositon and despite brake problems on the slower circuits, McLaren went a long way towards matching their 1984 successes. Prost won in Brazil and at Monaco, was third in Canada and France, won the British GP, was second at the Nürburgring, won in Austria, was second at Zandvoort, won at Monza, was third at Spa and fourth in the European GP and third at Kyalami. He was also first on the road at Imola, but disqualified. The result was a total of 72 points, sufficient to win the World Championship. Lauda, in his last season of racing, suffered from unreliability throughout the year and missed two races because of a wrist injury. He won at Zandvoort, but otherwise could manage only fourth at Imola and fifth at the Nürburgring. McLaren again won the Constructors' Cup, but by a much smaller margin, 92 points to the 80 gained by Ferrari.

MP4/2C – 1986

Changes to the cars for 1986 included reshaped rear bodywork, improved gear linkage, lower driving position and revised rear suspension geometry. Prost had now been joined in the team by Keke Rosberg. In the early part of the season Prost and Rosberg were third and fourth in Spain, Prost won at Imola despite running out of fuel on the last lap with Rosberg fifth and Prost and Rosberg were first and second at Monaco – it was Prost's third successive win in the race. At Spa Prost turned in a magnificent drive after a first-lap pile-up, working his way through the field to finish sixth. Prost and Rosberg finished second and fourth in Canada and a third place for Prost followed at Detroit; McLaren International were still very much in the hunt for the World Championship.

Merzario

(Italy)

A1 – 1978

In 1978 Italian Formula One and sports-car driver Arturo Merzario decided to construct his own Ford-powered contender, largely based on March 751 components, but with increased wheelbase and track. Two of these A1 cars were assembled, but they looked bulky and heavy and were hopelessly uncompetitive. Merzario entered a total of 16 races, qualified as a starter at eight, but finished in none.

A1B, A2 and A4 – 1979

Merzario qualified the slightly updated A1B in the Argentine, but was caught up in a first-lap pile-up and was unable to run when the race was restarted. After failing to qualify in Brazil he appeard at Kyalami with the A2 'wing-car' evolved with help from his mechanic Simon Hadfield, but again failed to qualify. He started at Long Beach with the A1B, failed to qualify the A2 in Spain and Belgium and, after an accident in which he broke his right arm, entered Gianfranco Brancatelli at Monaco, but Brancatelli was unable to qualify. At Silverstone Merzario produced yet another new car, the A4, designed with assistance from Gianpaolo Dallara of Lamborghini. The A4 incorporated parts from the abortive Kauhsen project which Merzario had bought and was a much improved design with slim monocoque, underwing side pods, rocker-arm suspension and a single fuel cell. It was all to no purpose, however, and the pattern of non-qualification as a starter continued for the rest of the year. By then Merzario had realized just how much the odds were stacked against him and withdrew from Formula One.

78. In the 1978 Swedish Grand Prix Arturo Merzario with the Merzario waves past Villeneuve's Ferrari.

Minardi

(Italy)

M85 – 1985

After running a number of Formula Two teams Giancarlo Minardi took the plunge into Formula One in 1985. Giacomo Caliri was commissioned to design the M85, which featured a carbon-composite monocoque with pull-rod-operated double wishbone suspension front and rear, 8 ft 6.6 in. wheelbase, 5 ft 11.3 in. front track and 5 ft 5.4 in. rear track. Although it had originally been planned to use the turbocharged V-8 Alfa Romeo engine, this all changed when Carlo Chiti left Alfa Romeo in 1984. Chiti set up Motori Moderni and developed a turbocharged V-6 1498.9 cc (80 × 49.7 mm) engine said to develop 720 bhp at 11,300 rpm, and Minardi became the first and so far only user of this engine. Because the new engine was not ready at the start of the season, Pierluigi Martini drove the M85 with Cosworth power in the first two races of the 1985 season. The Moderni engine was installed in the Minardi from the Imola race onwards. Both car and driver seemed hopelessly inadequate, engine failures were frequent and Martini had more than his fair share of accidents. The only race in which the Martini was still running when the flag fell was the Australian GP, in which Martini finished eighth and last.

M185B – 1986

Minardi carried on in 1986 with two slightly modified cars driven by Andrea de Cesaris and Alessandro Nannini. No finishes at all were gained in the early part of the season.

79. Little in the way of promise or hope for the future was displayed in 1985 by the Minardi, driven by Pierluigi Martini, and seen here in the Canadian Grand Prix.

Osella

(Italy)

Yet another small team forming part of the also-rans of Formula One, Osella first entered Grand Prix racing in 1980. Enzo Osella had acquired the Abarth company, renowned for their sports derivatives of production Fiats, and having achieved considerable success with sports/racing cars, entered Formula Two racing in 1976. In 1979 the team won three races with cars driven by Eddie Cheever and so the team decided to have a go at the premier category of racing.

FA1 and FA1B – 1980

The first Formula One Onsella was a 'wing-car' designed by Osella and Giorgio Stirano and was driven by Cheever. The design featured a Ferrari-inspired monocoque with aluminium stressed skins over a tubular steel internal frame and front and rear suspension by upper rocking arms, lower wishbones and inboard coil spring/damper units. Inevitably the Cosworth DFV engine was used with the Hewland FGB 5-speed gearbox. The wheelbase was a fraction under 9 ft, front track 5 ft 7.7 in. and rear track 5 ft 3.8 in. At the Italian GP at Imola the team introduced the lighter FA1B car with narrower monocoque and greater area of under-wings. Both types of Osella proved uncompetitive, Cheever failed to qualify at four races and his only finish, in 12th place, was at Imola.

FA1B and FA1C – 1981

During most of 1981 Osella fielded two slightly modified FA1B cars. Beppe Gabbiani drove for the team throughout the year, but he failed to qualify at 12 races and failed to finish in the three that he did start. Miguel Angel Guerra was entered in the first three races of the year, but failed to qualify at any, finally qualifying at Imola and retiring before he was dropped from the team. Piercarlo Ghinzani finished 13th at Zolder and failed to qualify at Monaco. Giorgio Francia failed to qualify in Spain and, after running one car in France, Osella engaged Jean-Pierre Jarier for the British GP onwards. Jarier consistently qualified and usually finished, albeit not in the first six, and at the Italian GP onwards drove the FA1C. This was a much improved car with the monocoque constructed from aluminium sheet with honeycomb outer skins.

FA1C and FA1D – 1982

Osella continued to field two cars, for Jarier and Riccardo Paletti. In the early part of the season Paletti consistently failed to qualify and Jarier qualified but achieved nothing. At Imola, with a very small field because of the FOCA teams' withdrawal, both drivers started and Jarier finished fourth (there were only five finishers). At Monaco neither driver qualifed and then disaster struck at Montreal. Both drivers qualified, but at the start of the warm-up lap Paletti, accelerating from the back of the grid and completely unsighted, drove into the back of the stalled Ferrari of pole-position man Pironi and suffered internal injuries from which he died. Jarier withdrew from the race and for the remainder of the year Osella entered only a single car. At the German GP Osella produced the FA1D with wider track and undertrays for the engine and gearbox. There were no further finishes in the points in 1982.

FA1D and FA1E – 1983

The team started the year with the FA1D cars modified to comply

80. Sadly the enthusiastic Osella team has always been amongst the also-rans. Cheever drove this Ford-powered FA1B in the 1980 Canadian Grand Prix, but retired because of fuel pressure problems.

with the 'flat bottom' rules, with Corrado Fabi and Piercarlo Ghinzani as drivers. At Imola the FA1E with the Tipo 1260 V-12 Alfa Romeo engine was driven by Ghinzani, but it did little to help him qualify. By the British GP a second FA1E was ready for Fabi, and this and a third car built were the work of Auto Racing Technology and featured Tony Southgate-designed slim carbon and alloy monocoque and new push-rod front suspension. By this time the turbocharged cars were completely dominant and the Osellas achieved nothing during the year.

FA1E and FA1F – 1984

Initially the team entered a single car for Ghinzani. Although bearing the FA1E designation, it was in fact based on a 1983 Alfa Romeo carbon-composite monocoque with Osella modifications and the turbocharged Alfa Romeo engine. At Kyalami, Ghinzani lost control of the Alfa-based car during the warm-up, crashed heavily and it was destroyed by fire. By the Belgian GP the Osella team had ready their own new FA1F car with turbocharged engine. Ghinzani consistently qualifed the FA1F (except at the San Marino GP), but the team's only

81. A fine view of Ghinzani with the turbocharged Alfa Romeo-powered Osella FA1G in practice at Detroit in 1985. He was eliminated in a first lap accident.

points were scored by Ghinzani fifth at Dallas and Jo Gartner, who joined Osella mid/season and finished fifth at Monza.

FA1F and FA1G – 1985

Ghinzani stayed with the team, driving the FA1F in the first two races and switching to the improved FA1G at Imola. There was a marginal improvement in Osella performances in that the cars quite often finished, but Ghinzani failed to qualify at Monaco. Later in the year he moved on to the Toleman team and his place was taken by Dutch driver Huub Rothengatter. There was not a single finish in the first six during the year.

FA1G – 1986

Osella had hoped to buy Motori Moderni engines for 1986, but simply could not afford them, so struggled on with the 1985 cars driven by Ghinzani once more and Christian Danner. Nothing at all was achieved during the early part of the year and it was only too obvious that Osella's Formula One future was even bleaker than its past.

Parnelli

(United States)

VPJ4 – 1974

The Parnelli was an ambitious American effort in Formula One that unfortunately soon petered out because of loss of enthusiasm and interest. The team was formed by Velco Miletich and R. Parnelli-Jones, who had a very good track record in USAC racing, and the cars were driven by Mario Andretti. The VPJ4 was designed by Maurice Phillipe and it displayed strong Lotus influence with wedge-shaped monocoque, side radiators, front suspension by double wishbones and torsion bars, rear suspension by single lower links, parallel upper links, twin radius rods and torsion bars, and inboard brakes front and rear. It was of course yet another car powered by the Cosworth DFV engine and with Hewland FG400 gearbox. The wheelbase was 8 ft 4 in., front track 4 ft 11 in. and rear track 5 ft 1 in. Andretti drove the VPJ4 into seventh place on its debut in the Canadian GP, but failed at the start of the United States GP because of electrical problems.

VPJ4 – 1975

By the start of the 1975 season the team was already in trouble, partly because the American team owners were losing interest in Formula One and partly because of the necessity to switch from Firestone to

Goodyear tyres (Firestone had withdrawn from racing at the end of 1974). Even so a measure of success was obtained. Andretti finished third in the International Trophy at Silverstone, after a collision with Lauda on the first lap of the Spanish GP he took the lead until he crashed as a result of suspension damage in the first-lap incident, and, because of Indianapolis, he missed the Belgian race. He finished fourth in Sweden, missed the Dutch GP and took fifth place in the French GP on the Paul Ricard circuit. There were no other finishes in the points. Development had continued through the year with the adoption of outboard front brakes and, at the last race of the season at Watkins Glen, coil spring rear suspension.

VPJ4B – 1976

In this slightly revised form the Parnelli used coil spring suspension front and rear and the rear bodywork had been modified. Andretti finished sixth in the South African GP and retired at Long Beach before the team finally withdrew. It had all been a great waste of money and talent.

82. One of two new cars to make its debut in the 1974 Canadian Grand Prix was the Parnelli VPJ4 which Mario Andretti drove into fourth place.

Pearce
(United Kingdom)

Wheel manufacturer and tyre stockist John Pearce had entered an old Cooper chassis with Ferrari V-12 engine for Chris Lawrence to drive in the 1966 British and German GPs and the Gold Cup race at Oulton Park. This encouraged him to build a simple space-frame Formula One car with the Martin V-8 engine for 1967 racing. The first car was exhibited at the Racing Car Show in 1967 with the Martin engine installed, but in fact was the car intended to take the Ferrari engine. The Martin engine was a light-alloy, 16-valve 2996 cc (85 × 66 mm) unit with single overhead camshafts. The engine was first raced in a Lotus 35 chassis entered by Charles Lucas for Roy Pike at Brands Hatch on Boxing Day 1966, and Pike finished third. The Lotus non-started at Brands Hatch in March and the engine was tested in a Pearce chassis at Brands Hatch until Lawrence crashed heavily, writing off the new car. After non-starting at the Race of Champions, Pearce entered three cars for the International Trophy at Silverstone, two Pearce-Martins for Peter Gethin and Tony Lanfranchi and the Cooper-Ferrari for Robin Darlington. In the words of *Autosport*, 'The entry for the International Trophy was cut drastically when the J. A. Pearce Engineering transporter inexplicably caught fire when unattended on Wednesday evening [before the race]. It was utterly destroyed, as were the new Pearce-Martin GP machines and the older Cooper-Ferrari. So intense was the blaze that considerable damage was done to the roadway, which forms the straight during club meetings.' The Southall-based team never attempted to build new cars.

Penske
(United Kingdom)

PC1 –1974

When Roger Penske entered Formula One, he already had a very experienced and successful racing record that had included entering Ferrari and Lola cars in International sports car racing, the turbocharged Porsche 917/30 in CanAm events and had also fielded a McLaren M19 for Mark Donohue. Penske set up a base at Poole in Dorset, and there Geoff Ferris, formerly with Brabham, designed the PC1 with wedge-shaped monocoque, side radiators, front suspension by double wishbones and semi-inboard coil spring/damper units and rear suspension by parallel lower links, single top links, twin radius rods and outboard coil spring/damper units. The wheelbase was 8 ft 4 in., and front and rear track 5 ft 0 in. The Cosworth DFV engine was used with the Hewland FGA400 gearbox. Donohue finished 12th on the Penske's debut in the Canadian GP and retired at Watkins Glen.

PC1 and PC3 – 1975

A second PC1 with rocker-arm inboard front suspension was ready by the start of the 1975 season, but it soon became clear that the Penskes were not competitive. At Kyalami the second car ran with the rear track widened by three inches and a spacer between engine and gearbox to increase the wheelbase by five inches. Donohue managed sixth place in the International Trophy at Silverstone and he finished fifth in the Swedish GP. These results were not good enough for Penske, who decided to buy a March 751 while a new car was being developed. Sadly Donohue crashed during race morning practice in Austria, when the left front tyre deflated, and suffered injuries that proved fatal. Penske missed the Italian race, but appeared at Watkins Glen with a new car, the PC3, and a new driver, John Watson. The PC3 featured a shorter wheelbase, more than passing similarity to the March 751 and the original PC1 rear suspension. Because of an engine misfire Watson drove the older PC1 in the race and finished ninth.

PC3 and PC4 – 1976

In the early part of the year Watson raced the PC3s, finishing fifth at Kyalami. At the Swedish GP Penske brought out the PC4 with low,

83. The second new contender to make its debut in Canada in 1974 was the Penske PC1 driven by Mark Donohue into twelfth place.

tapered monocoque, revised bodywork and, from the French race onwards, longer 8 ft 11 in. wheelbase. It soon became clear that the team was making real progress and Watson finished third in the French GP (only to be disqualifed because the side plates of the rear aerofoil were a centimetre too high, the result of the whole aerofoil bending during the race, and then reinstated on appeal), fourth in the British GP, winning after a fine drive in Austria and retiring at Zandvoort with gearbox problems when in second place. He rounded off the season with sixth place at Watkins Glen. Despite the promise shown in 1976, Penske withdrew at the end of the season to concentrate on American events, and although he retained the premises at Poole, the cars were sold to Hans Gunther Schmid to form the basis of the ATS team.

RAM
(United Kingdom)

Yet another team struggling against the odds with too little money and too much optimism, the RAM team run by John MacDonald and Mick Ralph fielded Brabham and March cars from 1976 onwards. In 1981 RAM raced cars specially built for them by March and, bearing RAM chassis numbers, driven by Derek Daly and Eliseo Salazar. These March 811s achieved nothing in the way of success, but for 1982 were updated as the 821 and raced with Jochen Mass and Raul Boesel as drivers. The best result was seventh place by Mass at Detroit and it was Mass who had an horrific crash at the Paul Ricard circuit when he collided with Baldi's Arrows, was launched over the catch-fencing, hit a tyre-lined barrier and ricocheted across a perimeter track into a fence at the edge of the spectator enclosure. Around a dozen onlookers suffered burns and abrasions, but the accident could have been so very much worse and was influential in the decision to outlaw the ground-effect wing cars.

01 – 1983

Although the team continued to use the March name in 1983, the cars were RAM-designed and built. The 01 was the work of Dave Kelly and was a simple DFV-powered car with suspension front and rear by upper and lower wishbones, pull-rods and with inboard springs. During the year the RAMs were handled by a number of drivers, Kenny Acheson, Eliseo Salazar, Jean-Louis Schlesser and Jacques Villeneuve, but they were hopelessly uncompetitive and failed to qualify at ten of the year's races.

02 – 1984

For 1984 the RAM team arranged to use the 4-cylinder Hart turbocharged engines developing around 600 bhp at 10,750 rpm. One of the 1983 cars was modified to take the Hart unit, but later in the year the team produced 02 cars proper with new carbon-composite monocoques. The RAM entries always looked good and were well prepared, but they were no more competitive than previously. Drivers during the year were Phillipe Alliot and Jonathan Palmer, while Mike Thackwell replaced Palmer at Montreal when he was driving at Le Mans. None of the RAM drivers finished in the first six during the year and there were no encouraging signs that the team was making headway.

03 – 1985

RAM ran the new 03 cars with carbon-composite monocoques and still with Hart engines for Manfred Winkelhock and Phillipe Alliot; the team suffered a bad blow when Winkelhock suffered fatal injuries in the endurance race at Mosport and his place in the team was taken by Kenny Acheson. By the end of the year the team had been obliged to miss the last two races, it had lost its sponsorship from Skoal Bandit tobacco and the situation looked even more hopeless than ever.

The team was still hoping to run a single car for Mike Thackwell in 1986 and appeared at the Rio testing with the 03 decked out in Swan lager colours. Unfortunately the sponsorship never emerged and the team was forced to withdraw from Formula One without running in any of the year's races.

84. Another successful Grand Prix contender, the RAM 03 with Hart turbocharged engine. Manfred Winkelhock is seen in the 1985 French Grand Prix in which he finished twelfth.

Rebaque

(Mexico)

HR100 – 1979

During 1978–79 this Mexican private entrant ran his own small private team with Lotus 78 and 79 cars. There was not much assistance from Lotus so far as spares and development were concerned and Rebaque decided to commission his own Formula One contender. The result was the HR100 designed and constructed by Penske Racing at Poole. The Rebaque featured a slim monocoque very similar to that of the Lotus, Williams-inspired side pods, front and rear suspension by upper rocking arms, bottom wishbones and inboard springs, 9 ft wheelbase, 5 ft 8 in. front track and 5 ft 4 in. rear track. Rebaque used the car as a spare at Zandvoort, failed to qualify at Monza, retired in Canada and failed to qualify at Watkins Glen. Although some development work was carried out over the winter, the HR100 was never again raced and Rebaque next appeared as number two in the Brabham team.

Renault

(France)

The state-owned French car manufacturer had become increasingly involved in motor racing through the engine development work of Amédée Gordini, racing entrant who later became a Renault employee, and through their connections with the Alpine concern that both built Renault-powered road cars and competition cars. When Renault decided to enter Formula One, they were also developing turbocharged engines for the Le Mans Prototypes, and so in their early days their efforts were divided. Development of the turbocharged engines was carried out at the Gordini works, while Alpine, taken over by Renault in 1976, developed the chassis. Renault's decision to build a turbocharged engine was bold and displayed foresight, but like so many pioneers the team never reaped the full benefit of its initiative, and when it withdrew from racing at the end of 1985 it had never won the World Championship.

RS01 – 1977

The Renault V-6 EF1 turbocharged engine had a capacity of 1492 cc (86 × 42.8 mm) and an initial claimed power output of 510 bhp at 11,000 rpm. It was installed in an slab-sided coke bottle-shaped aluminium monocoque stiffened by steel plates with front suspension by double wishbones and inboard springs and rear suspension by parallel lower links, single upper links, twin radius rods and outboard springs. Transmission was by a Hewland FGA400 6-speed gearbox. The RS01 had a wheelbase of 8 ft 2 in., front track of 5 ft 1.4 in. and rear track of 5 ft 3.3 in. It had a simple, rugged chassis and the smooth body, designed by Marcel Hubert, was finished a distinctive yellow.

Jean-Pierre Jabouille drove the RS01 on its debut in the British GP, starting from well back on the grid and retiring early in the race. The Renault ran in four other races in 1977, failing to finish in three and not qualifying at the fourth.

RS01 – 1978

Once again only a single car was entered in 1978, partly because the RS01 was still very much at the development stage and partly because much of Renault's efforts were concentrated on winning at Le Mans. Jabouille was still the driver, qualifying well up the field at most races, performing better on the faster circuits. Renault missed the first two races of the year in South America, but ran in the remaining 14, and Jabouille's best performance was at Watkins Glen, where he finished fourth.

RS01 and RS10 – 1979

With a victory at Le Mans under their belt Renault put far greater effort into their 1979 racing programme and fielded two cars for Jabouille and Réne Arnoux. Initially the RS01s were used, but at Jarama Renault fielded the RS10 for Jabouille. The RS10, designed by Michel Tétu, who had joined Renault from Ligier, was a ground-effect

85. The early days of the turbocharged engine. Arnoux with this Renault RS10 finished sixth in the 1979 Austrian Grand Prix.

car with much slimmer monocoque, curvaceous, louvred side-pods and end-plate mounted rear wing. The wheelbase had been increased to 9 ft 4.6 in. A second of these cars was ready for Arnoux by the Monaco race and in all four were built during the year, carrying the numbers RS10, RS11, RS12 and RS14 because of the new numbering system adopted by Renault. By Monaco the cars were fitted with twin KKK turbochargers instead of the single larger turbocharger previously installed. It was at this point that Renault development began to pay off, and in the next race, the French GP at Dijon, Jabouille and Arnoux took first and third places. A second place for Arnoux followed in the British GP, Arnoux was sixth in Austria and Arnoux rounded off the season with second place at Watkins Glen. The opposition began to take serious notice.

RE20 – 1980

New cars were built for 1980 in the series RE20–25 with the 'E' in the designation standing for Renault's main sponsor Elf. There were many minor changes, including a new skirt system and side-pods, and other changes were made as the season progressed. The Renaults held the first two places for much of the Brazilian GP and Arnoux went on to win after Jabouille's car suffered turbo failure. Arnoux scored another win at Kyalami, Arnoux was fourth at Zolder, the Renaults were withdrawn in Spain together with the Alfa Romeo and Ferrari entries and next ran at the Paul Ricard circuit, where Arnoux finished fifth. Jabouille scored a fine victory in Austria, Arnoux was second at Zandvoort, but otherwise success eluded the team in the latter part of the year. Because Jabouille crashed badly in Canada, only a single entry for Arnoux had run at Watkins Glen.

RE20B and RE30 – 1981

Renault found themselves in severe difficulties in 1981, mainly because of changes in the rules. The RE20B had been developed from the 1980 cars to comply with the ban on sliding skirts. When the Ford-powered teams developed suspension lowering devices that were accepted as legal, the Renaults driven by Alain Prost and René Arnoux were outclassed. The best performances were a third by Prost and fifth by Arnoux in the Argentine. At Zolder, Renault produced the new RE30 cars (numbered RE30–35) of much lighter construction than their predecessors, a new Renault gearbox with Hewland gears and shorter wheelbase. Arnoux failed to qualify at Zolder because of problems in practice, and when the race was restarted after a starting grid mêlée, Prost's clutch soon failed. Later in the year Prost won the French GP with Arnoux fourth, Prost was second at Hockenheim, Arnoux second in Austria, Prost won at Zandvoort and Monza and Prost finished

86. Alain Prost with the Renault RE30 was fastest in practice for the 1981 Dutch Grand Prix and apart from one lap when he missed a gear led throughout.

second at Las Vegas. Prost took fifth place in the Drivers' Championship and Renault was third in the Constructors' Cup. The team was steadily progressing to the top.

RE30B – 1982

For 1982 the Renault team relied on updated versions of the 1981 cars, but throughout the year the cars were developed and modified on a race-by-race basis. At Kyalami Prost and Arnoux took first and third places and Prost was first in Brazil, but both Renaults were eliminated at Long Beach, where they raced with water ballast because they were apparently underweight. Prost crashed whilst leading at Monaco with two laps to the finish, and although Prost finished sixth in the British GP the team went through a bleak period without success until Arnoux and Prost took the first two places in the French GP at the end of July. Arnoux finished second at Hockenheim and Prost was second in the Swiss GP at Dijon (Arnoux was about to take the lead when he retired because of fuel injection trouble), while at Monza Arnoux scored the team's fourth Championship race win of the season. At the year's final race at Las Vegas Prost took fourth place. Prost finished fourth in the World Championship and Renault third in the Constructors' Cup.

RE30C and RE40 – 1983

In the early races Renault entered the RE30 cars updated to comply with the new 'flat bottom' rules, power output was now around 650 bhp at 12,000 rpm and the drivers were now Prost and Eddie Cheever. The first of the RE40 cars with carbon-composite monocoque was driven by Prost at Long Beach. By the French GP the Renaults had found their form and Prost and Cheever took first and third places, Prost finished second to Tambay's Ferrari in the San Marino GP at Imola and he was third at Monaco, where the cars were fitted with revised exhaust systems exiting beneath extended full-width underwings and claimed by rivals to create ground effect by illegal means; the new Renault layout was subsequently confirmed to be legal and adopted by other teams. Prost and Cheever were first and third in the Belgian GP, newly returned to Spa-Francorchamps, Cheever was second in Canada, Prost won at Silverstone, was fourth at Hockenheim and won in Austria. Prost was leading the World Championship by 14 points from Nelson Piquet, but gradually his lead slipped away. Cheever was third at Monza while Prost suffered two more retirements before finishing second to Prost in the European GP at Brands Hatch. Piquet finished third in South Africa, while Prost retired yet again, so the Brazilian came out the Championship winner with 59 points to the 57 of the Renault driver.

RE50 – 1984

By 1984 the now rather elderly Renault engines were using alloy blocks as standard, they were fitted with Garrett AiResearch turbochargers, were developing around 750 bhp and were installed in new carbon-Kevlar monocoques. Prost had left to drive for McLaren, Cheever also departed and the new drivers were Patrick Tambay and Derek Warwick. The year proved to be the start of a decline from which Renault never recovered. The team failed to win a single race during the year and the best performances were sixth by Tambay in Brazil (Warwick had led until the suspension failed), third by Warwick at Kyalami, a really good second place by Warwick at Zolder and fourth at Imola and second by Tambay in the French GP. Later in the year Warwick was second in the British GP and third at Hockenheim, while Tambay took sixth place at Zandvoort.

RE60 and RE60B – 1985

At the end of the year Gérard Larrousse, who had been team

87. Renault, pioneers of the turbocharged engine in Formula One, retired from racing at the end of 1985. Derek Warwick with this RE60 finished fifth at Monaco in 1985.

manager for so many years, was sacked and he and Michel Tétu joined the Ligier team. Tétu had completed the design of the new and improved RE60 before he left and work on the much revised EF15 engine of 1494 cc (80.1 × 49.4 mm) developing 810 bhp at 11,500 rpm was well advanced. A further improved car, the RE60B, appeared during the year. The cars, however, no longer seemed either competitive or reliable. Tambay finished fifth in Brazil, third in Portugal and third at Imola, while Warwick was fifth at Monaco and Brands Hatch. Shortly after the German GP Renault announced that they would be withdrawing from racing at the end of the year and thereafter the team's performances went from bad to worse as they 'played out' the season. The only finish in the points was sixth place by Warwick in the Belgian GP.

Shadow

(United Kingdom)

Don Nicholls, founder of Advanced Vehicle Systems, had first caught the public eye with the Shadow sports car distinguished by its very small 10 in. and 12 in. wheels, which he had run in the 1970 CanAm races. The car achieved no success, but it brought him a lot of attention, and when he decided to enter Formula One he obtained major sponsorship from Universal Oil Products. Nicholls attracted a strong team that included Jack Oliver, Alan Rees and Tony Southgate and, initially, the team's prospects of success seemed to be excellent.

DN1 – 1973

The first cars designed by Tony Southgate featured a 'coke bottle'-shaped monocoque with chisel nose, front suspension by double wishbones and outboard coil spring/damper units and rear suspension by lower wishbones, single upper links, single radius rods and outboard coil spring/damper units. The Cosworth DFV engine was used with a modified Hewland FG400 gearbox The wheelbase was 8 ft 4 in., front track 4 ft 10 in. and rear track 5 ft 0 in. The first Shadows were driven by Jack Oliver and American George Follmer and made their debut in the South African GP. Follmer finished sixth at Kyalami on his Formula One debut and subsequently he was third in Spain and Oliver was third in Canada. One of the DN1 cars was sold to Graham Hill, who raced it without success under his Embassy Racing banner. Despite the tendency of the Shadows to shake themselves to bits, the results for the team's first season had been reasonably encouraging.

DN1 and DN3 – 1974

The DN1 was raced in both the Argentine and Brazil until a second new car was ready, and the DN3 was a vastly improved car with lengthened wheelbase, widened track, longer nose and generally improved aerodynamics. Oliver had retired from racing, but stayed with the team in a management role, and the new drivers were Jean-Pierre Jarier and Peter Revson. Revson took sixth place in the Race of Champions at Brands Hatch, but crashed with fatal results in pre-race testing at Kyalami as the result of suspension failure. Brian Redman drove for the team in Spain, Belgium and Monaco but withdrew from Formula One. In Sweden the second Shadow was driven by Bertil Roos and then Tom Pryce took over for the remainder of the season. Jarier finished third in the International Trophy at Silverstone and third at Monaco, he was fifth in Sweden and Pryce was sixth in the German GP, but in real terms not much progress had been made since 1973.

DN3B, DN5 and DN7 – 1975

For the first two races of the season in South Africa, Pryce drove the updated DN3B, moving on to the new DN5 at Kyalami, while Jarier raced the DN5 from the start of the year. The main changes on the new cars were aerodynamic, but the weight distribution was improved and the DN5s were lighter. Shadows' first win came with Tom Pryce and the DN5 in the Race of Champions at Brands Hatch. In the Championship series Jarier was classifed fourth in the Spanish GP, Pryce was sixth at Zolder and Zandvoort and fourth at the Nürburgring. In the Austrian GP Jarier drove the new DN7 with a Matra V-12 engine.

88. The Shadows DN3s in the 1974 Spanish Grand Prix; Redman, who finished seventh, leads Jarier, who was running at the end of the race but unclassified.

He retired because of problems with the fuel system, but Pryce was third in this race, stopped short because of bad weather. A sixth place for Pryce followed at Monza, where Jarier again drove the DN7 without success.

DN5B and DN8 – 1976

Nicholls suffered two bad blows before the start of 1976. Matra withdrew the V-12 engine in favour of supplying Ligier and, much more important, UOP withdrew its sponsorship. From now on the only way was down and survival was a very tough struggle. In the early part of the year the team raced the DN5Bs, improved versions of the 1975 cars, and although Tony Southgate had designed the lighter, more aerodynamic DN8 before leaving to join Lotus, it was not ready until later in the year. It was inevitably a bad year for the team, and whilst Pryce was third in Brazil and Jarier crashed when in second place, both at the wheel of DN5Bs, Pryce was also fourth in the British GP with a DN5B and fourth with the DN8 in Holland on its first race outing.

DN5B and DN8 – 1977

Lack of money inhibited new developments for 1977. Pryce was joined in the team by Renzo Zorzi. Zorzi finished sixth and last but one in Brazil. In South Africa, Shadow suffered a terrible blow with the death of Tom Pryce. Zorzi's Shadow stopped out on the circuit with a blown engine, and when leaking fuel ignited, a young marshall dashed across the track with a fire extinguisher straight into the path of Tom Pryce's car. The marshall was killed by the Shadow and Pryce

89. Tom Pryce with the 1975 Shadow DN5 in the 1976 Spanish Grand Prix in which he finished eighth. By this time the team had lost its UOP sponsorship.

was killed instantly by the impact of the extinguisher. With the driver already dead, the Shadow careered on to collide with Laffite's Ligier. Alan Jones was in the team from Long Beach onwards, while Riccardo Patrese drove for Shadow at Monaco in place of Zorzi (here Jones was sixth) and also at Zolder (where Jones was fifth). Oliver came out of retirement to partner Jones in Sweden and Patrese was back in the team for the French GP and drove for Shadow for the remainder of the season except when prevented by Formula Two commitments. In Austria, Jones achieved a magnificent one-off victory for the Shadow team, beating Lauda's Ferrari by 20 seconds. At this race Merzario was in the team. Jones turned in another fine performance at Monza to take third place. Jarier drove in place of Patrese at Watkins Glen. Jones rounded off the season with two satisfactory fourth places, in Canada and Japan. Shadow's temporary resurgence had been substantially due to the fact that early in the season they had gained sponsorship from Ambrosia, but this lasted only very briefly as it was withdrawn after the German GP.

DN9 – 1978

Before the start of the season Alan Rees, Jack Oliver, Tony Southgate and David Wass had left to form the Arrows team. Before he left Southgate had designed the new D9 'wing-car' and it was subsequently held in the High Court in an action brought by Nicholls that the new Arrows infringed Shadow copyright drawings to the extent of 40 per cent of the components. Although the Arrows, subsequently declared illegal, was racing at the start of 1978, Shadow struggled on with the DN8, and their DN9 'wing-car' completed by John Baldwin was not ready until Long Beach, where it was driven by Hans-Joachim Stuck. The second Shadow was driven in 1978 by Clay Regazzoni, Regazzoni finished fifth with a DN8 in Brazil, fifth with a DN9 in Sweden and Stuck was fifth in the British GP with a DN9

DN9B – 1979

Shadow struggled on with the existing cars modified to DN9B specification by Richard Owen and John Gentry. The drivers were Elio de Angelis and Jan Lammers. A number of further modifications were made to the cars during the season, including rocker-arm suspension and new side-pods, but nothing was gained during the year except for a fourth place by de Angelis at Watkins Glen.

DN11 and DN12 – 1980

It was only too evident that the end was near, but Shadow struggled on with the new DN11 driven by Stefan Johannson and David Kennedy, with Geoff Lees coming into the team in place of Johannson at Long Beach onwards. It was evident that the DN11 was a failure and at Zolder Shadow produced the first of the new short-wheelbase DN12 cars. A second DN12 was ready for the Spanish GP a month later. By the Belgian race Teddy Yip had bought into the Shadow team, which became known as Theodore Shadow. By the French GP he had decided that he was simply wasting money and the Shadow team did not race again. One of the DN12 cars raced briefly as a Theodore in 1981.

Shannon

(United Kingdom)

A rather unsatisfactory special resulting from the combined talents of mechanic Aiden Jones and vastly experienced constructor Paul Emery, the Shannon ran in only one Formula One race, the 1966 British GP. Jones built a rather flimsy riveted aluminium monocoque with rocker arm suspension. The power unit was the Coventry Climax V-8 FPE engine, originally built for the 2500 cc Grand Prix Formula of 1954 onwards but unraced, because the Climax directors concluded quite wrongly that it was insufficiently powerful to be competitive. Now, 12 years later, Emery enlarged one of the four engines which he had acquired to 3-litres, a move facilitated by the FPE's wet cylinder liners, developed it to run on pump fuel (it had been designed for alcohol fuels) and, mated with a Colotti gearbox, installed it in the Jones-designed monocoque. The Shannon was driven by Trevor Taylor, and despite the exhausts bottoming in practice, he lapped faster than Arundell's 2-litre Lotus BRM and Lawrence's Cooper-Ferrari, but retired on the first lap of the race because of a split fuel tank.

Spirit

(United Kingdom)

201 – 1983

Spirit Racing had been formed by John Wickham and Gordon Coppuck to run a team of Formula Two cars in 1982 with Honda 2-litre V-6 engines. At this time Honda had under development their RA163-E 1500 cc turbocharged engine and entered into an arrangement with Spirit to run a Honda-powered Formula One car at a number of races in 1983. The Formula One Spirit was a modified Formula Two car

90. Mauro Baldi with the Hart-powered Spirit 101D in the 1985 Brazilian Grand Prix. Spirit sold their tyre contract to Toleman early in the year.

with front and rear suspension by upper rocking arms, lower wishbones and inboard springs, the wheelbase was 8 ft 4 in., front track 5 ft 9 in. and rear track 5 ft 4 in. The team was well satisfied with the car in winter testing and ran it in a number of events with Stefan Johannson at the wheel. He qualified for all the races entered and the team gradually developed the chassis, entering an improved 201C car at Zandvoort. By the European GP at Brands Hatch Spirit had ready, but did not race, the 101 built from scratch as a Formula One car.

101B – 1984

Obviously Spirit hoped that Honda would go on supplying engines in 1984, but instead the Japanese company elected to support only the Williams team. Spirit carried on racing with the 101B, the car seen at Brands Hatch in 1983 modified to take the Hart 415T turbocharged engine. There was talk that the Spirit would be driven by Emerson Fittipaldi, who was thinking of returning to racing, and although he tested the 101B, this came to nothing. Instead the Spirit was driven by Mauro Baldi, who had bought the drive with finance supplied by his sponsor. Baldi drove in six races, his place was taken by Huub Rothengatter at Detroit, where the team was forced to run with a Cosworth engine because of a shortage of Hart units, and the Dutchman drove in six more races before Baldi resumed at the wheel for the last two races of the year. Sadly the Spirit never finished in the points.

101D – 1985

Spirit carried on into the 1985 season with the modified 101D with push-rod front suspension and repositioned radiators, running at three races before selling their tyre contract to Toleman and pulling out of racing altogether. It had been a gallant but hopeless effort.

Surtees
(United Kingdom)

During 1967–68 John Surtees had run a team of Lola sports cars in close liaison with the works, he had built the Len Terry-designed Surtees TS5 Formula 5000 cars in 1969 and, after his thoroughly miserable season with BRM in 1969, it was not a difficult decision to build his own Formula One cars. In the early part of 1970 he raced a McLaren M7C until his own new Ford-powered contender was ready.

TS7 – 1970

The TS7 featured an aluminium-alloy monocoque stiffened by three bulkheads, the front bulkhead fabricated from aluminium alloy and the other bulkheads from Reynolds 531 tubing. At the front suspension was by upper rocking arms, lower wishbones and inboard coil spring/damper units, while at the rear there were single upper links and radius arms, lower reversed wishbones and outboard coil spring/damper units. The Ford engine was used with the Hewland DG300 5-speed gearbox. The wheelbase was 8 ft 0 in., front track 4 ft 10 in. and rear track 5 ft 0 in. Painted red and white with the usual Surtees arrowhead on the nose, the new car made its debut in the British GP at Silverstone. Here Surtees retired with engine problems, but later in the year Surtees won the Gold Cup at Oulton Park and he finished fifth in the Canadian GP, while Derek Bell with a second car took sixth place at Watkins Glen.

TS9 – 1971

In 1971 Surtees received sponsorship from Brook Bond-Oxo and Rob Walker, while a second car driven by Rolf Stommelen was sponsored by the German magazine *Auto Motor und Sport* and Eifelland caravans. The TS7 was used for the first couple of races, but Team Surtees produced the new TS9 with lower and flatter monocoque, the wheelbase was three inches longer, the track an inch wider and, from Watkins Glen onwards, it had side-mounted radiators. Successes during the year were few and far between. Surtees finished third in the Race of Champions at Brands Hatch, third in the Jochen Rindt Memorial race at Hockenheim, fifth at Zandvoort, sixth in the British GP (Stommelen was fifth) and won the poorly supported Gold Cup at Oulton Park. At Monza Mike Hailwood appeared for the team; he was well up with the leaders all the way and finished fourth.

91. Andrea de Adamich with the Surtees TS9B on his way to fourth place in the 1972 Spanish Grand Prix.

TS9B and TS14 – 1972

Strictly, the 1971 car with side radiators was designated the TS9A and in slightly modified TS9B form was raced by Team Surtees throughout the year. Mike Hailwood was now team leader, backed up by Tim Schenken, and with a third red and white TS9B sponsored by Ceramica Pagnossin for Andrea de Adamich to drive. It was a largely unsuccessful year and the best performances were a fifth place by Schenken in the Argentine GP, whilst Hailwood finished second in the Race of Champions at Brands Hatch, fourth in the Belgian GP and second in the Italian GP. Surtees only raced twice during the year, in the International Trophy at Silverstone in which he finished third and at Monza, where he handled the new TS14 on its race debut. The TS14 was built to conform to the 1973 deformable structure regulations and featured a new monocoque of sandwich construction formed by aluminium sheet and foam and an inner layer of glass fibre, a rear bulkhead formed by a full-width tubular structure to which the Ford engine was attached and outboard suspension front and rear.

TS14 – 1973

1973 proved yet another season of failure. Team drivers were Hailwood and Carlos Pace. Hailwood crashed in the Race of Champions as the result of a failure of either a tyre or the suspension, Hailwood and Regazzoni (BRM) collided at Kyalami and the three team cars were badly damaged in the first-lap pile-up at Silverstone (here Surtees had entered a third car for Jochen Mass). All that was achieved during the year was a fourth place by Pace at the Nürburgring and a third by Pace in Austria.

TS16 – 1974

Mike Hailwood left to drive for McLaren, so the team drivers were Pace and Mass. The 1974 car differed little from its predecessor other than in reduction in weight by about 60 lb. Pace finished fourth in Brazil and Mass was second in the International Trophy at Silverstone, but nothing else worth while was gained, and after the Swedish GP Pace left the team, subsequently joining Brabham. Leo Kinnunen drove a TS16 for the AAW Racing team, but gave up after a succession of failures to qualify. Later Surtees entered cars for Bell, Dolhem, Jabouille, Koinigg and Quester. Koinigg crashed with fatal results, probably the result of tyre failure, in the last race of the year at Watkins Glen.

TS16 – 1975

Team Surtees soldiered on with the now outdated TS16 for another season, entering only a single slightly modified car for John Watson.

Although Watson failed to finish in the first six at any of the year's Championship races, he did take second place in the Race of Champions, fourth in the International Trophy at Silverstone and fifth in the Swiss GP at Dijon.

TS19 – 1976

New cars, the TS19s, with pyramid-section monocoques rather like the Brabham BT44s, were built for 1976. Suspension was by double wishbones and outboard springs at the front, by lower wishbones, parallel upper links, twin radius and outboard springs at the back and with very compact dimension: the wheelbase was 8 ft 2.8 in., front track 4 ft 10 in. and rear track 4 ft 11 in. Surtees missed the Brazilian GP, but a TS19 for Brett Lunger sponsored by Chesterfield appeared in South Africa and Alan Jones first drove a TS19 with Durex sponsorship in the Race of Champions, taking second place. In Belgium Jones took an excellent fifth place. He also finished fifth at Brands Hatch and rounded off the season with a fourth place in Japan. During the year Henri Pescarolo also competed with a TS19 entered by Norev Racing and in Japan the second team car was driven by Noritake Takahara.

92. This Surtees was driven by Carlos Pace in the 1974 Monaco Grand Prix, but was eliminated in a first-lap multiple accident.

TS19 – 1977

Surtees again entered two TS19s in 1977, one sponsored by Beta Tools for Vittorio Brambilla and the second with Durex sponsorship by quite a list of paying drivers: Hans Binder in the first six races, Larry Perkins at Zolder, Anderstorp and Dijon, Vern Schuppan at Silverstone, Hockenheim, the Österreichring and Zandvoort, Leoni Lambert at Monza and Hans Binder again for the last three races of the year. Brambilla was fourth in Belgium, fifth in Germany and sixth in Canada.

TS20 – 1978

Although the team campaigned througout 1978 with slightly improved TS20 cars driven by Brambilla and Rupert Keegan (the latter sponsored by British Air Ferries), not a single Championship point was gained. The team had been planning the TS21 for 1979, but there were no signs of sponsorship because of the team's poor record and Team Surtees was in danger of losing its membership of FOCA because it had not scored a Championship point during the year. This also meant the loss of subsidized travel outside Europe and so Team Surtees quietly disappeared from the Formula One scene.

Tecno

(Italy)

After building a sound reputation as constructors of, initially, karts and, later, Formula Three and Two cars, the Pederzani brothers, based in Bologna, decided to embark on a Formula One programme. It was well financed with sponsorship from Martini & Rossi (it was entered as the Martini Racing Team), well managed by David Yorke and with sound drivers, but design, construction and administration were so appalling that it remained in continual chaos and failure.

PA123 – 1972

In many respects the Tecno was inspired by Ferrari design practice. The team built its own flat-12 2995 cc (80.98 × 48.46 mm) engine, claimed optimistically to develop 460 bhp at 11,000 rpm and mated with the Hewland FG400 gearbox. The monocoque was also Ferrari-inspired, with a tubular frame and riveted-on aluminium skins. The engine formed a stressed unit and was bolted to the rear bulkhead. Suspension at the front was by double wishbones and outboard coil spring/damper units, while at the rear there were upper links, lower wishbones, radius rods and outboard coil spring/damper units. An unusual feature was that the coil springs were mounted in a near-

93. The flat-12 Tecno PA123 was a hopelessly unsuccessful project. Derek Bell is seen in practice for the 1972 French Grand Prix at Clermont-Ferrand.

vertical position. The wheelbase was 8 ft 4 in., and front and rear track 5 ft 1.4 in. As originally tested the Tecno featured twin side radiators and pannier tanks mounted on outriggers, but both these features had been abandoned by the time the car was first raced. Originally only one was entered, driven alternatively by 'Nanni' Galli and Derek Bell, and when it first appeared at the Belgian GP nothing depressed as much as its tatty appearance and poor construction. Although the PA123 was progressively modified as the season progressed, there seemed little improvement in performance and nothing was achieved apart from a third place (out of five finishers) in the non-Championship Vallelunga race – and there were only seven starters.

PA123 – 1973

For the 1973 Tecno a new chassis was designed by Alan McCall and Chris Amon was signed up to drive the new car, which was numbered 006. 006 featured double wishbone front suspension with semi-outboard springs and rear suspension by lower wishbones, single upper links and outboard springs. Amon was unhappy with the handling of 006, and by the time it first raced, a replacement was already on the drawing board. It made its debut in the Belgian GP at Zolder; it looked rough and the engine sounded clapped, but Amon struggled through the race to finish sixth. At this point Tecno withdrew to await the new car designed by Gordon Fowell and with the monocoque constructed by John Thompson. The new car, typed the E731, distinguished by its exceptionally low construction and cramped cockpit, was ready by the British GP. It was clearly not a raceworthy proposition at this stage and Amon drove the 006 at Silverstone and Zandvoort, retiring at both circuits. In Austria Amon practised with both cars, but by this time he was completely fed up with the Tecno project and left the circuit before the race. The Tecno never raced again.

Theodore

(United Kingdom)

TR1 – 1978

Although the Theodore was financed by 'Teddy' Yip based in Macau, the team itself was very British, design was by Ron Tauranac, management by Irishman Sidney Taylor and they occupied Ron Tauranac's old Ralt premises at Woking. Tauranac had devised a very odd-looking car with blunt lines, the space between the front and rear wheels occupied by bodywork, conventional suspension at the front by double wishbones and outboard springs and at the rear by parallel lower links, single upper links, twin radius and outboard springs. The wheelbase was 8 ft 4.2 in., front track 4 ft 10.8 in. and rear track 5 ft 4.8 in. Eddie Cheever failed to qualify the Theodore in the South American races, but Keke Rosberg came through to score a very surprising victory in the rain-soaked International Trophy at Silverstone. Rosberg failed to qualify at four Championship races and by the German GP the Theodore had been abandoned and Rosberg was entered at the wheel of a Wolf.

TR2 and TY01 – 1981

Three years later Yip was again racing cars bearing the Theodore name. The first of these was the Shadow DN12, renamed after Yip's aquisition of that ailing team, but this, now typed TR2, was crashed by Geoff Lees in the non-Championship South African GP at the beginning of the year. By Long Beach the new Tony Southgate-designed TY01 'wing-car' was ready and three of these were built. The TY01 was distinguished by its front wing mounted on a centre pylon and it featured front and rear suspension by upper rocking arms, lower wishbones and inboard springs. Patrick Tambay drove the TY01 into sixth place at Long Beach, but did not finish again in the points before leaving to drive for Ligier in mid-season. For the remainder of the season Marc Surer drove the Theodores, consistently but without success.

TY01 and TY02 – 1982

Although Theodore started the season at Kyalami with the TY01, two TY02s with aluminium-honeycomb monocoques were soon completed. Derek Daly drove for the team in early races, but by the fifth round of the Championship he had joined the Williams team and his place had been taken by Jan Lammers. Lammers failed to qualify in his three races and was duly replaced by Geoff Lees in Canada, but Lammers drove again at Zandvoort, scraping in on the back of the

94. Keke Rosberg with the Theodore TR1 in practice for the 1978 Belgian Grand Prix at Zolder.

grid, but failed to qualify at the next three races. Tommy Byrne took the drive at Hockenheim and stayed with the team for the rest of the year. Sadly, absolutely nothing was achieved.

N183 – 1983

Yip now combined Theodore with the struggling Ensign team in which he already had a financial interest. The 1983 Theodore was simply an updated version of the Ensign raced the previous year, although two cars were built with carbon-fibre cockpit stiffening. The team's drivers had to buy their entries. Johnny Cecotto stayed with the team throughout the year, omitting only the last two races, and managed a sixth place at Long Beach, while Robert Guerrero ran in every race except the final Grand Prix at Kyalami but never achieved anything worthwhile. In addition Brian Henton drove in the Race of Champions and finished fourth. By the end of the season Yip realized that there was little point in carrying on with the team, especially as it seemed unlikely that a turbocharged engine would be available, and he and Ensign's Maurice Nunn turned their attention to American CART racing.

Token

(United Kingdom)

RJ02 – 1974

Designed by Ray Jessop and built by Rondel Racing, the Formula Two team run by Ron Dennis and Neil Trundle, the RJ02 was disposed of by Rondel when they were unable to obtain sponsorship and sold to Tony Vlassopoulo and Ken Grob, who renamed it the Token. It was a simple conventional design with slim monocoque, front suspension by double wishbones and outboard springs, rear suspension by parallel lower links, single upper links, twin radius rods and outboard springs, 8 ft 0 in. wheelbase and with front track of 5 ft 2 in. and rear track of 5 ft 3 in. The Cosworth DFV engine was used with the Hewland FGA400 geabox. Entered by Token Racing, RJ02 was driven by Tom Pryce in the International Trophy at Silverstone and the Belgian GP, in which he crashed. David Purley drove at the British GP, but failed to qualify, and Ian Ashley qualified for both the German and Austrian GPs, finishing at the tail of the field. The Token did not run again in 1974.

RJ02 – 1975

By 1975 the Token had been acquired by John Thorpe of Safir Engineering, and so the car was renamed the Safir. It was driven by Tony Trimmer in the Race of Champions at Brands Hatch and the International Trophy at Silverstone, and at both races was still running, but last, when the flag fell. The RJ02 was not raced again.

Toleman

(United Kingdom)

Backed by Ted Toleman (who runs the largest car transporter business in the UK) and managed by Alex Hawkridge, the Toleman team won the European Formula Two Championship in 1980 with their own cars designed by Rory Byrne and John Gentry and powered by Brian Hart-developed engines. To enter Formula One in 1981 was a bold and risky step, but despite the many problems encountered, Toleman has come very close to major success.

95. Tom Pryce qualified well for the 1974 Belgian Grand Prix with the Token RJ02, but was eliminated in a collision with Scheckter's Tyrrell.

TG181 – 1981

Byrne and Gentry designed an aluminium monocoque of, compared to the team's rivals, rather bulky and ungainly appearance; front and rear suspension was by upper rocking arms, lower wishbones and with inboard springs. The wheelbase was 8 ft 10 in., front track 5 ft 7 in. and rear track 5 ft 6.3 in. Toleman commissioned the Hart 415T 4-cylinder 1494 cc (88 × 61.5 mm) turbocharged engine, and this was used with a Toleman/Hewland gearbox. At a time when most other teams were using the well-proven Cosworth DFV, Toleman faced all the development problems of a new engine, but it was an essential step to ensure the long-term future of the team. The drivers were Brian Henton and Derek Warwick, who had raced for the Toleman Formula Two team, but the year proved an uphill struggle. Toleman first ran at Imola, the fourth round in the Championship, but it was not until the thirteenth round at Monza that a Toleman qualified and Henton started from the back row of the grid to finish tenth and last. Warwick qualified at the last round at Las Vegas, but was eliminated by transmission problems.

TG181C and TG183 – 1982

For most of the year Toleman relied on the 1981 cars in slightly updated TG181C form, but at Monza the team produced the TG183 with carbon-fibre monocoque, pull-rod-operated suspension, the Hart engine (now developing around 580 bhp) was now a semi-stressed member and the whole car was much neater and looked more compact. Warwick remained with the team and was joined by Teo Fabi. Toleman withdrew from the Detroit and Montreal races, but showed consistent improvement throughout the year; Warwick failed to qualify at only three races and Fabi failed to qualify seven times. There was nothing achieved in the way of results, but Toleman did seem to be getting somewhere!

96. In 1981 Toleman were struggling with Hart-powered TG181. Here Derek Warwick tries unsuccessfully to qualify at the British Grand Prix.

TG183B – 1983

The existing design was developed to comply with the 1983 'flat-bottom' rules and the Hart engines were now fitted with British Holset turbochargers in place of the American Garretts previously installed. Warwick was joined in the team by Bruno Giacomelli and at long last some decent results were obtained. Whilst Warwick qualified as a starter at all the year's races, Giacomelli failed to qualify at Monaco only. At Zandvoort Warwick finished fourth, he took sixth place at Monza, finished fifth in the European GP at Brands Hatch (with Giacomelli sixth) and rounded off the season with fourth place at Kyalami. Toleman had achieved respectability.

TG183B and TG184 – 1984

Warwick left to drive for Renault, but Toleman were quick to sign up Ayrton Senna, and he was partnered by Johnny Cecotto. Toleman used the TG183B and Senna finished sixth in South Africa. By the French GP at Dijon, Toleman had switched from Pirelli to Michelin

97. Despite problems that kept them out of racing in the early part of 1985, Toleman showed continuing promise. Teo Fabi drives the Hart-powered TG185 in the Detroit race in which he retired with clutch failure.

tyres (which was to prove unfortunately significant) and the TG184 was ready to race. At Monaco Senna took a brilliant second place in heavy rain and was rapidly catching Prost's leading McLaren when the race was brought to a premature end. In the British GP at Brands Hatch Senna finished third, but the race was marred for Toleman by Cecotto's bad practice crash caused by a jammed throttle; the Venezuelan suffered severe leg and ankle injuries when the front of the carbon monocoque was crushed against the barriers. Only a single car for Senna was entered in Germany, Austria and Holland and at Monza he was suspended by the team for having signed up with Lotus for 1985, allegedly in breach of contract. Stefan Johansson had joined Toleman for the remainder of the season and at Monza the second car was driven by Pierluigi Martini. Johansson finished fourth at Monza, Senna returned to the team at the new Nürburgring and rounded off the season with third place in Portugal.

TG185 – 1985

For 1985 Toleman signed up Johansson and John Watson to drive the new TG185 cars. Michelin, however, withdrew from racing, Goodyear was not prepared to take on another team and after the team's open criticism of Pirelli in 1984 before they switched to Michelin, the Italian company refused to supply Toleman. Toleman missed the first three races of the season, but after buying out Spirit's tyre contract, Toleman fielded a single car with Benetton sponsorship at the Monaco GP onwards for Teo Fabi. From the Austrian GP a second car was entered for Ghinzani. Although Fabi took pole position at the new Nürburgring, the team failed to gain a single finish in the first six.

B186 – 1986

For 1986 the team was renamed Benetton Formula, reflecting the immense financial backing from the Italian knitwear company, and had obtained supplies of BMW turbocharged engines. Rory Byrne's new B186 cars were driven by Teo Fabi and Gerhard Berger, and they showed real promise once more. Berger finished sixth in Brazil, Fabi and Berger were fifth and sixth in Spain, Berger was third at Imola and Berger was second fastest in practice at Spa, but delayed by a first-lap multiple accident, and the Benettons led in Austria.

Trojan

(United Kingdom)

T103 – 1974

Trojan had built production McLarens until the end of 1972 and for 1973 asked Ron Tauranac to design a Trojan Formula 5000 car. This was built in two versions, and then Peter Agg of Trojan asked Tauranac to design a Formula One car. The result was the T103 with simple monocoque, split radiators in the nose and the centre-section of the car extended to fill the space between front and rear wheels. The Cosworth DFV engine was used with the Hewland DG300 gearbox. The wheelbase was 8 ft 6 in., front track 5 ft 1 in. and rear track 5 ft 4 in. Tim Schenken was the driver and the Trojan made its debut at the Spanish GP. The team was refused an entry at the Swedish GP, did not run in France and qualified at six out of the eight races at which it was entered. The best finishes were 10th places in Belgium and Austria. It was a very low-budget exercise and the Trojan team withdrew before the North American races.

Tyrrell

(United Kingdom)

Ken Tyrrell had enjoyed his own racing career with Cooper 500 cc cars before becoming a successful entrant in Formula Three and Two, a spotter of talent who gave early drives to Jacky Ickx and Jackie Stewart. His success with Formula Two Matras led to his collaboration in Formula One with the French company. At the end of 1969 Matra

98. Tim Schenken drove the Trojan T103 into tenth place in the 1974 Belgian Grand Prix.

told Tyrrell that they wanted him to run cars with their V-12 engines the following year, but he declined and ran a team of March 701 cars until his own new Tyrrell was ready.

001 – 1970

To design the car, Tyrrell commissioned Derek Gardner, project engineer for the Matra MS84 four-wheel drive car who had just left the Ferguson organization. Gardner evolved a 'coke-bottle' monocoque with more than a passing resemblance to that of the Matra MS80 and constructed in aluminium sheet, with fabricated steel bulkheads and the rear roll-over bar built as an integral part of the rear bulkhead. The fuel was carried in four bags concentrated well within the wheelbase and the 001 was distinguished by a very wide, flat nose fin surmounting the radiator air intake and with small adjustable flaps on the trailing edges. Front suspension was by double wishbones and outboard coil spring/damper units, while at the rear there were twin parallel lower links, single upper links and coil spring/damper units. The DFV engine was used with a Hewland FG400 5-speed gearbox. The wheelbase was 7 ft 10.2 in., front track 5 ft 3 in. and rear track 5 ft 2.9 in. Stewart drove the car on its debut in the Gold Cup at Oulton Park and the three North American races, but there were inevitable teething troubles and no success was gained.

001, 002 and 003 – 1971

At this time Tyrrell simply numbered the cars sequentially as they were built. By 1971 the design had been fully sorted and settled and two new cars were built with detail changes. Stewart and team-mate

99. Jackie Stewart with the Tyrrell 002 on his way to victory in the 1971 Monaco Grand Prix.

François Cevert embarked on a season of remarkable success, the result of superb preparation, excellent team management and the simple fact that Stewart was the World's finest driver at the time. Stewart finished second in the South African GP, second in the Race of Champions, second in the non-Championship Questor GP and, during the European season, had wins in Spain, Monaco, France, Britain and Germany. He also won the Canadian GP and Cevert was the winner at Watkins Glen. Stewart won the Drivers' Championship with 62 points to the 33 of second-place man Peterson. Tyrrell also won the Constructors' Cup with 73 points to the 36 of BRM. Changes to the cars during the year had included the adoption of full-width noses, high air-boxes and experiments with longer wheelbases.

005 and 006 – 1972

In the early part of the year the team raced the existing cars, while Gardner developed the new 005 and 006 cars. Stewart won the first of the Championship races in the Argentine, but generally the season was less successful than expected. Lotus and McLaren were able to match the speed of the Tyrrells, the cars suffered mechanical shortcomings which Tyrrell frankly attributed to 'inefficiency' and Stewart missed the Belgian GP because of ulcer trouble. Cevert had finished second at Nivelles and Stewart bounced back to win the French GP after Amon's Matra suffered a puncture.

Tyrrell revealed the new 005 at Clermont-Ferrand. Directly developed from the earlier Tyrrells, it featured a more slab-shaped monocoque, a 1.5 in. shorter wheelbase, complete enclosure of the mechanical parts, inboard front brakes and the oil radiators transferred

100. In 1972 Francois Cevert drove this Tyrrell 002 into second place in the Belgian Grand Prix.

to the sides of the car. At Brands Hatch Stewart practised with the new car, but suffered a minor accident in practice, the team was plagued by vibration under braking and in the race he drove 003 into second place. Stewart finally raced 005, now fitted with outboard brakes, in Austria, but no success came the team's way until the North American races, and with 005 Stewart won both the Canadian and United States GPs. By the Canadian race 006 had been completed for Cevert. Patrick Depailler also drove a third car for the team in the French and United States GPs. Stewart finished second in the Drivers' Championship with 45 points to the the 61 of Emerson Fittipaldi.

005 and 006 – 1973

The team continued with the 005 and 006 cars in 1973 building new cars with the conventional numbering 006/2 and 006/3, now with a revised inboard front brake layout. The Tyrrell drivers enjoyed formidable success during the year, with Cevert finishing second in the Argentine (Stewart was third), Stewart second in Brazil and then winning in South Africa, Belgium (with Cevert second) and Monaco and fifth in Sweden. Cevert was second in Spain and France and fifth at Silverstone, while Stewart won at Zandvoort (with Cevert second) and the Nürburgring (again Cevert was second), taking second place in Austria and fourth at Monza. For the two North American races Amon was brought into the team with a third car, but the cars failed in Canada. In the United States tragedy struck when Cevert crashed fatally in practice with a new car and the team withdrew from the race. Stewart, winner of the 1973 World Championship, retired with 25 Championship wins to his credit (equalling Jim Clark's record) and the team entered 1974 with new drivers.

007 – 1974

For 1974 Tyrrell signed up Jody Scheckter and Patrick Depailler and raced the 006 cars in the first three races, before switching to the new 007 at the Spanish GP. The new cars featured a longer 8 ft 6 in. wheelbase, torsion bar suspension, side radiators and inboard brakes front and rear. With the 006 cars Depailler finished sixth in the Argentine and fourth in South Africa. He also drove the 006 at Jarama, Monaco and Dijon, but otherwise the team used the 007 for the rest of the year. It was a year of moderate success, with Scheckter finishing fifth in Spain, third in Belgium, second at Monaco and winning the Swedish race with Depailler in second position. Fifth and sixth places for Scheckter and Depailler followed at Zandvoort, and Scheckter was fourth at Dijon and went on to score his second win of the season in the British GP at Brands Hatch. Another second place for the South African followed at the Nürburgring, with third place at Monza, and

Depailler was fifth in Canada and sixth in the United States GP. In the Drivers' Championship Scheckter took third place with 45 points.

007 – 1975

In 1975 Tyrrell relied on the 007 cars once more, but they had now reverted to coil spring suspension (inboard at the front and outboard at the rear) and the front brakes were again outboard. Scheckter and Depailler were again the drivers, and although the team fared reasonably well, it was beginning to slip. Depailler finished fifth in the Argentine, Scheckter won the South African GP (with Depailler third), Depailler was fifth at Monaco and then Scheckter bounced back with a fine second place in the Belgian GP at Zolder. Tyrrell did not feature in the points again until the French GP, where Depailler took sixth place, Scheckter was third in the abandoned British GP and Scheckter was sixth in the United States race. There had been a clear fall-off in results as the season progressed.

007 and P34 – 1976

In the early part of 1977 Tyrrell continued to rely on the 007 cars, but there soon appeared the revolutionary P34 six-wheel cars with four 10 in. diameter front wheels. Gardner could see many advantages for the layout, including increased tyre contact with the road, increased braking area and reduction of lift at the front, thereby increasing cornering speeds. The P34s had panels in the cockpit sides so that the drivers could observe the front wheels. From the front axle, the wheelbase was 8 ft 0.6 in., front track 4 ft 0 in. and rear track 4 ft 10 in.

With the 007 Depailler was second in Brazil, Scheckter fourth in

101. Jody Scheckter finished second in the 1974 German Grand Prix with this 007 Tyrrell.

102. The 1976 six-wheel Tyrrell Project 34 cars proved far more successful than most critics expected. This is Patrick Depailler on his way to second place behind team-mate Scheckter in the Swedish Grand Prix.

South Africa and Depailler third at Long Beach. The first of the P34s was driven by Depailler in Spain, and by the Belgian race both drivers had these cars. Scheckter was fourth in Belgium, Scheckter and Depailler second and third at Monaco and these drivers took first and second places in Sweden. Another second place by Depailler followed in the French GP, Scheckter was second in the British race and at the Nürburgring but crashed in Austria as a result of suspension failure whilst leading the race. A fifth for Scheckter followed at Zandvoort, Scheckter and Depailler took fifth and sixth places at Monza, Depailler was second in Canada, Scheckter second in the United States and Depailler finished the season with second place in Japan. Scheckter took third place in the Drivers' Championship. All in all it was a good season for the team, which had faced testing, development and construction problems throughout the year.

P34 – 1977

For 1977 Depailler was joined in the Tyrrell team by Ronnie Peterson. The expected Tyrrell domination never happened, for the P34s had grown bulkier and heavier and were plagued by tyre problems; the latest Goodyear tyres suited only the rear wheels of the Tyrrell and problems were inevitable. The year was not a complete disaster, however, because some worthwhile places were gained. Depailler finished third in South Africa and fourth at Long Beach, Peterson was third in Belgium, Depailler fourth in Sweden, Peterson finished fifth in Austria and sixth at Monza, while Depailler scored Tyrrell's best result of the year by finishing second in Canada and was third in the last race of the year in Japan.

008 – 1978

Derek Gardner left at the end of the year to work for Borg Warner and new designer Maurice Phillipe produced the 008 with conventional four wheels, shallow aluminium monocoque, front suspension by double wishbones and inboard springs and rear suspension by parallel lower links, single upper links, twin radius rods and outboard springs. It was a compact, neat and exceedingly well made car with 8 ft 10.3 in. wheelbase, 5 ft 7 in. front track 5 ft 2/3 in. rear track. The drivers were now Depailler and Didier Pironi.Tyrrell seemed to have recovered some of the ground lost. Depailler was third in the Argentine and in Brazil, Pironi finished sixth, and Depailler took second place in South Africa, third at Long Beach and scored a fine victory at Monaco. Another sixth place for Pironi followed in Belgium, but after this run of good finishes, a succession of retirements followed and the next finish in the points was at Brands Hatch, where Depailler was fourth. Pironi was fifth at Hockenheim and Depailler took a fine second place in Austria, but nothing else was achieved during the remainder of the year. Depailler finished fifth in the Drivers' Championship.

009 – 1979

Phillipe's next development was a close imitation of the Lotus 79 ground-effect design, with similar rocker-arm front suspension, but rear suspension by double wishbones, longer 9 ft 2 in. wheelbase and narrower track front and rear. Pironi stayed with the team and he was now joned by Jean-Pierre Jarier. The 009 never showed any prospects of winning and the Tyrrell team was beginning to find life financially difficult in Formula One. The best performances were a fourth place by Pironi in Brazil, a third by Jarier in South Africa, sixth by Jarier at Long Beach, fifth and sixth places by Jarier and Pironi in Spain, third by Pironi in Belgium, fifth by Jarier in France, third by Jarier in the British GP, sixth by Jarier at Monza and fifth by Pironi at Watkins Glen. Consistent – if not impressive! Geoff Lees drove for Tyrrell at Hockenheim and Derek Daly in Austria, while Jarier was incapacitated by hepatitis.

010 – 1980

It was only too indicative of the fact that Tyrrell had lost all initiative and their sense of direction that the 1980 010 cars were based on the Williams FW07. There were differences, of course, because the rear suspension was by upper rockers and lower wishbones, and whilst the wheelbase was identical, the front track was slightly narrower and the rear track, which was changed during the season, varied from being much the same to some 8 in. wider. Jarier was now joined in the team by Derek Daly and during the year Daly suffered two bad accidents that were attributable to structural failure rather than driver error. Nothing much was gained during the year, but Daly finished fourth in the Argentine, Jarier took fifth place in Belgium, Jarier was again fourth in Spain, Daly and Jarier fourth and fifth in the British race and Jarier was fifth at Zandvoort, the total sum of Tyrrell efforts which gave the team sixth place in the Constructors' Cup.

010 and 011 – 1981

By this time Tyrrell was very much on the slippery slope towards oblivion, and whilst a new 011 did appear in 1981, for much of the year the team relied on the 1980 cars. Eddie Cheever was the regular driver for the team in the early part of the year, but a second car was driven by Desiré Wilson in the non-Championship South African GP (she crashed), Kevin Cogan failed to qualify at Long Beach and Ricardo Zunino drove in the Brazilian and Argentine races before the second car was driven regularly from Imola onwards by Michele Alboreto.

The 011, broadly similar to the 010 but complying with the 1982 regulations relating to driver safety cells, was crashed by Cheever in practice for the British GP, Cheever drove it again at Hockenheim, and from Austria onwards (where Cheever failed to qualify) there was a second 011 for Alboreto. The result of the season's efforts all stood to the credit of Cheever, fifth at Long Beach, sixth in the Belgian GP, fifth at Monaco, fourth in the British GP and fifth in the German GP.

011 – 1982

Tyrrell continued to race the 011 cars in 1982, now modified by the adoption of pull-rod suspension and complying with the regulations as to fixed skirts. The wheelbase was increased to 9 ft 1 in. and a narrow track version of the 011 was used on the faster circuits. Alboreto remained with the team, joined by Slim Borgudd for the first three races, but thereafter by Brian Henton. Despite the lack of competitive machinery Alboreto, whose potential was obviously immense, turned in some fine drives, finishing fourth in the Brazilan GP, fourth at Long Beach, third at Imola, sixth in the French GP, fourth at Hockenheim, fifth at Monza and scoring a brilliant victory at Las Vegas, taking the lead as faster runners fell by the wayside.

011 and 012 – 1983

The 011 cars were modified and updated for the 1983 season to comply with the 'flat-bottom' rules, but it was not until the Austrian GP that the team produced the new 012 with carbon-fibre monocoque. Changes to the design included shorter wheelbase, narrower track and

103. By 1981 the great days of the Tyrrell team were over. Here Michele Alboreto struggles vainly to qualify with the 010 at Jarama.

revised rear suspension. Alboreto remained with the team and he was joined by Dannie Sullivan, who was later to achieve immense success in American racing. Tyrrell also adopted the new and much redesigned Cosworth DFY engine and there were no prospects of a turbocharged engine being available. During the year the sole finishes in the points were a fifth by Sullivan at Monaco and a sixth by Alboreto at Zandvoort. In addition Sullivan took an unexpected second place in the non-Championship Race of Champions at Brands Hatch.

012 – 1984

It was simply a case of plugging on with the old Cosworth-powered cars in 1984, hoping that something would turn up. Something did turn up, but it was far from pleasant. It was a dreadful year for the team and its drivers, newcomers to Formula One, Martin Brundle and Stefan Bellof. Bellof managed to finish sixth at Zolder, fifth at Imola and third at Monaco, while Brundle was fifth in Brazil and took a brilliant second place in the Detroit GP. At Detroit an analysis of water taken from the Tyrrell's water injection system allegedly revealed the presence of hydrocarbons and suggested the addition of illegal additives to the fuel. Tyrrell managed to run in the British race after a High Court injunction had been granted. FISA banned Tyrrell from the 1984 World Championship and foreited the points gained so far in 1984, but allowed the team to race whilst its appeal was heard. Brundle had crashed badly in practice at Dallas and for the time being his place in the team was taken by Stefan Johansson. Mike Thackwell drove for Tyrrell at Hockenheim (Bellof was driving a Porsche at Mosport) but failed to qualify. By Monza Tyrrell had lost his appeal and

104. Tyrrell were the last team still to use the Ford engine. Brundle with the 012 leads Warwick (Renault) and Boutsen (Arrows) at Detroit in 1985.

he was banned from running in the last three races of the year. It was clear that Tyrrell was less than popular in the stance that he had taken as his team slipped steadily downwards, but the real truth behind the allegations made by FISA is a matter for conjecture.

014 – 1985

By the start of 1985, Tyrrell was racing again and had managed to secure supplies of turbocharged Renault engines, but it was necessary to go on using the Cosworth in the early part of the year. The first of the Renault-powered 014s ran in the French GP early in July. The basic design remained unchanged, but the new car featured a longer wheelbase and wider track. The drivers were Brundle and Johansson until the Swedish driver joined Ferrari and Bellof rejoined the Tyrrell team. Sadly Bellof was killed at Spa at the wheel of a Porsche and in the Italian and Belgian races only a single car was entered for Brundle. Ivan Capelli drove a second car in the European GP at Brands Hatch and in the Australian GP, whilst Philippe Streiff drove for Tyrrell in South Africa. The only finishes in the points during the year were by Bellof with Cosworth-powered cars, sixth in the Portuguese and fourth at Detroit.

014 – 1986

In 1986 the 014s were driven by Martin Brundle and Philippe Streiff, Tyrrell was still very much fighting its way back to respectability and in the early part of the year Brundle finished fifth in Brazil. There were no other finishes in the points, but the team continued to make steady progress.

Williams

(United Kingdom)

Frank Williams has enjoyed a chequered history in Formula One. He first entered the category in 1969 with a Brabham BT26A for Piers Courage, fielded the de Tomaso 505 cars in 1970 and ran March cars in 1971–72. The first proper Williams cars competed in 1972

FX3 – 1972

Known as the Politoys FX3 (and named after its sponsor), Williams's first Formula One car was designed by Len Bailey and featured a shapely 'coke bottle' aluminium monocoque with the usual Ford DFV engine, Hewland FG400 gearbox, front suspension by double wishbones and outboard coil spring/damper units and rear suspension by parallel lower links, single top links, twin radius rods and outboard springs. The wheelbase was 8 ft 0 in., front track 5 ft 1 in. and rear track 5 ft 0 in. The car made its debut in the British GP, but was crashed heavily by Henri Pescarolo. After a rebuild it was driven in the John Player Challenge Trophy at Brands Hatch in October by Chris Amon, but was eliminated by an engine misfire.

FX3B and IR – 1973

For 1973 the Williams team received sponsorship from the Iso Rivolta car manufacturing concern, with additional sponsorship from Marlboro, and the cars were raced as Iso Marlboros. Initially the team fielded FX3B cars, slightly modified versions of the 1972 prototype, and from the Spanish GP onwards entered the broadly similar IR, which complied with the new deformable structure regulations and featured a slightly longer wheelbase. A number of different drivers handled the cars during the year, including Jackie Pretorius, Howard

105. Arturo Marzario with the Iso Marlboro Williams FW in practice for the 1974 Monaco Grand Prix. Merzario was eliminated in a first-lap multiple accident.

Ganley, Tony Trimmer (fourth in the Race of Champions at Brands Hatch), 'Nanni' Galli, Tom Belso, Henri Pescarolo, Graham McRae, Gijs van Lennep, Rikki von Opel, Tim Schenken and Jacky Ickx, but the only finish in the points was sixth places by van Lennep in Holland and by Howden Ganley in Canada.

FW – 1974

Although the 1974 cars were still the IRs, they appeared in the entry list as FWs! Arturo Merzario was the usual driver, but the second car was driven during the season by Tom Belso, Gijs van Lennep, Richard Robarts, Jean-Pierre Jabouille and Jacques Laffite (he ran in the last five races). Merzario finished third in the non-Championship President Medici Grand Prix, sixth in South Africa, and fourth at Monza, so at least there were signs of improvement.

FW03 and FW04 – 1975

During 1975 the old cars were known as FW02 and FW03, while a new variant with squarish monocoque, but broadly unchanged was known as the FW04. The regular drivers were Merzario and Jacques Laffite, but they were contracted to drive for Alfa Romeo in sports car races and so a number of other drivers handled the Williams cars during the year, including Tony Brise, Ian Scheckter, Vern Schuppan, François Migault, Ian Ashley, Jo Volanthen, Renzo Zorzi and Lella Lombardi. The one real success during the year came when Laffite took second place in the German GP, thanks to a considerable extent to a spate of punctures suffered by other drivers.

106. Merzario was still with the Wolf Williams team in 1976 and drove this FW05, in the Canadian Grand Prix.

FW06 – 1978

For 1976 Williams sold a 60 per cent interest in his team to Walter Wolf. By September of that year he was out and ex-Lola engineer Patrick Head joined him. Throughout 1977 Williams raced a March 761 car for Belgian Patrick Neve, but by the following year the first of many new Patrick Head-designed Williams cars was ready to race. The new FW06 was a compact and simple design with front suspension by upper rocking arms and inboard springs and rear suspension by lower wishbones and links, single upper links, single radius rods and outboard springs. The wheelbase was 8 ft 4 in., front track 5 ft 2 in. and rear track 5 ft 0 in. Throughout the year driver Alan Jones had the Williams well to the fore and despite many retirements when he was doing well he finished fifth in the French GP and second in the United States race.

FW07 – 1979

In the early part of the year Williams Grand Prix engineering fielded FW06 cars for Alan Jones and Glay Regazzoni, but no success was gained. By the Spanish GP the team was ready to field two of the new FW07 'wing' cars, inspired by the Lotus 79, but essentially an innovative new design. The FW07 was based on an aluminium honeycomb monocoque, front and rear suspension was by upper rocking arms, bottom wishbones and inboard springs, The wheelbase was 8 ft 10 in., front track 5 ft 8 in. and rear track 5 ft 3 in. The new cars were superbly designed with the most careful attention paid to aerodynamics and they were beautifully constructed. They soon proved their worth, with

107. By 1980 the Williams star was very much in the ascendant. Alan Jones was holding second place at Long Beach with this FW07B when he was eliminated in a collision with Giacomelli's Alfa Romeo.

second place by Regazzoni at Monaco and fourth by Jones in the French GP, but then came a succession of wins. Regazzoni was the winner in the British GP, Jones won at Hockenheim (with Regazzoni second), the Österreichring, Zandvoort and Montreal (with Regazzoni third). Jones finished third in the Drivers' Championship and Williams was second in the Constructors' Cup. Nevertheless Jones had won more Grands Prix during the year than Championship winner Scheckter.

FW07B – 1980

For 1980 Head developed the FW07B with stiffened monocoque and extended underwings. Because of porpoising problems (soon to be cured) Jones's car was restored to FW07 trim in the Argentine and he scored a fine win from Piquet's Brabham. Jones took third place in Brazil, retired in his next two races, finished second in Belgium (with team-mate Reutemann third), Reutemann won at Monaco, Jones won in Spain, France (Reutemann was sixth) and Britain (Reutemann was third). Reutemann was second at Hockenheim (Jones was third), Jones was second in Austria (with Reutemann third) and Reutemann was fourth at Zandvoort. The pattern continued at Monza, where Jones and Reutemann took second and third places and the team rounded off the season with first and second places in the order Jones, Reutemann in both Canada and the United States. It had been a season of brilliant success, with Jones winning the Drivers' Championship with 67 points, Reutemann third with 42 points and Williams winning the Constructors' Cup with 120 points to the 66 of second-place team Ligier.

FW07C – 1981

At the beginning of the year Reutemann won the non-Championship South African GP with an FW07B but for the main season and to comply with the ban on sliding skirts, Williams produced the FW07C and soon developed their own lowering suspension device as first used by Brabham and accepted as legal. It was to prove another year of substantial success, although the Williams drivers were pipped in the World Championship by Nelson Piquet (Brabham). Alan Jones won the first round of the Championship at Long Beach with Reutemann second and in Brazil these positions were reversed with Reutemann winning from Jones. In the Argentine Reutemann finished second behind Piquet with Jones fourth. Reutemann was third at Imola, he won at Zolder and Jones was second at Monaco. Reutemann was fourth in Spain and finished second in the British race. In Austria, Jones and Reutemann were fourth and fifth, Jones was third at Zandvoort and Jones and Reutemann were second and third at Monza. The team's final success of the year was at Las Vegas, where Jones was the winner. Thanks to the fine race performances of both team drivers Williams again took the Constructors' Cup with 95 points to the 61 gained by Brabham.

FW07C and FW08 – 1982

At the end of 1981 Alan Jones retired and the team was now led by Carlos Reutemann partnered by Keke Rosberg. In South Africa, Reutemann drove the FW07C into second place with Rosberg fifth, Rosberg was second on the road in Brazil but disqualified because his car was underweight at the finish and he was second again at Long Beach. By this race Reutemann had made the abrupt decision to retire and his place in the United States had been taken by Andretti. By the Belgian GP the Williams team had ready the new FW08 cars, a design that had originally been planned to race with four rear wheels, but proved exceptionally successful in conventional four-wheel form. Rosberg was now partnered in the team by Derek Daly. With the new car that was shorter, lighter and more rigid than its predecessor and with improved aerodynamics, Rosberg enjoyed a consistent run of success, finishing second at Zolder, fourth at Detroit (with Daly fifth), fifth in France, third in Germany, taking second place in Austria, winning the Swiss GP at Dijon and taking fifth place at Las Vegas. On the strength of these consistent performances Rosberg took the World Championship with 44 points to the 39 of Didier Pironi and John Watson, who were equal second. During the year Daly had also finished sixth at Monaco and fifth in the British GP.

FW08C and FW09 – 1983

Patrick Head updated one of the 1982 cars to comply with the new 'flat-bottom' regulations and two new cars built were designated the FW08C. Rosberg was now partnered by Jacques Laffite. Again Rosberg was second on the road in Brazil, but again disqualified, this time for receiving a push-start. Laffite finished fourth at Long Beach, Rosberg won the Race of Champions at Brands Hatch and Rosberg and Laffite were fifth and sixth in France, and this rather dismal standard continued throughout the year. At Imola, Rosberg was fourth, he scored a rare victory at Monaco, was fifth in Belgium, second at Detroit (with Laffite fifth) and took fourth place in Canada. Laffite finished fifth at Hockenheim. For the last race of the year, the South African GP, Williams had ready the new FW09 with Honda turbocharged RA163-E engine, and Rosberg drove one of the new cars into fifth place.

FW09 – 1984

During the year the FW09 was developed into the FW09B with longer wheelbase, modified bodywork and wider rear track. It was a McLaren-dominated year, but the Williams-Hondas grew in strength and reliability as the year progressed. Rosberg finished second in Brazil, fourth in Belgium, sixth in France and fifth at Monaco. Laffite was sixth at Detroit and the breakthrough finally came at Dallas, where Rosberg won from Arnoux's Ferrari with Laffite in fourth place. Unfortunately the team failed to finish in the points during the remainder of the year, but the results in 1985 would be very different.

FW10 – 1985

Rosberg was now joined in the team by Nigel Mansell and Williams raced the FW10 cars with carbon-composite monocoques. After a slow start to the year with Mansell finishing fifth in Portugal and Imola and Rosberg fourth in Canada, Rosberg scored the Honda engine's first 1985 win at Detroit. A second place followed in France, Mansell was sixth at the Nürburgring and Zandvoort, he was second again

108. Immensely powerful and likely to prove the greatest threat to McLaren supremacy, the Honda-powered Williams FW10s driven by Mansell and Rosberg in the 1985 Belgian Grand Prix.

in Belgium and at the end of the year scored two more fine wins in the European GP at Brands Hatch (with Rosberg third) and in South Africa (with Rosberg second).

FW11 – 1986

For 1986 Patrick Head produced the lower and smaller FW11 and the team drivers were Mansell and Piquet. A terrible blow to the team was Frank Williams's road accident, which caused him severe injuries and resulted in his absence from Williams's Didcot works and the circuits in the early part of the year. It was however a tribute to his organization and ability to delegate that the team went on winning without him. It showed every sign of being a Williams year with Piquet winning in Brazil, Mansell finishing second in Spain, Piquet second at Imola, Mansell fourth at Monaco and then scoring wins at Spa and in Canada.

Wolf

(United Kingdom)

Although financed and run by Walter Wolf, an Austrian-born Canadian, the team was firmly British in that it was based on Wolf's acquisition of the Hesketh equipment and on Frank Williams's business, 60 per cent of which was acquired by Wolf. The team operated from Williams's premises in Reading. Hesketh designer Harvey Postlethwaite joined the team, but Frank Williams departed from the team he had created in September 1976.

FW05 – 1976

Entered as the Wolf-Williams, the FW05s were in fact the old Hesketh 308C cars and were driven by Jacky Ickx and Michel Leclère. Attempts to strengthen the structure of the 308C resulted in it becoming greatly overweight and it was hopelessly uncompetitive. Ickx was dismissed from the team after he had failed to qualify for the British GP and his place was taken by Arturo Merzario. For the remainder of the European races only the single car was entered, but Chris Amon drove a second car for Wolf in Canada, non-starting after a practice accident, and Warwick Brown drove in the United States GP.

WR1–3 – 1977

For 1977 Harvey Postlethwaite designed a completely new car, designated WR, and three examples were built bearing chassis numbers 1 to 3. The WR featured a distinctive arrow-shaped nose and wedge-shaped monocoque, front suspension by double wishbones and outboard springs and rear suspension by parallel lower links, single upper links, twin radius rods and outboard springs. The Cosworth DFV engine was used with the Hewland FGA400 gearbox. The wheelbase was 8 ft 2 in. (also raced in 8 ft 7 in. form), with front track 4 ft 7.5 in. and rear track 5 ft 0 in. The WR was an exceptionally rugged and reliable car and driver Ian Scheckter enjoyed a very successful season. He won the Argentine GP on the car's debut, finished second in South Africa, third at Long Beach and in Spain and won again at Monaco. Six non-finishes followed, but Scheckter came back to take third place at Zandvoort and Watkins Glen and win in Canada. The South African finished second in the Drivers' Championship with 55 points to the 72 of Niki Lauda.

WR5–6 – 1978

Scheckter raced the existing cars in the early part of 1978, but it was soon obvious that they were no match for the latest 'ground-effects' Lotus 79s and Postlethwaite responded with the WR5 and WR6 cars. Team management was now the responsibility of Peter Warr. The WR5 was a 'wing-car' design with wedge-shaped monocoque, but exceptionally ugly, angular appearance. The new cars featured lengthened 8 ft 7 in. wheelbase, widened 5 ft 4 in. track front and rear and new front suspension by upper rocking arms, lower wishbones and inboard springs. Scheckter first drove WR5 in practice at Monaco and raced it in the Belgian GP at Zolder. Two of the 1977 cars were sold to Theodore racing for Keke Rosberg to drive. Scheckter finished fourth in Spain, sixth in the French GP, second at Hockenheim, third

109. Jody Scheckter with the Wolf leads Watson's Brabham at Monaco in 1977.

in the United States and second in Canada. Bobby Rahal drove WR5 in the United States GP and one of the 1977 cars in Canada. It was clear that Wolf's star was waning rapidly.

WR7–9 – 1979

For 1979 Postlethwaite designed the WR7–9 cars with folded aluminium honeycomb sheet construction monocoques and slightly longer wheelbase. In the Argentine the car appeared with clutch-driven impeller blades to draw air through the oil cooler, but this was quickly banned as a moving aerodynamic device. Scheckter had now left to drive for Ferrari and his place in the team was taken by James Hunt. Two weeks after the Monaco GP Hunt decided to retire from racing and his place in the team was taken by Keke Rosberg. Neither driver finished in the first six, and during the winter of 1979–80 the Wolf team was merged with Fittipaldi.

Zakspeed

(West Germany)

841 – 1985

It was a bold decision by Erich Zakowski, renowned developer of Ford-based saloons for competition work and with vast experience of turbocharged engines, when he decided to enter Formula One. Zakspeed had developed a 1495 cc turbocharged 4-cylinder engine claimed to produce around 700 bhp at 11,500 rpm and this was

110. The Zakspeed driven by Jonathan Palmer showed considerable promise throughout 1985 and the team's prospects for 1986 looked encouraging.

installed in a chassis designed by Paul Brown. Brown devised a moulded carbon-composite monocoque with front suspension by double wishbones and inboard springs and with pull-rod-operated rear suspension. The wheelbase was 9 ft 3 in., front track 5 ft 10.8 in. and rear track 5 ft 3 in. The team made its debut at the Portuguese GP and the driver was Jonathan Palmer. The Zakspeed non-started at Imola because of an engine misfire on the warm-up lap and not long after the Dutch GP Palmer crashed badly with a Porsche at Spa and a broken leg put him out of racing. The Zakspeed was driven in the Belgian GP and the European GP at Brands Hatch by Christian Danner. Zakspeed did not contest the races outside Europe. No success was gained in 1985, but it was clear that the team was making steady progress.

861 – 1985

In 1986 Zakspeed fielded improved 861 cars, initially fielding a single car for Palmer, but from Imola onwards running a second car with Huub Rothengatter at the wheel. The entry of the second car seemed to dissipate the team's efforts and the marked progress that Zakspeed had been making now showed a marked deterioration.